# Celestial Navigation in a Nutshell

# Celestial Navigation in a Nutshell

**Hewitt Schlereth**

SHERIDAN HOUSE

First published 2000 by
Sheridan House Inc.
145 Palisade Street
Dobbs Ferry, NY 10522
www.sheridanhouse.com

*Library of Congress Cataloging-in-Publication Data*

Schlereth, Hewitt.
Celestial navigation in a nutshell / Hewitt Schlereth.
   p.    cm.
    Includes index.
    ISBN 1-57409-058-5 (alk. paper)
    1. Nautical astronomy. I. Title.
  VK555 .S339 2000
  527—dc21
                        99-049975
                        CIP

Editor: Catherine Degnon
Production Management: Quantum Publishing Services, LLC, Bellingham, WA
Composition/Design: Jill Mathews

Printed in the United States of America

ISBN 1-57409-058-5

# Contents

# Preface

Why celestial navigation? In this, the day of the hand-held GPS when the hand-held sextant is often regarded as some antiquated artifact, the usual answer to the question is that celestial is a nice backup. This quaint old art, it is argued, does not depend on batteries or fragile circuits or what is euphemistically called *selective availability* (which seems to mean, "The satellite can be turned off"). These are sound, practical reasons, to be sure. And true. But they aren't quite it, are they? There is something more to celestial than plain old utility.

Think back: From just about the first moment you set foot on a boat you heard two things talked of in hushed tones; Cape Horn, and celestial navigation. With the passage of time you likely as not came to see the Horn as the mariner's Everest and celestial as one of the higher Alps. At this stage you may not be dreaming about the Great Cape any more. But, hey, there's still the Matterhorn.

Why learn celestial navigation?

Because it will satisfy your soul.

# Introduction

I have often thought that if a pagan could be a saint, Ariadne would be the patron saint of navigators. When she handed the end of that skein of twine to Theseus as he entered the maze to find the Minotaur, she not only found the key to a labyrinth, she also hit upon the fundamental principle of navigation: If you know your way back, you are not lost. Taking her precept a step further, to navigate at sea you not only attach a thread to your starting point, you also keep track of the amount you pay out and take note of any twists or turns you happen to make.

What I am talking about here, of course, is what is customarily called *DR navigation*—knowing where you are by the dead-simple practice of keeping an account of the courses steered and distances run from a known departure point and not breaking the "thread" until another known point is established.

So, contrary to general belief, you do not begin navigating by first getting lost. That's the way Theseus would have done it. You know where you are because you know where you started from, the direction you went, the speed you went, and the length of time you went. It takes only the most basic application of arithmetic and common sense to pause now and then, lay out the course and distance on a chart, and mark the spot—your position by *deduced reckoning,* or what some refer to as *dead reckoning.* Most often, however, this position is called simply called the DR.

Here's the point. Navigation, taken as a whole, has two steps: (1) keeping the DR, and (2) periodically checking it by other means. In reality, navigation is a process of the one checking the other. It's extremely risky to leave out either step. Where's your check then?

Nowadays, if you are on a passage and using GPS and celestial in addition to your DR, a normal spread between the GPS, celestial, and

DR positions soon emerges. Any sudden change—a celestial or GPS fix twice its usual distance from the DR, for example—means something is out of whack *with the celestial or GPS*. Should you lose celestial to bad weather or GPS to accident or selective availability, you will by then have acquired a sure sense of your DR and can carry on with it until the weather clears or the satellites are back on.

Whatever you do, never give up the DR.

# Part I

☉  ♃  ♂  ♄  ♀  ☆  ☾

# Our Star:
# Navigation by the Sun

# 1

# The Big Picture

If navigation as a whole has two steps, celestial navigation has four:

1. Taking a sight with a sextant
2. Establishing a secondary reference, or benchmark, sight
3. Comparing the two sights
4. Putting the result of the comparison on a chart

Virtually everyone is familiar with the first sight, the so-called shot of the sun. That's where the navigator puts his or her eye to the telescope of a spindly black instrument, aims the contraption at the sun, twiddles a knob on its lower edge, and hollers "mark" to a crewmember hovering nearby with watch, pencil, and notebook to jot down the exact time the sun in the navigator's telescope touches the rim of the sea.

What virtually no one except the navigator is familiar with is the second sight—the one used as a benchmark for comparison with the first. The navigator generates this sight either by thumbing through a succession of books whose entire contents are rows and columns of numbers set in the tiniest type or by punching numbers into a pocket computer. This mathematically derived reference sight is what navigators talk about when they get together, because it is the *sine qua non* of modern celestial navigation and there are so many ways to get it, varying from the ridiculously easy to the absurdly arcane.

Taking the first sight is easy. Learning to use a sextant is a lot like learning to shoot a rifle, and the obvious analogy is the reason sights are usually called shots. Everyone learns to use a sextant very well, very quickly.

The benchmark sight, on the other hand, is what makes learning celestial difficult. It's not the concept; that's straightforward. The difficulties lie in the materials: the books of columns of numbers, the work forms, and the rigid protocols of pocket computers and calculators. For me, learning my way around the columns of figures and work forms was a lot like learning to dance the Charleston; I simply had to go through the steps many, many times before they finally became automatic. The process is the same for everyone. You can read about celestial navigation till the cows come home, but you won't learn it until you *do* it.

That's the bad news—you have to work a bit. The good news is that once you've got it, you never forget it, just as you never forget how to ride a bike.

# 2

# Mirror, Mirror

The marine sextant is a device for measuring angles. Virtually the symbol of celestial navigation, it is normally used at sea to measure the angle between the sun (or the moon, planets, or stars) and the horizon, but you can use it to measure any sort of angle. As a matter of fact, as a first step in learning celestial, I suggest you buy or borrow a sextant (the cheapest plastic one is fine), read the instruction manual, sit down in your living room, and practice measuring the angles between the lamps and the floor. Then take the sextant outside and measure the angles between the street lights and the road.

Once you have a sextant in your hand, you can easily see how it works; it's all done with mirrors (fig. 2-1). The mirrors allow you to keep an eye on two things at once: the body in the sky and a reference line. The reference line is the sea horizon if you're doing celestial at sea, the floor or street if you're practicing at home. You see the horizon in the fixed, lower mirror. The sun is reflected onto this mirror from the higher mirror attached to the sextant's hinged arm. As you move the arm and fine-tune with the adjustment knob, the sun and horizon are brought together in the fixed mirror.

There are two basic tricks to using the sextant: getting the sun and horizon in your field of view at the same time and making sure that when you measure the angle between horizon and sun your sextant is vertical. If it's not vertical, you will not be measuring the angle between the sun and the point on the horizon directly under it, but a slightly larger one.

To get the sun in your field of view, you need to estimate its angle above the horizon—its *altitude.* For a quick estimation, face the sun and look at the horizon. If the sun seems to be sending beams through your eyebrows, the altitude is about 30°; if the rays seem to be coming through your forehead, it's about 45°. Alternatively, taking into account that the average spread hand held at arm's length covers about 15°, hold out your hands, stack one on top of the other until you reach the sun, and then convert the hand spans to degrees. Either way, set your sextant to the estimated altitude, put down the filters so that you won't be blinded, and see if both sun and horizon are in the scope. If you can't find the sun either of these ways, set the sextant to 0°, put down the filters, and aim directly at the sun. Now push the arm of the sextant away from you, and the sun will appear to come down.

Keep moving the arm forward and bringing the sun down until you set its lower edge on the horizon. Now pause and just watch for a moment. The sun will either rise above the horizon or sink into it. Put it back on the horizon. Do this a couple of times to get the feel of it. Now look at your watch, second hand first. Note the time. Read the angle you have measured and write it down. That's all there is to a sight. Any sight, ever.

To ensure that you have the sextant vertical when you set it on the horizon and take the time, *rotate* the sextant about the axis of the telescope by cocking your wrist to the left and right a little. As you do so, the sun will appear to rise off the horizon and swing through an arc, just as though it were the pendulum bob of an old-fashioned grandfather clock (fig. 2-2). When the sun is at the bottom of its swing so that it is just touching the horizon, the sextant is vertical. *That's* when you take the time or holler "mark." *Then* read the angle you have measured. Remember: Time comes first. It's the number that's constantly changing. Unless you drop the sextant, the instrument will hold the altitude you measured forever.

You don't need the sea horizon to practice. Any straight line underneath the sun will do: the roof of a house, the top of an oil tank, a railroad track, a bridge. Learning celestial is like learning a

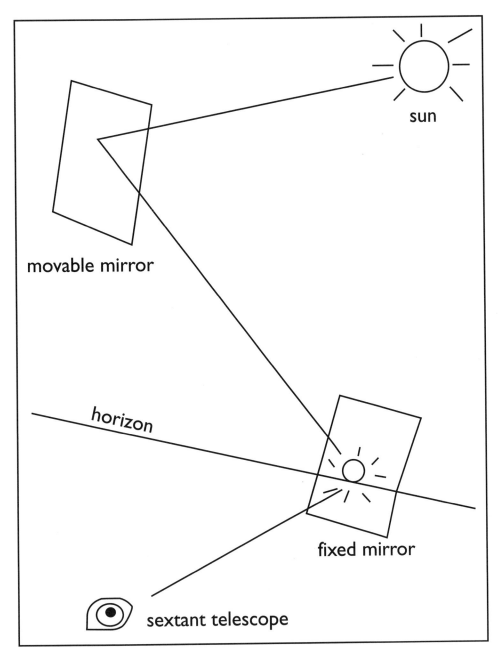

*Figure 2–1.* Bringing the sun down to the horizon

new dance; what's important is practicing the motions. Get used to cocking your wrist to "swing the arc" and "kiss" the sun's disk to the horizon. Acquire the habit of taking the time *before* reading the altitude, because, as you'll learn in the chapters ahead, without the time, the angle is useless.

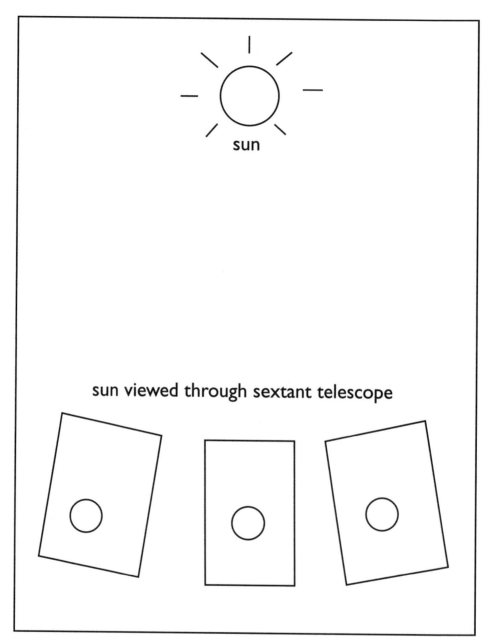

*Figure 2–2.* Swinging the arc

# Celestial Navigation in Theory

Okay, you've measured the altitude of the sun and written down the time you did it. Why?

Look at figure 3-1. Whenever you take a sight of the sun you are one point of a large right triangle. The difference between a conventional right triangle and this one is that the base of yours is not a straight line but an arc. It's not just any old arc. This particular arc is the great-circle track between you and the point on the earth that is directly under the sun, a point known as the *geographical position,* but usually written as an abbreviation, GP.

Great-circle arcs can be measured in degrees, and it is a happy fact that in this bulgy-bottomed triangle the number of degrees in the bulge equals the number of degrees in the angle at the apex. Because the two acute angles of a right triangle add up to 90° (remember, the angles of a triangle must add up to 180° and a right angle equals 90°), the angle at the apex must equal 90° minus the angle at your point—the angle you measured with your sextant. So, by taking a sextant shot of the sun and subtracting the angle from 90°, you can find out how far you are from the point on earth that is directly underneath the sun. Isn't it amazing what you can do with a couple of mirrors and a little trig?

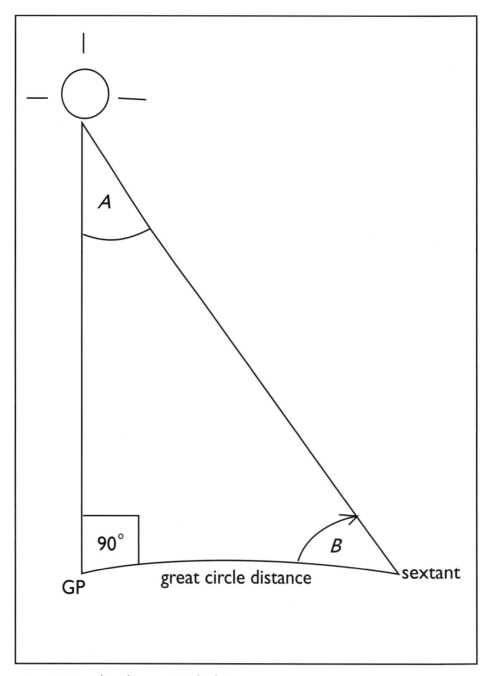

*Figure 3–1.* Finding the great-circle distance

Take a moment to nail down this concept with some simple numbers. Say you measure the altitude of the sun, and it's 60°. That means the angle at the apex of the triangle is 30°, which means that you are 30 great-circle degrees from the point on the earth that is right under the sun, the GP. By long-standing convention, 1 degree on a terrestrial great circle equals 60 nautical miles of distance. In this example, therefore, you are 1,800 nautical miles from the geographical position of the sun.

To make things a bit more realistic, imagine the measured altitude is 59°30′—that is, 59 1/2 degrees. In this case, the apex angle and corresponding great-circle arc are 30°30′, and the distance is 1,830 nautical miles (1 degree is 60 minutes of arc, which equals 60 nautical miles, so 1 minute of arc on a great circle equals 1 nautical mile; therefore, an additional 30 minutes adds 30 nautical miles to the previous example).

If you know the latitude and longitude of the GP you can now go to a chart or a globe, stick in a pin at that point, and draw a circle around it with a radius of 1,830 miles (fig. 3-2). You're somewhere on that circle, and if you've kept any sort of DR, the odds are very good you're at the spot on the circle closest to your DR. And that, you may be glad to know, is the entire theory of celestial navigation. However, theory is not the hard part of celestial navigation. Getting the data you need is.

For instance, it's all very well to know how far you are from the GP, but how do you know where the GP is? You don't. But you can look it up.

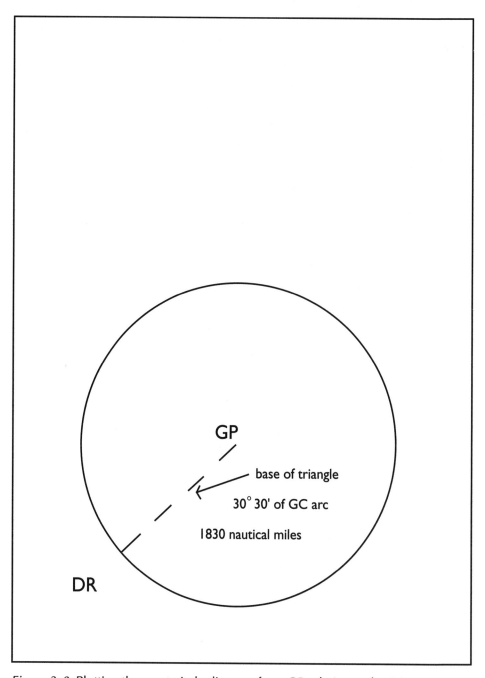

GP

base of triangle

30° 30' of GC arc

1830 nautical miles

DR

*Figure 3–2.* Plotting the great-circle distance from GP relative to the DR

# Columns of Numbers

If you know the time you take your sight—and of course you do—
you can look up the geographical position in the *Nautical Almanac,* a
book listing GPs for every hour of the entire year for not only the sun
but also the moon and the major planets and stars used in celestial
navigation. Figure 4-1 is a reproduction of what you see when you
open the almanac. The left-hand page displays three days' worth of
data for the planets and stars; the right-hand page, three days' worth
for the sun and moon. These pages are for June 18, 19, and 20, 1999.
Each day begins with an entry for midnight and continues in 1-hour
increments through the entry for 11 P.M., or 2300 hours (the almanac
uses the 24-hour system of expressing time).

Obviously, the times noted in this table have to be standardized
for use anywhere in the world, so by another long-standing custom,
*Nautical Almanac* time is Greenwich mean time (GMT). One way to
*get* the current GMT is to listen for the time signals on a shortwave
radio. They are broadcast continuously on the frequencies of 5, 10,
15, 20, and 25 MHz (where they are announced as "Coordinated
Universal Time," which is identical to GMT). Note that shortwave
reception is best at night. The simplest way to *keep* GMT is to buy a
digital watch, set it to the time and date you hear a broadcast, and

## 1999 JUNE 18, 19, 20 (FRI., SAT., SUN.)

| UT | ARIES GHA | VENUS −4.4 GHA | Dec | MARS −0.7 GHA | Dec | JUPITER −2.2 GHA | Dec | SATURN +0.4 GHA | Dec | STARS Name | SHA | Dec |
|---|---|---|---|---|---|---|---|---|---|---|---|---|
| **18 00** | 265 47.5 | 131 14.3 | N19 08.3 | 62 18.9 | S10 37.5 | 239 07.5 | N 9 44.7 | 224 36.4 | N13 35.8 | Acamar | 315 26.9 | S40 18.4 |
| 01 | 280 50.0 | 146 14.6 | 07.5 | 77 21.0 | 37.7 | 254 09.6 | 44.8 | 239 38.6 | 35.9 | Achernar | 335 35.2 | S57 14.2 |
| 02 | 295 52.5 | 161 14.8 | 06.7 | 92 23.1 | 38.0 | 269 11.6 | 45.0 | 254 40.8 | 35.9 | Acrux | 173 21.3 | S63 06.0 |
| 03 | 310 54.9 | 176 15.0 | .. 05.9 | 107 25.2 | .. 38.2 | 284 13.6 | .. 45.1 | 269 43.0 | .. 36.0 | Adhara | 255 21.4 | S28 58.4 |
| 04 | 325 57.4 | 191 15.2 | 05.1 | 122 27.2 | 38.4 | 299 15.7 | 45.3 | 284 45.2 | 36.1 | Aldebaran | 291 02.2 | N16 30.3 |
| 05 | 340 59.9 | 206 15.4 | 04.3 | 137 29.3 | 38.6 | 314 17.7 | 45.4 | 299 47.4 | 36.1 | | | |
| 06 | 356 02.3 | 221 15.7 | N19 03.6 | 152 31.4 | S10 38.8 | 329 19.8 | N 9 45.6 | 314 49.6 | N13 36.2 | Alioth | 166 30.1 | N55 58.1 |
| 07 | 11 04.8 | 236 15.9 | 02.8 | 167 33.5 | 39.1 | 344 21.8 | 45.8 | 329 51.8 | 36.3 | Alkaid | 153 07.2 | N49 19.3 |
| 08 | 26 07.2 | 251 16.1 | 02.0 | 182 35.6 | 39.3 | 359 23.8 | 45.9 | 344 54.0 | 36.4 | Al Na'ir | 27 57.1 | S46 57.6 |
| F 09 | 41 09.7 | 266 16.3 | .. 01.2 | 197 37.7 | .. 39.5 | 14 25.9 | .. 46.1 | 359 56.2 | .. 36.4 | Alnilam | 275 57.7 | S 1 12.3 |
| R 10 | 56 12.2 | 281 16.6 | 19 00.4 | 212 39.7 | 39.7 | 29 27.9 | 46.2 | 14 58.4 | 36.5 | Alphard | 218 06.9 | S 8 39.4 |
| I 11 | 71 14.6 | 296 16.8 | 18 59.6 | 227 41.8 | 39.9 | 44 30.0 | 46.4 | 30 00.6 | 36.6 | | | |
| D 12 | 86 17.1 | 311 17.0 | N18 58.8 | 242 43.9 | S10 40.2 | 59 32.0 | N 9 46.5 | 45 02.8 | N13 36.7 | Alphecca | 126 19.9 | N26 43.2 |
| A 13 | 101 19.6 | 326 17.3 | 58.0 | 257 46.0 | 40.4 | 74 34.1 | 46.7 | 60 05.1 | 36.7 | Alpheratz | 357 54.8 | N29 05.0 |
| Y 14 | 116 22.0 | 341 17.5 | 57.2 | 272 48.1 | 40.6 | 89 36.1 | 46.8 | 75 07.3 | 36.8 | Altair | 62 18.5 | N 8 52.1 |
| 15 | 131 24.5 | 356 17.7 | .. 56.4 | 287 50.1 | .. 40.8 | 104 38.1 | .. 47.0 | 90 09.5 | .. 36.9 | Ankaa | 353 26.5 | S42 18.4 |
| 16 | 146 27.0 | 11 18.0 | 55.6 | 302 52.2 | 41.0 | 119 40.2 | 47.1 | 105 11.7 | 36.9 | Antares | 112 39.2 | S26 25.8 |
| 17 | 161 29.4 | 26 18.2 | 54.8 | 317 54.3 | 41.3 | 134 42.2 | 47.3 | 120 13.9 | 37.0 | | | |
| 18 | 176 31.9 | 41 18.4 | N18 54.0 | 332 56.3 | S10 41.5 | 149 44.3 | N 9 47.4 | 135 16.1 | N13 37.1 | Arcturus | 146 05.4 | N19 11.3 |
| 19 | 191 34.3 | 56 18.7 | 53.2 | 347 58.4 | 41.7 | 164 46.3 | 47.6 | 150 18.3 | 37.2 | Atria | 107 50.3 | S69 01.6 |
| 20 | 206 36.8 | 71 18.9 | 52.4 | 3 00.5 | 41.9 | 179 48.3 | 47.7 | 165 20.5 | 37.2 | Avior | 234 22.9 | S59 30.7 |
| 21 | 221 39.3 | 86 19.2 | .. 51.6 | 18 02.6 | .. 42.2 | 194 50.4 | .. 47.9 | 180 22.7 | .. 37.3 | Bellatrix | 278 44.0 | N 6 20.8 |
| 22 | 236 41.7 | 101 19.4 | 50.8 | 33 04.6 | 42.4 | 209 52.4 | 48.0 | 195 24.9 | 37.4 | Betelgeuse | 271 13.4 | N 7 24.3 |
| 23 | 251 44.2 | 116 19.7 | 50.0 | 48 06.7 | 42.6 | 224 54.5 | 48.2 | 210 27.1 | 37.5 | | | |
| **19 00** | 266 46.7 | 131 19.9 | N18 49.2 | 63 08.7 | S10 42.8 | 239 56.5 | N 9 48.3 | 225 29.3 | N13 37.5 | Canopus | 264 01.5 | S52 41.9 |
| 01 | 281 49.1 | 146 20.2 | 48.4 | 78 10.8 | 43.1 | 254 58.6 | 48.5 | 240 31.5 | 37.6 | Capella | 280 51.0 | N45 59.7 |
| 02 | 296 51.6 | 161 20.4 | 47.6 | 93 12.9 | 43.3 | 270 00.6 | 48.6 | 255 33.8 | 37.7 | Deneb | 49 38.5 | N45 16.6 |
| 03 | 311 54.1 | 176 20.7 | .. 46.8 | 108 14.9 | .. 43.5 | 285 02.7 | .. 48.8 | 270 36.0 | .. 37.7 | Denebola | 182 44.7 | N14 34.7 |
| 04 | 326 56.5 | 191 20.9 | 46.0 | 123 17.0 | 43.8 | 300 04.7 | 48.9 | 285 38.2 | 37.8 | Diphda | 349 06.9 | S17 59.4 |
| 05 | 341 59.0 | 206 21.2 | 45.2 | 138 19.1 | 44.0 | 315 06.7 | 49.1 | 300 40.4 | 37.9 | | | |
| 06 | 357 01.5 | 221 21.4 | N18 44.4 | 153 21.1 | S10 44.2 | 330 08.8 | N 9 49.2 | 315 42.6 | N13 38.0 | Dubhe | 194 05.2 | N61 45.6 |
| 07 | 12 03.9 | 236 21.7 | 43.6 | 168 23.2 | 44.4 | 345 10.8 | 49.4 | 330 44.8 | 38.0 | Elnath | 278 26.7 | N28 36.3 |
| S 08 | 27 06.4 | 251 21.9 | 42.8 | 183 25.2 | 44.7 | 0 12.9 | 49.5 | 345 47.0 | 38.1 | Eltanin | 90 50.6 | N51 29.4 |
| A 09 | 42 08.8 | 266 22.2 | .. 42.0 | 198 27.3 | .. 44.9 | 15 14.9 | .. 49.7 | 0 49.2 | .. 38.2 | Enif | 33 57.6 | N 9 52.3 |
| T 10 | 57 11.3 | 281 22.5 | 41.2 | 213 29.3 | 45.1 | 30 17.0 | 49.8 | 15 51.4 | 38.2 | Fomalhaut | 15 35.8 | S29 37.4 |
| U 11 | 72 13.8 | 296 22.7 | 40.3 | 228 31.4 | 45.4 | 45 19.0 | 50.0 | 30 53.6 | 38.3 | | | |
| R 12 | 87 16.2 | 311 23.0 | N18 39.5 | 243 33.4 | S10 45.6 | 60 21.1 | N 9 50.1 | 45 55.8 | N13 38.4 | Gacrux | 172 12.9 | S57 06.8 |
| D 13 | 102 18.7 | 326 23.3 | 38.7 | 258 35.5 | 45.8 | 75 23.1 | 50.3 | 60 58.1 | 38.5 | Gienah | 176 03.4 | S17 32.4 |
| A 14 | 117 21.2 | 341 23.5 | 37.9 | 273 37.5 | 46.0 | 90 25.1 | 50.4 | 76 00.3 | 38.5 | Hadar | 149 02.9 | S60 22.3 |
| Y 15 | 132 23.6 | 356 23.8 | .. 37.1 | 288 39.6 | .. 46.3 | 105 27.2 | .. 50.6 | 91 02.5 | .. 38.6 | Hamal | 328 13.2 | N23 27.3 |
| 16 | 147 26.1 | 11 24.1 | 36.3 | 303 41.6 | 46.5 | 120 29.2 | 50.7 | 106 04.7 | 38.7 | Kaus Aust. | 83 57.8 | S34 23.0 |
| 17 | 162 28.6 | 26 24.4 | 35.5 | 318 43.7 | 46.7 | 135 31.3 | 50.9 | 121 06.9 | 38.8 | | | |
| 18 | 177 31.0 | 41 24.6 | N18 34.7 | 333 45.7 | S10 47.0 | 150 33.3 | N 9 51.0 | 136 09.1 | N13 38.8 | Kochab | 137 18.8 | N74 09.8 |
| 19 | 192 33.5 | 56 24.9 | 33.9 | 348 47.8 | 47.2 | 165 35.4 | 51.2 | 151 11.3 | 38.9 | Markab | 13 49.1 | N15 12.0 |
| 20 | 207 36.0 | 71 25.2 | 33.1 | 3 49.8 | 47.4 | 180 37.4 | 51.3 | 166 13.5 | 39.0 | Menkar | 314 26.7 | N 4 05.1 |
| 21 | 222 38.4 | 86 25.5 | .. 32.3 | 18 51.8 | .. 47.7 | 195 39.5 | .. 51.5 | 181 15.7 | .. 39.0 | Menkent | 148 20.1 | S36 22.1 |
| 22 | 237 40.9 | 101 25.7 | 31.5 | 33 53.9 | 47.9 | 210 41.5 | 51.6 | 196 17.9 | 39.1 | Miaplacidus | 221 42.5 | S69 43.2 |
| 23 | 252 43.3 | 116 26.0 | 30.6 | 48 55.9 | 48.1 | 225 43.6 | 51.8 | 211 20.1 | 39.2 | | | |
| **20 00** | 267 45.8 | 131 26.3 | N18 29.8 | 63 58.0 | S10 48.4 | 240 45.6 | N 9 51.9 | 226 22.4 | N13 39.3 | Mirfak | 308 56.3 | N49 51.3 |
| 01 | 282 48.3 | 146 26.6 | 29.0 | 79 00.0 | 48.6 | 255 47.7 | 52.1 | 241 24.6 | 39.3 | Nunki | 76 11.4 | S26 17.7 |
| 02 | 297 50.7 | 161 26.9 | 28.2 | 94 02.0 | 48.8 | 270 49.7 | 52.2 | 256 26.8 | 39.4 | Peacock | 53 35.8 | S56 44.0 |
| 03 | 312 53.2 | 176 27.2 | .. 27.4 | 109 04.1 | .. 49.1 | 285 51.8 | .. 52.4 | 271 29.0 | .. 39.5 | Pollux | 243 41.3 | N28 01.7 |
| 04 | 327 55.7 | 191 27.5 | 26.6 | 124 06.1 | 49.3 | 300 53.8 | 52.5 | 286 31.2 | 39.5 | Procyon | 245 11.4 | N 5 13.5 |
| 05 | 342 58.1 | 206 27.7 | 25.8 | 139 08.1 | 49.6 | 315 55.9 | 52.7 | 301 33.4 | 39.6 | | | |
| 06 | 358 00.6 | 221 28.0 | N18 25.0 | 154 10.2 | S10 49.8 | 330 57.9 | N 9 52.8 | 316 35.6 | N13 39.7 | Rasalhague | 96 16.2 | N12 33.7 |
| 07 | 13 03.1 | 236 28.3 | 24.1 | 169 12.2 | 50.0 | 345 59.9 | 52.9 | 331 37.8 | 39.8 | Regulus | 207 55.2 | N11 58.3 |
| 08 | 28 05.5 | 251 28.6 | 23.3 | 184 14.2 | 50.3 | 1 02.0 | 53.1 | 346 40.0 | 39.8 | Rigel | 281 22.8 | S 8 12.3 |
| S 09 | 43 08.0 | 266 28.9 | .. 22.5 | 199 16.3 | .. 50.5 | 16 04.0 | .. 53.2 | 1 42.3 | .. 39.9 | Rigil Kent. | 140 06.2 | S60 50.0 |
| U 10 | 58 10.4 | 281 29.2 | 21.7 | 214 18.3 | 50.7 | 31 06.1 | 53.4 | 16 44.5 | 40.0 | Sabik | 102 24.6 | S15 43.3 |
| N 11 | 73 12.9 | 296 29.5 | 20.9 | 229 20.3 | 51.0 | 46 08.1 | 53.5 | 31 46.7 | 40.0 | | | |
| D 12 | 88 15.4 | 311 29.8 | N18 20.1 | 244 22.3 | S10 51.2 | 61 10.2 | N 9 53.7 | 46 48.9 | N13 40.1 | Schedar | 349 53.0 | N56 31.7 |
| A 13 | 103 17.8 | 326 30.1 | 19.2 | 259 24.4 | 51.5 | 76 12.2 | 53.8 | 61 51.1 | 40.2 | Shaula | 96 36.2 | S37 06.1 |
| Y 14 | 118 20.3 | 341 30.4 | 18.4 | 274 26.4 | 51.7 | 91 14.3 | 54.0 | 76 53.3 | 40.2 | Sirius | 258 43.6 | S16 43.0 |
| 15 | 133 22.8 | 356 30.7 | .. 17.6 | 289 28.4 | .. 51.9 | 106 16.3 | .. 54.1 | 91 55.5 | .. 40.3 | Spica | 158 42.6 | S11 09.5 |
| 16 | 148 25.2 | 11 31.0 | 16.8 | 304 30.4 | 52.2 | 121 18.4 | 54.3 | 106 57.7 | 40.4 | Suhail | 223 00.7 | S43 26.0 |
| 17 | 163 27.7 | 26 31.3 | 16.0 | 319 32.4 | 52.4 | 136 20.4 | 54.4 | 121 59.9 | 40.5 | | | |
| 18 | 178 30.2 | 41 31.7 | N18 15.2 | 334 34.5 | S10 52.7 | 151 22.5 | N 9 54.6 | 137 02.2 | N13 40.5 | Vega | 80 45.9 | N38 47.0 |
| 19 | 193 32.6 | 56 32.0 | 14.3 | 349 36.5 | 52.9 | 166 24.5 | 54.7 | 152 04.4 | 40.6 | Zuben'ubi | 137 17.2 | S16 02.3 |
| 20 | 208 35.1 | 71 32.3 | 13.5 | 4 38.5 | 53.1 | 181 26.6 | 54.9 | 167 06.6 | 40.7 | | SHA | Mer. Pass. |
| 21 | 223 37.6 | 86 32.6 | .. 12.7 | 19 40.5 | .. 53.4 | 196 28.6 | .. 55.0 | 182 08.8 | .. 40.7 | | | |
| 22 | 238 40.0 | 101 32.9 | 11.9 | 34 42.5 | 53.6 | 211 30.7 | 55.2 | 197 11.0 | 40.8 | Venus | 224 33.2 | 15 14 |
| 23 | 253 42.5 | 116 33.2 | 11.1 | 49 44.5 | 53.9 | 226 32.7 | 55.3 | 212 13.2 | 40.9 | Mars | 156 22.1 | 19 45 |
| | h m | | | | | | | | | Jupiter | 333 09.8 | 7 59 |
| Mer. Pass. 6 11.9 | v 0.3 d 0.8 | v 2.1 d 0.2 | | v 2.0 d 0.1 | | v 2.2 d 0.1 | | | | Saturn | 318 42.7 | 8 57 |

*Figure 4–1.* GP tables, from the *Nautical Almanac*

## 1999 JUNE 18, 19, 20 (FRI., SAT., SUN.)

| UT | SUN GHA | Dec | MOON GHA | v | Dec | d | HP |
|---|---|---|---|---|---|---|---|
| **18 00** | 179 46.2 | N23 23.2 | 120 00.4 | 9.4 | N14 34.5 | 8.3 | 58.1 |
| 01 | 194 46.1 | 23.3 | 134 28.8 | 9.5 | 14 26.2 | 8.4 | 58.0 |
| 02 | 209 45.9 | 23.4 | 148 57.3 | 9.6 | 14 17.8 | 8.5 | 58.0 |
| 03 | 224 45.8 | .. 23.4 | 163 25.9 | 9.7 | 14 09.3 | 8.6 | 58.0 |
| 04 | 239 45.7 | 23.5 | 177 54.6 | 9.8 | 14 00.7 | 8.6 | 57.9 |
| 05 | 254 45.5 | 23.5 | 192 23.4 | 9.9 | 13 52.1 | 8.6 | 57.9 |
| 06 | 269 45.4 | N23 23.6 | 206 52.3 | 9.9 | N13 43.5 | 8.8 | 57.9 |
| **F** 07 | 284 45.3 | 23.7 | 221 21.2 | 10.1 | 13 34.7 | 8.8 | 57.8 |
| **R** 08 | 299 45.1 | 23.7 | 235 50.3 | 10.1 | 13 25.9 | 8.8 | 57.8 |
| **I** 09 | 314 45.0 | .. 23.8 | 250 19.4 | 10.3 | 13 17.1 | 8.9 | 57.7 |
| **D** 10 | 329 44.9 | 23.8 | 264 48.7 | 10.3 | 13 08.2 | 9.0 | 57.7 |
| **A** 11 | 344 44.7 | 23.9 | 279 18.0 | 10.4 | 12 59.2 | 9.0 | 57.7 |
| **Y** 12 | 359 44.6 | N23 24.0 | 293 47.4 | 10.5 | N12 50.2 | 9.1 | 57.6 |
| 13 | 14 44.4 | 24.0 | 308 16.9 | 10.6 | 12 41.1 | 9.1 | 57.6 |
| 14 | 29 44.3 | 24.1 | 322 46.5 | 10.6 | 12 32.0 | 9.2 | 57.5 |
| 15 | 44 44.2 | .. 24.1 | 337 16.1 | 10.8 | 12 22.8 | 9.3 | 57.5 |
| 16 | 59 44.0 | 24.2 | 351 45.9 | 10.8 | 12 13.5 | 9.3 | 57.5 |
| 17 | 74 43.9 | 24.2 | 6 15.7 | 10.9 | 12 04.2 | 9.3 | 57.4 |
| 18 | 89 43.8 | N23 24.3 | 20 45.6 | 11.0 | N11 54.9 | 9.4 | 57.4 |
| 19 | 104 43.6 | 24.3 | 35 15.6 | 11.1 | 11 45.5 | 9.5 | 57.3 |
| 20 | 119 43.5 | 24.4 | 49 45.7 | 11.2 | 11 36.0 | 9.4 | 57.3 |
| 21 | 134 43.4 | .. 24.5 | 64 15.9 | 11.2 | 11 26.6 | 9.6 | 57.3 |
| 22 | 149 43.2 | 24.5 | 78 46.1 | 11.4 | 11 17.0 | 9.6 | 57.2 |
| 23 | 164 43.1 | 24.6 | 93 16.5 | 11.4 | 11 07.4 | 9.6 | 57.2 |
| **19 00** | 179 42.9 | N23 24.6 | 107 46.9 | 11.4 | N10 57.8 | 9.6 | 57.2 |
| 01 | 194 42.8 | 24.6 | 122 17.3 | 11.6 | 10 48.2 | 9.7 | 57.1 |
| 02 | 209 42.7 | 24.7 | 136 47.9 | 11.6 | 10 38.5 | 9.8 | 57.1 |
| 03 | 224 42.5 | .. 24.7 | 151 18.5 | 11.8 | 10 28.7 | 9.8 | 57.0 |
| 04 | 239 42.4 | 24.8 | 165 49.3 | 11.8 | 10 18.9 | 9.8 | 57.0 |
| 05 | 254 42.3 | 24.8 | 180 20.1 | 11.8 | 10 09.1 | 9.9 | 57.0 |
| 06 | 269 42.1 | N23 24.9 | 194 50.9 | 12.0 | N 9 59.2 | 9.9 | 56.9 |
| **S** 07 | 284 42.0 | 24.9 | 209 21.9 | 12.0 | 9 49.3 | 9.9 | 56.9 |
| **A** 08 | 299 41.9 | 25.0 | 223 52.9 | 12.1 | 9 39.4 | 9.9 | 56.9 |
| **T** 09 | 314 41.7 | .. 25.0 | 238 24.0 | 12.1 | 9 29.5 | 10.0 | 56.8 |
| **U** 10 | 329 41.6 | 25.1 | 252 55.1 | 12.3 | 9 19.5 | 10.1 | 56.8 |
| **R** 11 | 344 41.4 | 25.1 | 267 26.4 | 12.3 | 9 09.4 | 10.0 | 56.7 |
| **D** 12 | 359 41.3 | N23 25.1 | 281 57.7 | 12.3 | N 8 59.4 | 10.1 | 56.7 |
| **A** 13 | 14 41.2 | 25.2 | 296 29.0 | 12.5 | 8 49.3 | 10.1 | 56.7 |
| **Y** 14 | 29 41.0 | 25.2 | 311 00.5 | 12.5 | 8 39.2 | 10.2 | 56.6 |
| 15 | 44 40.9 | .. 25.3 | 325 32.0 | 12.5 | 8 29.0 | 10.2 | 56.6 |
| 16 | 59 40.8 | 25.3 | 340 03.5 | 12.7 | 8 18.8 | 10.2 | 56.6 |
| 17 | 74 40.6 | 25.3 | 354 35.2 | 12.7 | 8 08.6 | 10.2 | 56.5 |
| 18 | **89 40.5 N23 25.4** | | 9 06.9 | 12.8 | N 7 58.4 | 10.3 | 56.5 |
| 19 | 104 40.4 | 25.4 | 23 38.7 | 12.8 | 7 48.1 | 10.2 | 56.5 |
| 20 | 119 40.2 | 25.4 | 38 10.5 | 12.9 | 7 37.9 | 10.3 | 56.4 |
| 21 | 134 40.1 | .. 25.5 | 52 42.4 | 13.0 | 7 27.6 | 10.4 | 56.4 |
| 22 | 149 39.9 | 25.5 | 67 14.4 | 13.0 | 7 17.2 | 10.3 | 56.4 |
| 23 | 164 39.8 | 25.5 | 81 46.4 | 13.1 | 7 06.9 | 10.4 | 56.3 |
| **20 00** | 179 39.7 | N23 25.6 | 96 18.5 | 13.1 | N 6 56.5 | 10.3 | 56.3 |
| 01 | **194 39.5** | 25.6 | 110 50.6 | 13.2 | 6 46.2 | 10.4 | 56.3 |
| 02 | 209 39.4 | 25.6 | 125 22.8 | 13.3 | 6 35.8 | 10.5 | 56.2 |
| 03 | 224 39.3 | .. 25.7 | 139 55.1 | 13.3 | 6 25.3 | 10.4 | 56.2 |
| 04 | 239 39.1 | 25.7 | 154 27.4 | 13.4 | 6 14.9 | 10.4 | 56.2 |
| 05 | 254 39.0 | 25.7 | 168 59.8 | 13.4 | 6 04.5 | 10.5 | 56.1 |
| 06 | 269 38.9 | N23 25.7 | 183 32.2 | 13.5 | N 5 54.0 | 10.5 | 56.1 |
| 07 | 284 38.7 | 25.8 | 198 04.7 | 13.5 | 5 43.5 | 10.5 | 56.1 |
| 08 | 299 38.6 | 25.8 | 212 37.2 | 13.6 | 5 33.0 | 10.5 | 56.0 |
| **S** 09 | 314 38.4 | .. 25.8 | 227 09.8 | 13.6 | 5 22.5 | 10.5 | 56.0 |
| **U** 10 | 329 38.3 | 25.8 | 241 42.4 | 13.7 | 5 12.0 | 10.5 | 56.0 |
| **N** 11 | 344 38.2 | 25.9 | 256 15.1 | 13.7 | 5 01.5 | 10.6 | 55.9 |
| **D** 12 | 359 38.0 | N23 25.9 | 270 47.8 | 13.8 | N 4 50.9 | 10.5 | 55.9 |
| **A** 13 | 14 37.9 | 25.9 | 285 20.6 | 13.9 | 4 40.4 | 10.6 | 55.9 |
| **Y** 14 | 29 37.8 | 25.9 | 299 53.5 | 13.8 | 4 29.8 | 10.6 | 55.8 |
| 15 | 44 37.6 | .. 26.0 | 314 26.3 | 14.0 | 4 19.2 | 10.5 | 55.8 |
| 16 | 59 37.5 | 26.0 | 328 59.3 | 13.9 | 4 08.7 | 10.6 | 55.8 |
| 17 | 74 37.4 | 26.0 | 343 32.2 | 14.0 | 3 58.1 | 10.6 | 55.7 |
| 18 | 89 37.2 | N23 26.0 | 358 05.2 | 14.1 | N 3 47.5 | 10.6 | 55.7 |
| 19 | 104 37.1 | 26.0 | 12 38.3 | 14.1 | 3 36.9 | 10.6 | 55.7 |
| 20 | 119 37.0 | 26.1 | 27 11.4 | 14.1 | 3 26.3 | 10.6 | 55.7 |
| 21 | 134 36.8 | .. 26.1 | 41 44.5 | 14.2 | 3 15.7 | 10.6 | 55.6 |
| 22 | 149 36.7 | 26.1 | 56 17.7 | 14.3 | 3 05.1 | 10.6 | 55.6 |
| 23 | 164 36.5 | 26.1 | 70 51.0 | 14.2 | N 2 54.5 | 10.6 | 55.5 |
| | SD 15.8 | d 0.0 | SD 15.7 | | 15.5 | | 15.2 |

### Twilight / Moonrise

| Lat. | Twilight Naut. | Civil | Sunrise | Moonrise 18 | 19 | 20 | 21 |
|---|---|---|---|---|---|---|---|
| N 72 | ☐ | ☐ | ☐ | 07 06 | 09 05 | 10 53 | 12 36 |
| N 70 | ☐ | ☐ | ☐ | 07 33 | 09 20 | 11 00 | 12 36 |
| 68 | ☐ | ☐ | ☐ | 07 53 | 09 32 | 11 06 | 12 37 |
| 66 | ☐ | ☐ | ☐ | 08 09 | 09 42 | 11 11 | 12 37 |
| 64 | //// | //// | 01 31 | 08 22 | 09 50 | 11 15 | 12 38 |
| 62 | //// | //// | 02 09 | 08 33 | 09 57 | 11 19 | 12 38 |
| 60 | //// | 00 50 | 02 36 | 08 42 | 10 03 | 11 22 | 12 38 |
| N 58 | //// | 01 40 | 02 56 | 08 51 | 10 09 | 11 25 | 12 38 |
| 56 | //// | 02 10 | 03 13 | 08 58 | 10 14 | 11 27 | 12 39 |
| 54 | 00 45 | 02 33 | 03 27 | 09 04 | 10 18 | 11 29 | 12 39 |
| 52 | 01 32 | 02 50 | 03 39 | 09 10 | 10 22 | 11 31 | 12 39 |
| 50 | 02 00 | 03 06 | 03 50 | 09 15 | 10 25 | 11 33 | 12 39 |
| 45 | 02 46 | 03 35 | 04 13 | 09 26 | 10 33 | 11 37 | 12 39 |
| N 40 | 03 16 | 03 58 | 04 31 | 09 35 | 10 39 | 11 40 | 12 40 |
| 35 | 03 44 | 04 16 | 04 46 | 09 43 | 10 44 | 11 43 | 12 40 |
| 30 | 03 58 | 04 31 | 04 59 | 09 50 | 10 49 | 11 46 | 12 40 |
| 20 | 04 27 | 04 56 | 05 21 | 10 02 | 10 57 | 11 50 | 12 41 |
| N 10 | 04 50 | 05 17 | 05 40 | 10 12 | 11 04 | 11 54 | 12 41 |
| 0 | 05 09 | 05 35 | 05 58 | 10 22 | 11 11 | 11 57 | 12 41 |
| S 10 | 05 26 | 05 52 | 06 15 | 10 32 | 11 18 | 12 01 | 12 42 |
| 20 | 05 42 | 06 10 | 06 34 | 10 42 | 11 25 | 12 04 | 12 42 |
| 30 | 05 59 | 06 28 | 06 55 | 10 54 | 11 33 | 12 09 | 12 42 |
| 35 | 06 07 | 06 39 | 07 07 | 11 01 | 11 38 | 12 11 | 12 43 |
| 40 | 06 17 | 06 51 | 07 21 | 11 08 | 11 43 | 12 14 | 12 43 |
| 45 | 06 27 | 07 04 | 07 38 | 11 17 | 11 49 | 12 17 | 12 43 |
| S 50 | 06 39 | 07 20 | 07 59 | 11 28 | 11 56 | 12 21 | 12 44 |
| 52 | 06 44 | 07 28 | 08 09 | 11 33 | 12 00 | 12 23 | 12 44 |
| 54 | 06 50 | 07 36 | 08 20 | 11 39 | 12 03 | 12 25 | 12 44 |
| 56 | 06 56 | 07 45 | 08 33 | 11 45 | 12 07 | 12 27 | 12 44 |
| 58 | 07 03 | 07 55 | 08 47 | 11 51 | 12 12 | 12 29 | 12 45 |
| S 60 | 07 10 | 08 07 | 09 05 | 11 59 | 12 17 | 12 32 | 12 45 |

### Sunset / Twilight / Moonset

| Lat. | Sunset | Twilight Civil | Naut. | Moonset 18 | 19 | 20 | 21 |
|---|---|---|---|---|---|---|---|
| N 72 | ☐ | ☐ | ☐ | 01 28 | 01 13 | 01 01 | 00 50 |
| N 70 | ☐ | ☐ | ☐ | 01 00 | 00 56 | 00 51 | 00 47 |
| 68 | ☐ | ☐ | ☐ | 00 38 | 00 42 | 00 44 | 00 44 |
| 66 | ☐ | ☐ | ☐ | 00 21 | 00 31 | 00 37 | 00 42 |
| 64 | 22 32 | //// | //// | 00 07 | 00 21 | 00 32 | 00 40 |
| 62 | 21 54 | //// | //// | 24 13 | 00 13 | 00 27 | 00 38 |
| 60 | 21 27 | 23 13 | //// | 24 06 | 00 06 | 00 23 | 00 37 |
| N 58 | 21 07 | 22 22 | //// | 24 00 | 00 00 | 00 19 | 00 35 |
| 56 | 20 50 | 21 52 | //// | 23 55 | 24 16 | 00 16 | 00 34 |
| 54 | 20 36 | 21 30 | 23 18 | 23 50 | 24 13 | 00 13 | 00 33 |
| 52 | 20 23 | 21 12 | 22 31 | 23 45 | 24 10 | 00 10 | 00 32 |
| 50 | 20 12 | 20 57 | 22 03 | 23 41 | 24 08 | 00 08 | 00 31 |
| 45 | 19 50 | 20 27 | 21 17 | 23 32 | 24 02 | 00 02 | 00 29 |
| N 40 | 19 32 | 20 05 | 20 46 | 23 25 | 23 58 | 24 28 | 00 28 |
| 35 | 19 17 | 19 46 | 20 23 | 23 18 | 23 54 | 24 26 | 00 26 |
| 30 | 19 04 | 19 31 | 20 04 | 23 13 | 23 50 | 24 25 | 00 25 |
| 20 | 18 42 | 19 06 | 19 35 | 23 03 | 23 44 | 24 22 | 00 22 |
| N 10 | 18 23 | 18 46 | 19 13 | 22 54 | 23 39 | 24 20 | 00 20 |
| 0 | 18 05 | 18 27 | 18 54 | 22 46 | 23 33 | 24 19 | 00 19 |
| S 10 | 17 47 | 18 10 | 18 37 | 22 38 | 23 28 | 24 17 | 00 17 |
| 20 | 17 29 | 17 53 | 18 20 | 22 29 | 23 23 | 24 14 | 00 14 |
| 30 | 17 08 | 17 34 | 18 04 | 22 19 | 23 16 | 24 12 | 00 12 |
| 35 | 16 55 | 17 23 | 17 55 | 22 13 | 23 13 | 24 11 | 00 11 |
| 40 | 16 41 | 17 12 | 17 46 | 22 06 | 23 09 | 24 09 | 00 09 |
| 45 | 16 24 | 16 58 | 17 35 | 21 58 | 23 04 | 24 07 | 00 07 |
| S 50 | 16 03 | 16 42 | 17 24 | 21 49 | 22 58 | 24 05 | 00 05 |
| 52 | 15 54 | 16 35 | 17 18 | 21 44 | 22 55 | 24 04 | 00 04 |
| 54 | 15 42 | 16 26 | 17 13 | 21 39 | 22 52 | 24 03 | 00 03 |
| 56 | 15 30 | 16 17 | 17 06 | 21 34 | 22 49 | 24 01 | 00 01 |
| 58 | 15 15 | 16 07 | 17 00 | 21 28 | 22 45 | 24 00 | 00 00 |
| S 60 | 14 58 | 15 55 | 16 52 | 21 21 | 22 41 | 23 58 | 25 14 |

### SUN / MOON

| Day | SUN Eqn. of Time 00h | 12h | Mer. Pass. | MOON Mer. Pass. Upper | Lower | Age | Phase |
|---|---|---|---|---|---|---|---|
| | m s | m s | h m | h m | h m | d % | |
| 18 | 00 55 | 01 01 | 12 01 | 16 34 | 04 09 | 05 27 | |
| 19 | 01 09 | 01 14 | 12 01 | 17 22 | 04 59 | 06 37 | |
| 20 | 01 21 | 01 28 | 12 01 | 18 08 | 05 45 | 07 48 | |

*Figure 4–1 (continued).*

use it as your navigation timepiece. If you're a worrier, buy two. Buy three. They're cheap. (Of course, you can always read GMT right off your GPS.)

Return to figure 4-1. Read down the time column (UT) to 1800 hours (6 P.M.) on Saturday, June 19, and across to the figures for the sun: 89°40.5′ and N 23°25.4′. The almanac is telling you that at 1800 hours GMT the sun is directly over longitude 89°40.5′ W and latitude 23°25.4′ N—a point in the Gulf of Mexico about 100 miles north of the Yucatán Peninsula and about 360 miles south of New Orleans, Louisiana. If you take a sight of the sun at exactly 1800 GMT on this day, that point in the Gulf is where you mark your GP.

Now look at the next day in the almanac extract (June 20), and notice what happens after midnight. At midnight the longitude of the sun is about 180°, which is just what you'd expect; it's midnight at the Greenwich meridian (0°), so the sun is near the date line. The next entry reads 194°39.5′. If the sun has crossed the date line, shouldn't its longitude be around 165°*E?* Yes, it should, and in fact, it is, but the almanac is compiled by astronomers, and astronomers don't work in longitudes and latitudes; they calculate *hour angles* and *declinations.*

Fortunately, declination and latitude are exact equivalents. That's why the N (for North) is given in the listings. If you look at the column headings under sun, however, you'll see that the second word actually reads "Dec." for *declination,* and the figures that at first appear to be longitudes are headed "GHA." The abbreviation for *Greenwich hour angle,* GHA is the number of degrees the sun is *west* of the Greenwich meridian. It is measured *westward* right around the globe from 0°, when the sun crosses the prime meridian near Greenwich, England, to 360°, when it arrives back there 24 hours later.

It's easy enough to convert from GHA to longitude (for example, 90° E is GHA 270°), but it's rarely done because celestial navigation is not practiced by sticking pins in charts and drawing circles around GPs. Instead, the GP is used to mathematically construct the second sight, the reference sight on which the actual practice of celestial depends (see chapter 5).

Glance down the sun columns again. Notice that the GHA (longitude) of the sun's GP increases about 15° an hour and its declination (latitude), 0.1′ (one-tenth of a minute) in three hours. Obviously, if you happen to take a sight at a time other than exactly on the hour, you have to interpolate to find the intermediate values.

Declination is clearly a lot easier to interpolate than GHA, and even if you don't bother, you lose only a fraction of a nautical mile. In fact, declination never changes more than 1´ in 1 hour, so you can ignore it without much peril or do an eyeball interpolation. If you are going to fiddle with declination, it's important to notice which way it's going. From March 21 to June 22 the sun is going north, so its declination is increasing. After the June solstice, the sun starts south, and its declination decreases until it crosses the equator on September 23; then declination increases in a southerly direction until the solstice on December 22, when the sun starts north and its declination again decreases. Simply scanning down the declination column tells you what's happening.

GHA, however, changes at a great rate; 15° every 1 hour amounts to 1´ every 4 seconds. Because the customary working unit in celestial navigation is 1 minute of arc (1´), you need to interpolate GHA to the nearest 4 seconds of time. For that exact a calculation you need help, which is provided by a special GHA interpolation table in the back of the *Nautical Almanac.* Printed on thirty buff-colored pages, this table allows interpolation to the nearest second of time.

Figure 4-2 is a copy of the columns in the interpolation table for 36 and 37 minutes of change in GHA. Assume that you shoot the sun at 18-36-49 GMT on June 19, 1999. Read down the 36´ column to 49 seconds and across to the number under the sun heading: add this figure—9°12.3´—to the GHA at 1800 hours of 89°40.5´ to get a GHA for the time of your sight of 98°52.8´.

It's an indication of the speed of things celestial to consider that in a bit over a half-hour the longitude of the sun's GP moves from New Orleans to Mexico City. Its latitude, however, does not change enough to be noticed by the table. That's because of the time of year, near the June solstice. It's not until 2100 hours that the table gives declination another tenth of a minute.

As just noted, it is usual in celestial navigation to work to the nearest 1´ of arc, so now return to the sextant to deal with factors that can introduce inaccuracies of that magnitude or more to your sight.

The first, *index error,* is common to all sextants and results from the mirrors being slightly out of alignment. To find your index error, first set the sextant to read exactly zero (0°00´) and look at the horizon. Depending on the type of horizon mirror in the sextant, you usually see either a step in the horizon or overlapping horizons. To

## 36ᵐ / 37ᵐ — INCREMENTS AND CORRECTIONS

### 36ᵐ

| 36 (s) | SUN PLANETS | ARIES | MOON | v or Corrⁿ d | v or Corrⁿ d | v or Corrⁿ d |
|---|---|---|---|---|---|---|
| 00 | 9 00·0 | 9 01·5 | 8 35·4 | 0·0 0·0 | 6·0 3·7 | 12·0 7·3 |
| 01 | 9 00·3 | 9 01·7 | 8 35·6 | 0·1 0·1 | 6·1 3·7 | 12·1 7·4 |
| 02 | 9 00·5 | 9 02·0 | 8 35·9 | 0·2 0·1 | 6·2 3·8 | 12·2 7·4 |
| 03 | 9 00·8 | 9 02·2 | 8 36·1 | 0·3 0·2 | 6·3 3·8 | 12·3 7·5 |
| 04 | 9 01·0 | 9 02·5 | 8 36·4 | 0·4 0·2 | 6·4 3·9 | 12·4 7·5 |
| 05 | 9 01·3 | 9 02·7 | 8 36·6 | 0·5 0·3 | 6·5 4·0 | 12·5 7·6 |
| 06 | 9 01·5 | 9 03·0 | 8 36·8 | 0·6 0·4 | 6·6 4·0 | 12·6 7·7 |
| 07 | 9 01·8 | 9 03·2 | 8 37·1 | 0·7 0·4 | 6·7 4·1 | 12·7 7·7 |
| 08 | 9 02·0 | 9 03·5 | 8 37·3 | 0·8 0·5 | 6·8 4·1 | 12·8 7·8 |
| 09 | 9 02·3 | 9 03·7 | 8 37·5 | 0·9 0·5 | 6·9 4·2 | 12·9 7·8 |
| 10 | 9 02·5 | 9 04·0 | 8 37·8 | 1·0 0·6 | 7·0 4·3 | 13·0 7·9 |
| 11 | 9 02·8 | 9 04·2 | 8 38·0 | 1·1 0·7 | 7·1 4·3 | 13·1 8·0 |
| 12 | 9 03·0 | 9 04·5 | 8 38·3 | 1·2 0·7 | 7·2 4·4 | 13·2 8·0 |
| 13 | 9 03·3 | 9 04·7 | 8 38·5 | 1·3 0·8 | 7·3 4·4 | 13·3 8·1 |
| 14 | 9 03·5 | 9 05·0 | 8 38·7 | 1·4 0·9 | 7·4 4·5 | 13·4 8·2 |
| 15 | 9 03·8 | 9 05·2 | 8 39·0 | 1·5 0·9 | 7·5 4·6 | 13·5 8·2 |
| 16 | 9 04·0 | 9 05·5 | 8 39·2 | 1·6 1·0 | 7·6 4·6 | 13·6 8·3 |
| 17 | 9 04·3 | 9 05·7 | 8 39·5 | 1·7 1·0 | 7·7 4·7 | 13·7 8·3 |
| 18 | 9 04·5 | 9 06·0 | 8 39·7 | 1·8 1·1 | 7·8 4·7 | 13·8 8·4 |
| 19 | 9 04·8 | 9 06·2 | 8 39·9 | 1·9 1·2 | 7·9 4·8 | 13·9 8·5 |
| 20 | 9 05·0 | 9 06·5 | 8 40·2 | 2·0 1·2 | 8·0 4·9 | 14·0 8·5 |
| 21 | 9 05·3 | 9 06·7 | 8 40·4 | 2·1 1·3 | 8·1 4·9 | 14·1 8·6 |
| 22 | 9 05·5 | 9 07·0 | 8 40·6 | 2·2 1·3 | 8·2 5·0 | 14·2 8·6 |
| 23 | 9 05·8 | 9 07·2 | 8 40·9 | 2·3 1·4 | 8·3 5·0 | 14·3 8·7 |
| 24 | 9 06·0 | 9 07·5 | 8 41·1 | 2·4 1·5 | 8·4 5·1 | 14·4 8·8 |
| 25 | 9 06·3 | 9 07·7 | 8 41·4 | 2·5 1·5 | 8·5 5·2 | 14·5 8·8 |
| 26 | 9 06·5 | 9 08·0 | 8 41·6 | 2·6 1·6 | 8·6 5·2 | 14·6 8·9 |
| 27 | 9 06·8 | 9 08·2 | 8 41·8 | 2·7 1·6 | 8·7 5·3 | 14·7 8·9 |
| 28 | 9 07·0 | 9 08·5 | 8 42·1 | 2·8 1·7 | 8·8 5·4 | 14·8 9·0 |
| 29 | 9 07·3 | 9 08·7 | 8 42·3 | 2·9 1·8 | 8·9 5·4 | 14·9 9·1 |
| 30 | 9 07·5 | 9 09·0 | 8 42·6 | 3·0 1·8 | 9·0 5·5 | 15·0 9·1 |
| 31 | 9 07·8 | 9 09·2 | 8 42·8 | 3·1 1·9 | 9·1 5·5 | 15·1 9·2 |
| 32 | 9 08·0 | 9 09·5 | 8 43·0 | 3·2 1·9 | 9·2 5·6 | 15·2 9·2 |
| 33 | 9 08·3 | 9 09·8 | 8 43·3 | 3·3 2·0 | 9·3 5·7 | 15·3 9·3 |
| 34 | 9 08·5 | 9 10·0 | 8 43·5 | 3·4 2·1 | 9·4 5·7 | 15·4 9·4 |
| 35 | 9 08·8 | 9 10·3 | 8 43·8 | 3·5 2·1 | 9·5 5·8 | 15·5 9·4 |
| 36 | 9 09·0 | 9 10·5 | 8 44·0 | 3·6 2·2 | 9·6 5·8 | 15·6 9·5 |
| 37 | 9 09·3 | 9 10·8 | 8 44·2 | 3·7 2·3 | 9·7 5·9 | 15·7 9·6 |
| 38 | 9 09·5 | 9 11·0 | 8 44·5 | 3·8 2·3 | 9·8 6·0 | 15·8 9·6 |
| 39 | 9 09·8 | 9 11·3 | 8 44·7 | 3·9 2·4 | 9·9 6·0 | 15·9 9·7 |
| 40 | 9 10·0 | 9 11·5 | 8 44·9 | 4·0 2·4 | 10·0 6·1 | 16·0 9·7 |
| 41 | 9 10·3 | 9 11·8 | 8 45·2 | 4·1 2·5 | 10·1 6·1 | 16·1 9·8 |
| 42 | 9 10·5 | 9 12·0 | 8 45·4 | 4·2 2·6 | 10·2 6·2 | 16·2 9·9 |
| 43 | 9 10·8 | 9 12·3 | 8 45·7 | 4·3 2·6 | 10·3 6·3 | 16·3 9·9 |
| 44 | 9 11·0 | 9 12·5 | 8 45·9 | 4·4 2·7 | 10·4 6·3 | 16·4 10·0 |
| 45 | 9 11·3 | 9 12·8 | 8 46·1 | 4·5 2·7 | 10·5 6·4 | 16·5 10·0 |
| 46 | 9 11·5 | 9 13·0 | 8 46·4 | 4·6 2·8 | 10·6 6·4 | 16·6 10·1 |
| 47 | 9 11·8 | 9 13·3 | 8 46·6 | 4·7 2·9 | 10·7 6·5 | 16·7 10·2 |
| 48 | 9 12·0 | 9 13·5 | 8 46·9 | 4·8 2·9 | 10·8 6·6 | 16·8 10·2 |
| 49 | [9 12·3] | 9 13·8 | 8 47·1 | 4·9 3·0 | 10·9 6·6 | 16·9 10·3 |
| 50 | 9 12·5 | 9 14·0 | 8 47·3 | 5·0 3·0 | 11·0 6·7 | 17·0 10·3 |
| 51 | 9 12·8 | 9 14·3 | 8 47·6 | 5·1 3·1 | 11·1 6·8 | 17·1 10·4 |
| 52 | 9 13·0 | 9 14·5 | 8 47·8 | 5·2 3·2 | 11·2 6·8 | 17·2 10·5 |
| 53 | 9 13·3 | 9 14·8 | 8 48·0 | 5·3 3·2 | 11·3 6·9 | 17·3 10·5 |
| 54 | 9 13·5 | 9 15·0 | 8 48·3 | 5·4 3·3 | 11·4 6·9 | 17·4 10·6 |
| 55 | 9 13·8 | 9 15·3 | 8 48·5 | 5·5 3·3 | 11·5 7·0 | 17·5 10·6 |
| 56 | 9 14·0 | 9 15·5 | 8 48·8 | 5·6 3·4 | 11·6 7·1 | 17·6 10·7 |
| 57 | 9 14·3 | 9 15·8 | 8 49·0 | 5·7 3·5 | 11·7 7·1 | 17·7 10·8 |
| 58 | 9 14·5 | 9 16·0 | 8 49·2 | 5·8 3·5 | 11·8 7·2 | 17·8 10·8 |
| 59 | 9 14·8 | 9 16·3 | 8 49·5 | 5·9 3·6 | 11·9 7·2 | 17·9 10·9 |
| 60 | 9 15·0 | 9 16·5 | 8 49·7 | 6·0 3·7 | 12·0 7·3 | 18·0 11·0 |

### 37ᵐ

| 37 (s) | SUN PLANETS | ARIES | MOON | v or Corrⁿ d | v or Corrⁿ d | v or Corrⁿ d |
|---|---|---|---|---|---|---|
| 00 | 9 15·0 | 9 16·5 | 8 49·7 | 0·0 0·0 | 6·0 3·8 | 12·0 7·5 |
| 01 | 9 15·3 | 9 16·8 | 8 50·0 | 0·1 0·1 | 6·1 3·8 | 12·1 7·6 |
| 02 | 9 15·5 | 9 17·0 | 8 50·2 | 0·2 0·1 | 6·2 3·9 | 12·2 7·6 |
| 03 | 9 15·8 | 9 17·3 | 8 50·4 | 0·3 0·2 | 6·3 3·9 | 12·3 7·7 |
| 04 | 9 16·0 | 9 17·5 | 8 50·7 | 0·4 0·3 | 6·4 4·0 | 12·4 7·8 |
| 05 | 9 16·3 | 9 17·8 | 8 50·9 | 0·5 0·3 | 6·5 4·1 | 12·5 7·8 |
| 06 | 9 16·5 | 9 18·0 | 8 51·1 | 0·6 0·4 | 6·6 4·1 | 12·6 7·9 |
| 07 | 9 16·8 | 9 18·3 | 8 51·4 | 0·7 0·4 | 6·7 4·2 | 12·7 7·9 |
| 08 | 9 17·0 | 9 18·5 | 8 51·6 | 0·8 0·5 | 6·8 4·3 | 12·8 8·0 |
| 09 | 9 17·3 | 9 18·8 | 8 51·9 | 0·9 0·6 | 6·9 4·3 | 12·9 8·1 |
| 10 | 9 17·5 | 9 19·0 | 8 52·1 | 1·0 0·6 | 7·0 4·4 | 13·0 8·1 |
| 11 | 9 17·8 | 9 19·3 | 8 52·3 | 1·1 0·7 | 7·1 4·4 | 13·1 8·2 |
| 12 | 9 18·0 | 9 19·5 | 8 52·6 | 1·2 0·8 | 7·2 4·5 | 13·2 8·3 |
| 13 | 9 18·3 | 9 19·8 | 8 52·8 | 1·3 0·8 | 7·3 4·6 | 13·3 8·3 |
| 14 | 9 18·5 | 9 20·0 | 8 53·1 | 1·4 0·9 | 7·4 4·6 | 13·4 8·4 |
| 15 | 9 18·8 | 9 20·3 | 8 53·3 | 1·5 0·9 | 7·5 4·7 | 13·5 8·4 |
| 16 | 9 19·0 | 9 20·5 | 8 53·5 | 1·6 1·0 | 7·6 4·8 | 13·6 8·5 |
| 17 | 9 19·3 | 9 20·8 | 8 53·8 | 1·7 1·1 | 7·7 4·8 | 13·7 8·6 |
| 18 | 9 19·5 | 9 21·0 | 8 54·0 | 1·8 1·1 | 7·8 4·9 | 13·8 8·6 |
| 19 | 9 19·8 | 9 21·3 | 8 54·3 | 1·9 1·2 | 7·9 4·9 | 13·9 8·7 |
| 20 | 9 20·0 | 9 21·5 | 8 54·5 | 2·0 1·3 | 8·0 5·0 | 14·0 8·8 |
| 21 | 9 20·3 | 9 21·8 | 8 54·7 | 2·1 1·3 | 8·1 5·1 | 14·1 8·8 |
| 22 | 9 20·5 | 9 22·0 | 8 55·0 | 2·2 1·4 | 8·2 5·1 | 14·2 8·9 |
| 23 | 9 20·8 | 9 22·3 | 8 55·2 | 2·3 1·4 | 8·3 5·2 | 14·3 8·9 |
| 24 | 9 21·0 | 9 22·5 | 8 55·4 | 2·4 1·5 | 8·4 5·3 | 14·4 9·0 |
| 25 | 9 21·3 | 9 22·8 | 8 55·7 | 2·5 1·6 | 8·5 5·3 | 14·5 9·1 |
| 26 | 9 21·5 | 9 23·0 | 8 55·9 | 2·6 1·6 | 8·6 5·4 | 14·6 9·1 |
| 27 | 9 21·8 | 9 23·3 | 8 56·2 | 2·7 1·7 | 8·7 5·4 | 14·7 9·2 |
| 28 | 9 22·0 | 9 23·5 | 8 56·4 | 2·8 1·8 | 8·8 5·5 | 14·8 9·3 |
| 29 | 9 22·3 | 9 23·8 | 8 56·6 | 2·9 1·8 | 8·9 5·6 | 14·9 9·3 |
| 30 | 9 22·5 | 9 24·0 | 8 56·9 | 3·0 1·9 | 9·0 5·6 | 15·0 9·4 |
| 31 | 9 22·8 | 9 24·3 | 8 57·1 | 3·1 1·9 | 9·1 5·7 | 15·1 9·4 |
| 32 | 9 23·0 | 9 24·5 | 8 57·4 | 3·2 2·0 | 9·2 5·8 | 15·2 9·5 |
| 33 | 9 23·3 | 9 24·8 | 8 57·6 | 3·3 2·1 | 9·3 5·8 | 15·3 9·6 |
| 34 | 9 23·5 | 9 25·0 | 8 57·8 | 3·4 2·1 | 9·4 5·9 | 15·4 9·6 |
| 35 | 9 23·8 | 9 25·3 | 8 58·1 | 3·5 2·2 | 9·5 5·9 | 15·5 9·7 |
| 36 | 9 24·0 | 9 25·5 | 8 58·3 | 3·6 2·3 | 9·6 6·0 | 15·6 9·8 |
| 37 | 9 24·3 | 9 25·8 | 8 58·5 | 3·7 2·3 | 9·7 6·1 | 15·7 9·8 |
| 38 | 9 24·5 | 9 26·0 | 8 58·8 | 3·8 2·4 | 9·8 6·1 | 15·8 9·9 |
| 39 | 9 24·8 | 9 26·3 | 8 59·0 | 3·9 2·4 | 9·9 6·2 | 15·9 9·9 |
| 40 | 9 25·0 | 9 26·5 | 8 59·3 | 4·0 2·5 | 10·0 6·3 | 16·0 10·0 |
| 41 | 9 25·3 | 9 26·8 | 8 59·5 | 4·1 2·6 | 10·1 6·3 | 16·1 10·1 |
| 42 | 9 25·5 | 9 27·0 | 8 59·7 | 4·2 2·6 | 10·2 6·4 | 16·2 10·1 |
| 43 | 9 25·8 | 9 27·3 | 9 00·0 | 4·3 2·7 | 10·3 6·4 | 16·3 10·2 |
| 44 | 9 26·0 | 9 27·5 | 9 00·2 | 4·4 2·8 | 10·4 6·5 | 16·4 10·3 |
| 45 | 9 26·3 | 9 27·8 | 9 00·5 | 4·5 2·8 | 10·5 6·6 | 16·5 10·3 |
| 46 | 9 26·5 | 9 28·1 | 9 00·7 | 4·6 2·9 | 10·6 6·6 | 16·6 10·4 |
| 47 | 9 26·8 | 9 28·3 | 9 00·9 | 4·7 2·9 | 10·7 6·7 | 16·7 10·4 |
| 48 | 9 27·0 | 9 28·6 | 9 01·2 | 4·8 3·0 | 10·8 6·8 | 16·8 10·5 |
| 49 | 9 27·3 | 9 28·8 | 9 01·4 | 4·9 3·1 | 10·9 6·8 | 16·9 10·5 |
| 50 | 9 27·5 | 9 29·1 | 9 01·6 | 5·0 3·1 | 11·0 6·9 | 17·0 10·6 |
| 51 | 9 27·8 | 9 29·3 | 9 01·9 | 5·1 3·2 | 11·1 6·9 | 17·1 10·7 |
| 52 | 9 28·0 | 9 29·6 | 9 02·1 | 5·2 3·3 | 11·2 7·0 | 17·2 10·8 |
| 53 | 9 28·3 | 9 29·8 | 9 02·4 | 5·3 3·3 | 11·3 7·1 | 17·3 10·8 |
| 54 | 9 28·5 | 9 30·1 | 9 02·6 | 5·4 3·4 | 11·4 7·1 | 17·4 10·9 |
| 55 | 9 28·8 | 9 30·3 | 9 02·8 | 5·5 3·4 | 11·5 7·2 | 17·5 10·9 |
| 56 | 9 29·0 | 9 30·6 | 9 03·1 | 5·6 3·5 | 11·6 7·3 | 17·6 11·0 |
| 57 | 9 29·3 | 9 30·8 | 9 03·3 | 5·7 3·6 | 11·7 7·3 | 17·7 11·1 |
| 58 | 9 29·5 | 9 31·1 | 9 03·6 | 5·8 3·6 | 11·8 7·4 | 17·8 11·1 |
| 59 | 9 29·8 | 9 31·3 | 9 03·8 | 5·9 3·7 | 11·9 7·4 | 17·9 11·2 |
| 60 | 9 30·0 | 9 31·6 | 9 04·0 | 6·0 3·8 | 12·0 7·5 | 18·0 11·3 |

*Figure 4–2.* Interpolation tables for GHA, from the *Nautical Almanac*

figure the size of the index error, or *index correction* (IC), move the index arm until the step or lap disappears. Then read the angle. The norm is a few minutes (2´, 3´, 4´). If these minutes are to the left of the zero mark, your sextant is measuring a positive angle when it should be measuring none (that is, the micrometer drum reads 2´, 3´, 4´, and so on), so you subtract those minutes from whatever the sextant reads. If these minutes are to the right of the zero mark, the sextant is reading a negative angle when it should be reading zero (the micrometer drum shows 58´ for an error of –2´, 57´ for –3´, 56´ for –4´, and so on); therefore you add those minutes to whatever altitude you measure. With plastic sextants, I have found this error changes from sight to sight. Index error is more stable in metal sextants, but it's good practice to check it anyway every time you take a sight.

The second factor that introduces an error of several minutes between the altitude the sextant measures and the true angle derives from your position relative to the horizon. When you take a sight, you stand or sit some distance above the horizon and are actually looking *down* at it, which *increases* the angle you measure. How much depends on how far above the surface of the water your eyes are; the addition is about 3 minutes (3´) for heights of eye between 9 and 12 feet. A table inside the front cover of the *Nautical Almanac* (fig. 4-3) presents the corrections for this phenomenon, called *dip*. Since dip increases the measured angle, it is subtracted from the sextant reading.

Two other factors that cause a mismeasurement of altitudes of the sun result from facets of the environment. When you set the edge of the sun on the horizon, you don't measure all the way to the GP, which is a *point* under the *center* of the solar disk; you measure to the edge of a small circle *around* the GP. Your sextant reading is shy of the one you want by one-half the diameter of the solar disk. Therefore, you have to add what is called the *semidiameter* of the sun. The size of the sun's disk varies a bit in the course of the year because the sun's distance from earth changes, but for practical purposes it is 16´. In any case, its actual value is printed at the bottom of the GHA columns. For the three days in June shown in figure 4-1, the exact semidiameter (SD) is 15.8´. Since measuring to the lower edge of the disk means you measure too small an angle, semidiameter is added to the sextant reading.

## ALTITUDE CORRECTION TABLES 10°–90°—SUN, STARS, PLANETS

| OCT.—MAR. SUN APR.—SEPT. | | | | | | STARS AND PLANETS | | | | DIP | | | | | |
|---|---|---|---|---|---|---|---|---|---|---|---|---|---|---|---|
| App. Alt. | Lower Limb | Upper Limb | App. Alt. | Lower Limb | Upper Limb | App. Alt. | Corrⁿ | App. Alt. | Additional Corrⁿ | Ht. of Eye | Corrⁿ | Ht. of Eye | Ht. of Eye | Corrⁿ | |

| ° ′ | ′ | ′ | ° ′ | ′ | ′ | ° ′ | ′ | | | m | | ft. | m | | ′ |
|---|---|---|---|---|---|---|---|---|---|---|---|---|---|---|---|
| 9 34 | +10·8 | −21·5 | 9 39 | +10·6 | −21·2 | 9 56 | −5·3 | **1999** | | 2·4 | −2·8 | 8·0 | 1·0 | − | 1·8 |
| 9 45 | +10·9 | −21·4 | 9 51 | +10·7 | −21·1 | 10 08 | −5·2 | **VENUS** | | 2·6 | −2·9 | 8·6 | 1·5 | − | 2·2 |
| 9 56 | +11·0 | −21·3 | 10 03 | +10·8 | −21·0 | 10 20 | −5·1 | Jan. 1–May 8 | | 2·8 | −3·0 | 9·2 | 2·0 | − | 2·5 |
| 10 08 | +11·1 | −21·2 | 10 15 | +10·9 | −20·9 | 10 33 | −5·0 | Dec. 9–Dec. 31 | | 3·0 | −3·1 | 9·8 | 2·5 | − | 2·8 |
| 10 21 | +11·2 | −21·1 | 10 27 | +11·0 | −20·8 | 10 46 | −4·9 | ° ′ | | 3·2 | −3·2 | 10·5 | 3·0 | − | 3·0 |
| 10 34 | +11·3 | −21·0 | 10 40 | +11·1 | −20·7 | 11 00 | −4·8 | 60 +0·1 | | 3·4 | −3·3 | 11·2 | | | |
| 10 47 | +11·4 | −20·9 | 10 54 | +11·2 | −20·6 | 11 14 | −4·7 | | | 3·6 | −3·4 | 11·9 | See table | | |
| 11 01 | +11·5 | −20·8 | 11 08 | +11·3 | −20·5 | 11 29 | −4·6 | May 9–June 26 | | 3·8 | −3·5 | 12·6 | ← | | |
| 11 15 | +11·6 | −20·7 | 11 23 | +11·4 | −20·4 | 11 45 | −4·5 | Oct. 18–Dec. 8 | | 4·0 | −3·6 | 13·3 | m | | ′ |
| 11 30 | +11·7 | −20·6 | 11 38 | +11·5 | −20·3 | 12 01 | −4·4 | ° ′ | | 4·3 | −3·7 | 14·1 | 20 | − | 7·9 |
| 11 46 | +11·8 | −20·5 | 11 54 | +11·6 | −20·2 | 12 18 | −4·3 | 41 +0·2 | | 4·5 | −3·8 | 14·9 | 22 | − | 8·3 |
| 12 02 | +11·9 | −20·4 | 12 10 | +11·7 | −20·1 | 12 35 | −4·2 | 76 +0·1 | | 4·7 | −3·9 | 15·7 | 24 | − | 8·6 |
| 12 19 | +12·0 | −20·3 | 12 28 | +11·8 | −20·0 | 12 54 | −4·1 | June 27–July 19 | | 5·0 | −4·0 | 16·5 | 26 | − | 9·0 |
| 12 37 | +12·1 | −20·2 | 12 46 | +11·9 | −19·9 | 13 13 | −4·0 | Sept. 24–Oct. 17 | | 5·2 | −4·1 | 17·4 | 28 | − | 9·3 |
| 12 55 | +12·2 | −20·1 | 13 05 | +12·0 | −19·8 | 13 33 | −3·9 | ° ′ | | 5·5 | −4·2 | 18·3 | | | |
| 13 14 | +12·3 | −20·0 | 13 24 | +12·1 | −19·7 | 13 54 | −3·8 | 34 +0·3 | | 5·8 | −4·3 | 19·1 | 30 | − | 9·6 |
| 13 35 | +12·4 | −19·9 | 13 45 | +12·2 | −19·6 | 14 16 | −3·7 | 60 +0·2 | | 6·1 | −4·4 | 20·1 | 32 | −10·0 | |
| 13 56 | +12·5 | −19·8 | 14 07 | +12·3 | −19·5 | 14 40 | −3·6 | 80 +0·1 | | 6·3 | −4·5 | 21·0 | 34 | −10·3 | |
| 14 18 | +12·6 | −19·7 | 14 30 | +12·4 | −19·4 | 15 04 | −3·5 | July 20–Aug. 4 | | 6·6 | −4·6 | 22·0 | 36 | −10·6 | |
| 14 42 | +12·7 | −19·6 | 14 54 | +12·5 | −19·3 | 15 30 | −3·4 | Sept. 7–Sept. 23 | | 6·9 | −4·7 | 22·9 | 38 | −10·8 | |
| 15 06 | +12·8 | −19·5 | 15 19 | +12·6 | −19·2 | 15 57 | −3·3 | ° ′ | | 7·2 | −4·8 | 23·9 | | | |
| 15 32 | +12·9 | −19·4 | 15 46 | +12·7 | −19·1 | 16 26 | −3·2 | 29 +0·4 | | 7·5 | −4·9 | 24·9 | 40 | −11·1 | |
| 15 59 | +13·0 | −19·3 | 16 14 | +12·8 | −19·0 | 16 56 | −3·1 | 51 +0·3 | | 7·9 | −5·0 | 26·0 | 42 | −11·4 | |
| 16 28 | +13·1 | −19·2 | 16 44 | +12·9 | −18·9 | 17 28 | −3·0 | 68 +0·2 | | 8·2 | −5·1 | 27·1 | 44 | −11·7 | |
| 16 59 | +13·2 | −19·1 | 17 15 | +13·0 | −18·8 | 18 02 | −2·9 | 83 +0·1 | | 8·5 | −5·2 | 28·1 | 46 | −11·9 | |
| 17 32 | +13·3 | −19·0 | 17 48 | +13·1 | −18·7 | 18 38 | −2·8 | Aug. 5–Sept. 6 | | 8·8 | −5·3 | 29·2 | 48 | −12·2 | |
| 18 06 | +13·4 | −18·9 | 18 24 | +13·2 | −18·6 | 19 17 | −2·7 | ° ′ | | 9·2 | −5·4 | 30·4 | ft. | | |
| 18 42 | +13·5 | −18·8 | 19 01 | +13·3 | −18·5 | 19 58 | −2·6 | 26 +0·5 | | 9·5 | −5·5 | 31·5 | 2 | − | 1·4 |
| 19 21 | +13·6 | −18·7 | 19 42 | +13·4 | −18·4 | 20 42 | −2·5 | 46 +0·4 | | 9·9 | −5·6 | 32·7 | 4 | − | 1·9 |
| 20 03 | +13·7 | −18·6 | 20 25 | +13·5 | −18·3 | 21 28 | −2·4 | 60 +0·3 | | 10·3 | −5·7 | 33·9 | 6 | − | 2·4 |
| 20 48 | +13·8 | −18·5 | 21 11 | +13·6 | −18·2 | 22 19 | −2·3 | 73 +0·2 | | 10·6 | −5·8 | 35·1 | 8 | − | 2·7 |
| 21 35 | +13·9 | −18·4 | 22 00 | +13·7 | −18·1 | 23 13 | −2·2 | 84 +0·1 | | 11·0 | −5·9 | 36·3 | 10 | − | 3·1 |
| 22 26 | +14·0 | −18·3 | 22 54 | +13·8 | −18·0 | 24 11 | −2·1 | **MARS** | | 11·4 | −6·0 | 37·6 | See table | | |
| 23 22 | +14·1 | −18·2 | 23 51 | +13·9 | −17·9 | 25 14 | −2·0 | Jan. 1–Feb. 21 | | 11·8 | −6·1 | 38·9 | ← | | |
| 24 21 | +14·2 | −18·1 | 24 53 | +14·0 | −17·8 | 26 22 | −1·9 | July 28–Dec. 31 | | 12·2 | −6·2 | 40·1 | ft. | | |
| 25 26 | +14·3 | −18·0 | 26 00 | +14·1 | −17·7 | 27 36 | −1·8 | ° ′ | | 12·6 | −6·3 | 41·5 | 70 | − | 8·1 |
| 26 36 | +14·4 | −17·9 | 27 13 | +14·2 | −17·6 | 28 56 | −1·7 | 60 +0·1 | | 13·0 | −6·4 | 42·8 | 75 | − | 8·4 |
| 27 52 | +14·5 | −17·8 | 28 33 | +14·3 | −17·5 | 30 24 | −1·6 | | | 13·4 | −6·5 | 44·2 | 80 | − | 8·7 |
| 29 15 | +14·6 | −17·7 | 30 00 | +14·4 | −17·4 | 32 00 | −1·5 | Feb. 22–Apr. 22 | | 13·8 | −6·6 | 45·5 | 85 | − | 8·9 |
| 30 46 | +14·7 | −17·6 | 31 35 | +14·5 | −17·3 | 33 45 | −1·4 | May 11–July 27 | | 14·2 | −6·7 | 46·9 | 90 | − | 9·2 |
| 32 26 | +14·8 | −17·5 | 33 20 | +14·6 | −17·2 | 35 40 | −1·3 | ° ′ | | 14·7 | −6·8 | 48·4 | 95 | − | 9·5 |
| 34 17 | +14·9 | −17·4 | 35 17 | +14·7 | −17·1 | 37 48 | −1·2 | 41 +0·2 | | 15·1 | −6·9 | 49·8 | | | |
| 36 20 | +15·0 | −17·3 | 37 26 | +14·8 | −17·0 | 40 08 | −1·1 | 76 +0·1 | | 15·5 | −7·0 | 51·3 | 100 | − | 9·7 |
| 38 36 | +15·1 | −17·2 | 39 50 | +14·9 | −16·9 | 42 44 | −1·0 | | | 16·0 | −7·1 | 52·8 | 105 | − | 9·9 |
| 41 08 | +15·2 | −17·1 | 42 31 | +15·0 | −16·8 | 45 36 | −0·9 | Apr. 23–May 10 | | 16·5 | −7·2 | 54·3 | 110 | −10·2 | |
| 43 59 | +15·3 | −17·0 | 45 31 | +15·1 | −16·7 | 48 47 | −0·8 | ° ′ | | 16·9 | −7·3 | 55·8 | 115 | −10·4 | |
| 47 10 | +15·4 | −16·9 | 48 55 | +15·2 | −16·6 | 52 18 | −0·7 | 34 +0·3 | | 17·4 | −7·4 | 57·4 | 120 | −10·6 | |
| 50 46 | +15·5 | −16·8 | 52 44 | +15·3 | −16·5 | 56 11 | −0·6 | 60 +0·2 | | 17·9 | −7·5 | 58·9 | 125 | −10·8 | |
| 54 49 | +15·6 | −16·7 | 57 02 | +15·4 | −16·4 | 60 28 | −0·5 | 80 +0·1 | | 18·4 | −7·6 | 60·5 | | | |
| 59 23 | +15·7 | −16·6 | 61 51 | +15·5 | −16·3 | 65 08 | −0·4 | | | 18·8 | −7·7 | 62·1 | 130 | −11·1 | |
| 64 30 | +15·8 | −16·5 | 67 17 | +15·6 | −16·2 | 70 11 | −0·3 | | | 19·3 | −7·8 | 63·8 | 135 | −11·3 | |
| 70 12 | +15·9 | −16·4 | 73 16 | +15·7 | −16·1 | 75 34 | −0·2 | | | 19·8 | −7·9 | 65·4 | 140 | −11·5 | |
| 76 26 | +16·0 | −16·3 | 79 43 | +15·8 | −16·0 | 81 13 | −0·1 | | | 20·4 | −8·0 | 67·1 | 145 | −11·7 | |
| 83 05 | +16·1 | −16·2 | 86 32 | +15·9 | −15·9 | 87 03 | 0·0 | | | 20·9 | −8·1 | 68·8 | 150 | −11·9 | |
| 90 00 | | | 90 00 | | | 90 00 | | | | 21·4 | | 70·5 | 155 | −12·1 | |

App. Alt. = Apparent altitude = Sextant altitude corrected for index error and dip.

*Figure 4–3.* Altitude correction tables, from the *Nautical Almanac*

The final sextant correction factor arises from the properties of air and light. Light rays bend as they pass through air, making the sun appear higher in the sky than it is in fact. The more air a ray passes through, the more pronounced the bending, or *refraction.* At altitudes above 65° there is no refraction for practical purposes. The lower the altitude, the greater the refraction. At 0° altitude refraction amounts to 35´, which is greater than the diameter of the sun. Thus, at sunset, even though you see the sun squashed on the horizon like a red-hot tomato, it is actually below the edge of the earth.

The *Nautical Almanac* combines refraction and the semidiameter of the sun into one correction in a table printed in two parts on the inside of the front cover. The right-hand part of the table is for altitudes from 0° to 10° (not shown), the left for the rest—in practice, the normal range of altitudes (fig. 4-3). Note that this section is further divided into two parts, the columns on the left for the months October through March, when the sun is closest to the earth and its disk appears larger, and those on the right for April through September, when the sun is farther away and its semidiameter is a few tenths of a minute smaller.

The left half of the refraction/semidiameter table and the dip table are what are called *critical-type,* which simply means that the values of refraction/semidiameter and dip are valid for a range of altitudes and eye heights, respectively. For example, dip is –3.0´ for heights-of-eye from 9.2 feet *through* 9.8 feet (or 2.8 meters *through* 3.0 meters), and the combined refraction/semidiameter correction from April through September is +14.3´ for altitudes of the lower limb (edge) of the sun from 28°33´ through 30°00´. The more lightly printed number to the right of +14.3´ (–17.5´) is the combined correction if you need a sight of the sun when its lower edge is in a cloudbank. You bring the upper limb (edge) to the horizon; now the semidiameter has to be subtracted because you've measured too large an angle. Therefore, the correction is negative.

By now it should be perfectly obvious that the practice of celestial navigation involves keeping track of a lot of tiny bits of information. That, naturally, suggests you need a work sheet. Celestial navigation is no exception to the rule that the hardest part of any job is the paperwork.

Figure 4-4 is such a work sheet. I have taken a hypothetical sextant sight of 29°36´ and filled out the sheet on the basis of what

Date: 6-19-99

| | | | |
|---|---|---|---|
| Sextant Reads | [Hs] | | 29° 36′ |
| Index Corr. | [IC] | | + 04′ |
| Dip Corr. | [C] | | − 03′ |
| Apparent Alt. | [Ha] | | 29° 37′ |
| Ref/SD | | | + 14.3′ |
| Observed Alt. | [Ho] | | 29° 51.3′ |

| | | | |
|---|---|---|---|
| GHA   1800 UT | 89° 40.5′ | Dec. | N 23° 25.4′ |
| + 36m − 49s | 9° 12.3′ | | |
| GHA  18-36-49 | 98° 52.8′ | Dec. | N 23° 25.4′ |

*Figure 4–4.* Work sheet for finding the GHA and declination of the GP

has been covered in this chapter, using the conventional terms and abbreviations. The two key points to remember are: Your sextant measures your distance from the GP; and the *Nautical Almanac* tells you where the GP is at the moment your sextant measures that distance.

# 5

# Celestial Navigation in Practice

If the previous chapter roused the experimental scientist in you, and you actually found a chart and pushed a pin into the Gulf of Mexico at the GP, you know firsthand why direct application of the so-simple principle of celestial navigation won't work—you need a very long string, and the string stretches!

A normal working scale for celestial navigation in small boats is 1 nautical mile to about 1 millimeter. At this scale, if your observed altitude is 60°, the GP is 30 great-circle degrees, or 1,800 nautical miles, away—that distance requires 6 feet of string! A sight of 30° makes the GP 3,600 miles away and requires 12 feet of string— clearly impossible in any small craft. These very practical difficulties with scale and strings are why celestial navigators had to develop another approach, and about one hundred and fifty years ago, they did.

They approached the problem from the other direction. Instead of thinking *outward* from a GP far away across the globe, they thought *toward* the GP from their patch of ocean. Since the dead-reckoning position was the closest known point in their stretch of sea, they asked, How far is the DR from the GP? Stated another way, the question became, What is the great-circle distance from the DR to the GP?

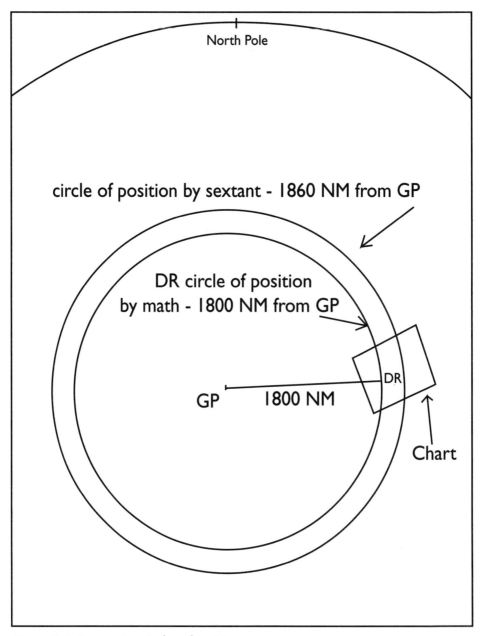

*Figure 5–1.* Comparing circles of position

Of course, mariners have known for hundreds of years how to use mathematics to find the great-circle distance between any two points on the surface of the earth. The new element is this: If navigators know how far the DR is from the GP and also know from their sextants how far *they* are from the GP, they can use the DR as the starting point from which to lay out the rim of the particular circle around the GP on which they are. The problem then becomes simply a matter of comparing the two distances and marking off the difference between them. The GP does not have to be on the chart at all. Navigators can work from the chart that covers the patch of water where they actually are. The problems of scale and string vanish. The DR becomes a signpost in the sea, a benchmark in the brine.

Imagine, for example, that computation shows your DR to be 1,800 nautical miles from the GP of the sun at the time you take a sight and that your observed altitude is 59°. Subtracting 59° from 90° gives a great-circle distance of 31° between you and the GP—1,860 nautical miles. The math says the DR is on the rim of a circle 1,800 miles from the GP. Your sextant has you on the rim of a circle 1,860 miles from the GP (fig. 5-1). Relative to the DR, therefore, you are 60 nautical miles *farther away* from the GP and can use the DR to lay out the circle on which your sextant measurement places you. You don't need to plot the GP at all, because you can locate yourself relative to the DR. And since you don't need the GP on the chart, you can work to any scale you find convenient.

That's the principle: The sextant tells how far you are from the GP; mathematics determines how far the DR is from the GP; you compare the two distances and use the DR to locate the arc you are on. As with the first so-simple principle of celestial navigation, however, applying this one also presents practical difficulties.

For instance, how do you orient the arcs? Are they horizontal, vertical, at a slant? How much of a slant?

Obviously what you need is the *bearing* —the so-called initial great-circle course—to the GP. It should come as no surprise to learn that math can supply the direction as well as the distance to the GP. The bearing—that is, the true, not magnetic, direction—from the DR to the GP is found by formula and conventionally marked on the chart as an arrow. In effect, the arrow is a little piece of the great-circle radius from the GP.

There remains the problem of drawing the arcs with the proper amount of bend. If you can come up with a way to do this, ad hoc and quickly while aboard a boat, go to the head of the class. No one before you has managed it. Instead, for nearly two centuries navigators have substituted straight lines—tangents to the edges of the circles, really—for the arcs themselves (fig. 5-2). The lines introduce an inaccuracy, but it is generally small, because, as you have seen, the circles around the GPs usually have enormous radii, so their rims

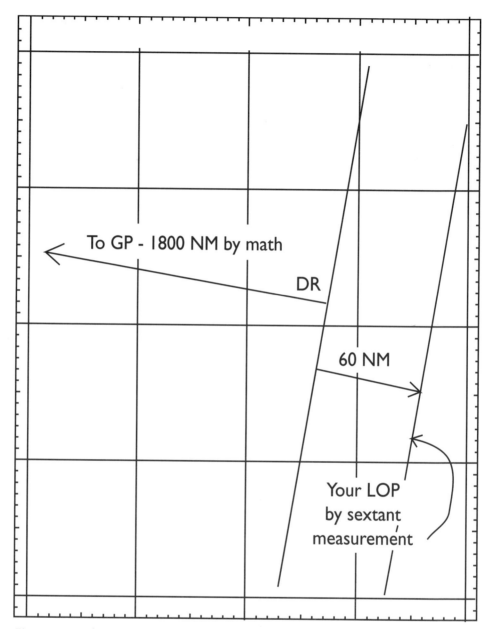

*Figure 5–2*. Substituting tangents for arcs

are very, very shallow arcs. Like the assumption that the GHA changes at precisely 15° per hour, the substitution of straight lines for arcs is done for practical reasons and is one of the many elements that makes celestial navigation an art of useful approximations, not an exact science.

In the few years I taught celestial navigation I found that the main difficulty people had in accepting the DR as a starting point is the tendency to think of the DR as rather nebulous and uncertain. It is not. The DR is a specific point on the surface of the earth. You can mark it on a chart and specify its latitude and longitude to any level of exactitude you like. As such, it can be used as the starting point for any great circle to any other place on earth. What is nebulous and uncertain when you are at sea is *your* location. It's somewhere near the DR, but you can never put a pencil point on it until you arrive at your destination (or hit a charted rock).

The great-circle bearing and the distance between two points on earth are calculated by means of two long mathematical formulas, which for more than a century navigators solved with pencil, paper, and tables of logarithms (talk about *tedious!*). On sailing ships and even steamers, there is time for this sort of plodding plotting, but with the advent of trans-oceanic aircraft a faster method of arriving at these values had to be found.

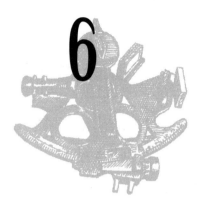

# 6

# More Columns of Numbers

To simplify the calculations needed to determine the great-circle bearing and distance between two points on earth, navigators stopped using DRs as reference points in favor of a much smaller number of special, selected points called *assumed positions,* or APs. With fewer reference points, it became possible for computers to presolve the formulas for all the possible AP–GP bearings and to compile these precomputed solutions in published *sight reduction tables* (yes, more columns of numbers). With these tables, navigators discovered that if they used an AP instead of a DR, they no longer had to grind away with logarithms to find great-circle courses and distances; they could simply look them up.

If you imagine there was a stampede to the assumed-position method, you are quite right. The older method lives on, and the formulas, which are given in the back of the *Nautical Almanac,* can be solved with a basic scientific calculator, but that turns out to be almost as tedious as working with logarithms.

To understand the AP method and to use celestial navigation intelligently, you need to know something of how the formulas for great-circle course and distance work. Basically, the formulas need three pieces of information: latitude of the benchmark, latitude of the

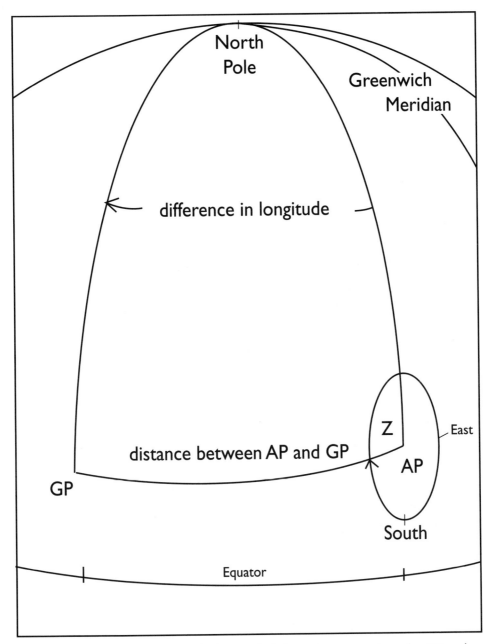

*Figure 6–1.* Spherical triangle with the North Pole as the apex, where the GP and AP are in the same hemispheres

GP, and the difference in longitude between the benchmark and GP.

What the formulas do with this data is solve an enormous *spherical triangle* whose points are a pole of the earth, a GP, and a benchmark. Which pole is used depends on whether the benchmark is in the northern or southern hemisphere. Figure 6-1 shows one such triangle drawn with the North Pole as the apex. The sides of the triangle are the two longitudes, the meridian of the benchmark and the meridian of the GP. The angle at the pole is the difference between the longitudes of the GP and the benchmark. The base of the triangle is one of the two values a navigator wants to know, the great-circle distance between the benchmark and the GP. The other—the direction to the GP—is the angle at the benchmark's point labeled Z.

If you use DRs as benchmarks, the formulas produce an almost infinite number of solutions, because each 1´ change in latitude or longitude at that point of the triangle makes a new triangle and produces a new great-circle distance and direction when plugged into the equations. Therefore, if you use DRs, you have to solve each triangle as it occurs, which is what navigators did for a long time.

The AP method, however, curtails the number of reference points by allowing the benchmarks to be located only on exact, whole degrees of latitude *and* at an exact integral number of degrees from the GP in longitude. In essence, this means the three variables in the formulas are changed in 1° leaps, not tiny, 1´ steps. Leaping by degrees still allows a lot of APs—there's always one within 30´ or so of any DR—but their number is vastly fewer (so many fewer that all the possible AP–GP distances and bearings to the sun for the entire earth fit onto the 600 printed pages of a sight reduction table).

With the AP method, therefore, after you take your sight, the procedure is to find the AP that is closest to your DR, look in the sight reduction table for the distance and bearing from that AP to the sun, and compare the distances and lay down the tangent line using the AP as your point of reference rather than the DR.

Figure 6-2 is a sketch using an AP to locate the tangent to the circle of position, given the same situation as shown previously in figure 5-2, where the sextant-measured distance is 31°, or 1,860 nautical miles. Assume that calculation shows this AP to be 1,820 nautical miles from the GP. Instead of being 60 miles from the DR, you are 40 miles from the AP. But you still end up on the same line.

Although the AP is a different distance from the GP, the line representing the edge of the circle on which you must be—the *line of position*, or LOP—is the same. It has to be. You are there. You are that distance from the GP and on that line by actual measurement with your sextant, so whatever reference point you choose to use, be it DR or AP, has to put you that distance from the GP and, therefore, produce that line. Your measured distance from the sun can't

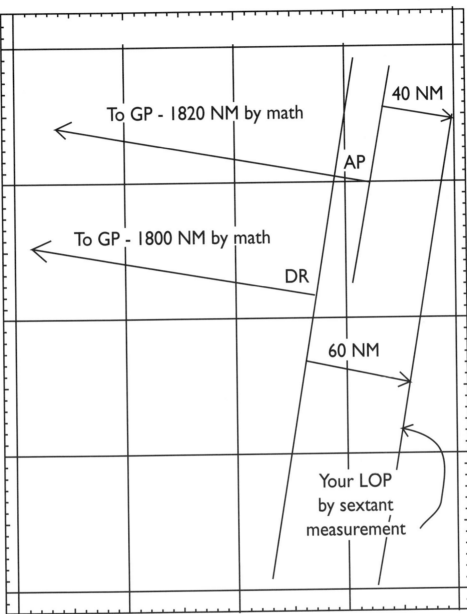

*Figure 6–2.* Using the AP to locate the tangent to the circle of position

change, so what does change with a change of reference point is the distance from the point to you, or more correctly speaking, the string of points you could be on, the LOP. Notice also that the direction—that is, the bearing—from the AP to the GP is essentially the same, as the parallel arrows in the sketch indicate. As you practice celestial, you'll find that because the GP is so far away, it takes a big change of position to produce a 1° change in the bearing to the sun.

You may be annoyed about now by the constant converting of sextant altitudes to great-circle distances. You are not alone, and the table-makers have responded, programming their computers to convert the great-circle distances back to degrees and minutes and subtract them from 90° to produce a table of precomputed sextant *altitudes* rather than great-circle distances. That way you, the navigator, can directly compare your observed altitude with the one in the table instead of horsing around with more arithmetic.

For example, in figure 5-2, if you were told a sextant on the arc through the DR measures an angle of 60°, that indicates what circle you are on just as surely as learning the circle through the DR is 1,800 miles from the GP. You would then compare your observed altitude of 59° and correctly deduce that you must be on the rim of a circle 1°, or 60 nautical miles, farther away from the GP than the one through the DR. Similarly, if you were told that by calculation a sextant at the AP measures 59°40´, that is the same as telling you the AP is 1,820 nautical miles from the GP. But given an altitude for the benchmark instead of a distance, you can immediately compare your observed altitude of 59° to it and see that you must be 40´ farther from the GP of the sun than the AP is, because that's the only way you can measure a smaller angle. That 40´ difference between the altitude calculated for the AP and the altitude you measure is 40 nautical miles. Moreover, it is away from the sun relative to the benchmark AP, so again you end up with the same LOP.

And that's the way celestial navigation works in practice. You don't compare great-circle distances, you compare altitudes. You compare your observed altitude to one precomputed for an assumed position and then printed in a table, and you use the *difference* in the altitudes to lay off an LOP. If the altitude at the AP is larger than the one you measure with your sextant, you are farther from the sun than the AP is, and vice versa. Look back to figure 3-1. If you move toward the GP by 1°, the great-circle distance *decreases* by 1° and the altitude of the sun *increases* 1°. Move away 1° or 1´, and the great-circle distance *increases* 1° or 1´ and the altitude *decreases*. A catch-phrase can help you remember this relationship: Computed Greater, Away. In other words, if the altitude in the table is greater than the one you observe, then, relative to the assumed benchmark, you are farther away from the GP of the sun (and vice versa).

So much for the infrastructure. Now move on to the hard part, the paperwork.

Date: 6-19-99                    DR:    41°12´ N
                                        28°42´ W

| Sextant reads | [Hs] | 29°36´ |
|---|---|---|
| Index corr. | [IC] | + 04´ |
| Dip corr. | [D] | – 03´ |
| Apparent alt. | [Ha] | 29°37´ |
| Ref/SD | | + 14.3´ |
| Observed alt. | [Ho] | 29°51.3´ |

GHA  1800 UT   89°40.5´   Dec.  N 23°25.4´

+ 36m, 49s        9°12.3´

**GHA** 18-36-49   98°52.8´   Dec.  N 23°25.4´

*Figure 6–3.* Work sheet for finding the GHA and declination of the GP, with DR coordinates added

As an example, again assume it is June 19, 1999. You are in the eastern Atlantic not far from the Azores at a DR position of 41°12´ N, 28°42´ W. Figure 6-3 is a reprise of the work sheet from chapter 4, with the DR added. The final, observed altitude (Ho) after corrections and compensations is 29°51.3´. The Greenwich hour angle for the time of the sight is 98°52.8´, and declination is 23°25.4´ N.

Before starting your calculations, round these numbers to the nearest minute, the usual working precision for practical celestial navigation, so that Ho is 29°51´; GHA, 98°53´; and declination, 23°25´ N.

Remember that the three variables in the spherical triangle formulas are the latitude of the benchmark, the latitude of the GP, and the difference in longitude between the benchmark and GP. These are the same pieces of data you need to use the AP sight reduction table, but the numerical part of each piece has to be a whole number of degrees, with no dangling minutes.

First compute the latitude of the AP. That's easy. The DR is 41°12′ N, so locating the AP on 41° exactly satisfies that requirement.

Finding the longitude of the AP is a little trickier, but look at figure 6-1 again to see what you need to do. The GHA of the sun is 98°53′, or 98°53′ W longitude—the left side of the triangle. The AP's longitude is the right side of the triangle. If you make the longitude of the AP 28°53′ W, the minutes subtract away and leave a difference of exactly 70°.

Now you have a benchmark or an assumed position, AP, whose coordinates are 41°00′ N, 28°53′ W. This is the point for which the sight reduction table provides you a *computed altitude* (Hc) to compare with the one you observed.

The latitude of the GP is the same as the sun's declination: 23°25′ N. For the sake of the table, round to 23° N.

Figure 6-4 is the work form with the new data added. At this point notice that the line you would expect to be called *difference in longitude* is instead labeled LHA. Remember that to astronomers longitude is hour angle; the difference in longitude is thus termed *local hour angle,* or LHA.

Also notice the two rows at the bottom available for writing down both the data you need *for* the sight reduction table and the data you get *from* it. The data you need to use the table are: latitude of the AP, 41° N; declination of the sun (latitude of the GP), 23° N; and LHA (difference in longitude between AP and GP), 70°.

With those three scraps of information you are now ready to use the sight reduction table. There are two currently being printed by the United States Defense Mapping Agency, the most compact being Publication No. 249, *Sight Reduction Tables for Air Navigation,* more commonly called *HO 249*. The tables are divided into three 8 ¹/₂ by 11-inch volumes of about 300 pages each. The spine of Volume 1 is red; of Volume 2, white; of Volume 3, blue. To navigate by the sun you need only volumes 2 and 3 (white and blue spines). Since sight reduction tables contain precomputed solutions of eternal triangles, unlike the almanac they don't go out of date. They also work when wet, when dropped, and without batteries.

Date: 6-19-99                    DR:    41°12′ N
                                        28°42′ W

| | | |
|---|---|---|
| Sextant reads | [Hs] | 29°36′ |
| Index corr. | [IC] | + 04′ |
| Dip corr. | [D] | – 03′ |
| Apparent alt. | [Ha] | 29°37′ |
| Ref/SD | | + 14.3′ |
| Observed alt. | [Ho] | 29°51.3′ |

| | | | |
|---|---|---|---|
| GHA   1800 UT | 89°40.5′ | Dec. | N 23°25.4′ |
| + 36m, 49s | 9°12.3′ | | |
| **GHA**  18-36-49 | 98°52.8′ | Dec. | N 23°25.4′ |

| | | | |
|---|---|---|---|
| **GHA**  18-36-49 | 98°53′ | Dec. | N 23°25′ |
| AP longitude | – 28°53′ W | AP latitude = 41° N | |
| **LHA** | 70°00′ | | |

Data for HO 249:   lat. = 41° (Same / Contr) | LHA = 70°   Dec. = 23°

Data from HO 249: Hc =    d = $^+_-$ | Z =

*Figure 6–4.* Work sheet for entering the sight reduction tables to find the computed altitude (Hc) of the AP

To use the tables you need to find the correct page. For the example, first find the volume with information for latitude 41°. It's Volume 3 (blue spine). There are six pages of data for every degree of latitude, so now thumb through till you find the cluster for 41°, pages 14 through 19.

Now you need to pick the correct page out of the six. For declination 23°, it's page 18 (fig. 6-5). Notice that the heading LAT 41° in the upper right corner is not accompanied by any designation for hemisphere, N or S. That's because which hemisphere the AP is in is not important; what is important is whether the AP and GP are in hemispheres of the *same* name (both north or both south) or of *contrary* name (one north, the other south). You can stand a spherical triangle

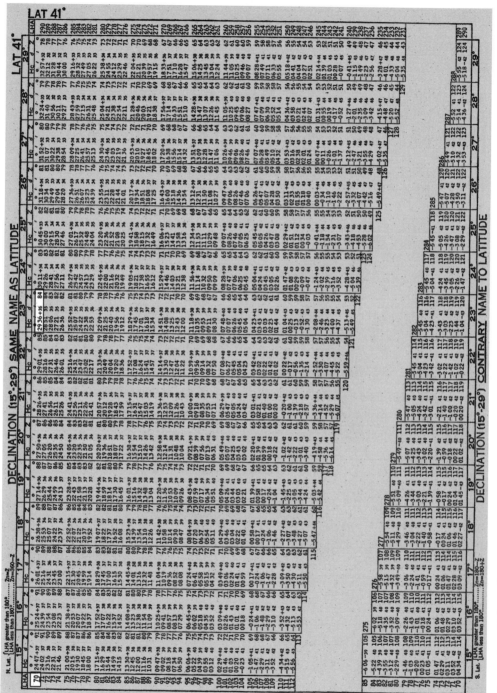

Figure 6–5. Sight reduction page for latitude 41°, from *HO 249*

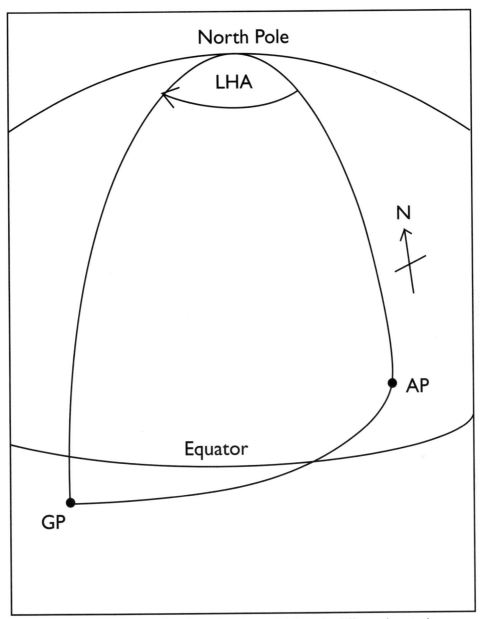

*Figure 6–6.* Spherical triangle where the GP and AP are in different hemispheres, so declination is contrary to latitude

like the one in figure 6-1 on its head, labeling the apex as the South Pole, and nothing changes in the mathematical solution; the angles and the sides remain the same. If the GP is across the equator from the AP, however, you have a different triangle (fig. 6-6).

In the example, declination is north and so is the latitude of the AP, so it falls under the heading "Declination (15°–29°) **Same** Name as Latitude." Notice that the word *same* is printed in boldface and underlined to indicate its importance.

The pages with solutions for the cross-equator triangles are headed "Declination (15°–29°) **Contrary** Name to Latitude"; the beginning of one starts at the bottom of figure 6-5. The word *latitude* in the headings refers, of course, to the latitude of the AP.

At this point you're on the correct page: latitude 41° and same name as the declination, 23°, both north. The third piece of information you need to enter the table is the difference in longitude, or local hour angle.

LHA is found in the column on the left margin; your LHA of 70° happens to be the first entry. Follow across this top row until you reach the column for declination 23°. Write down on the work form *all* the numbers you find at this cell in the table: 29°36´, +35´, and 84°. Obviously, these are the data *from* the table. You put in three numbers and you got out three. Fair enough.

The first number, 29°36´, is called the computed altitude and abbreviated in the table and on the work sheet Hc. This is the altitude that would have been observed from the AP at the time you took your sight had there been a navigator at the AP to take it. Comparing it to your sight of 29°51´, you can tell you must be 15´, or 15 nautical miles, closer to the sun, relative to the benchmark AP, because your observed altitude is 15´ larger than the computed one. You also know something else; you and the AP are in the same general vicinity.

You will find as you do more celestial that when you are using the AP method the difference in altitudes doesn't tell you an awful lot right away. Because an AP can be as much as 30´ of latitude or longitude from the DR, you need to plot the difference, called the *intercept,* on a chart before you can see how the resulting LOP squares up with the DR. However, it's always comforting to know when you get to this stage that you haven't fouled up in some major way and put yourself into the next ocean, so an altitude from the table that looks similar to the one from your sextant tends to be soothing to the spirit.

The second of the three numbers from the table, +35´, is the amount the altitude as observed from the AP changes as a result of a 1° change in the declination. Remember that the actual declination for the time of your sight is 23°25´. But the example is working the solution for a triangle whose declination corner is at 23° N, precisely.

Refer again to the table, reading across at 70° LHA and down from 24° declination. The computed altitude is 30°11´. That's what the altitude at the AP would be if the declination were 24° precisely. Your actual declination is about halfway between the two columns in the table, so the actual altitude at the AP is about halfway between 29°36´ and 30°11´. The difference between them is 35´; it's shown in the table to help you interpolate between the columns. And yes, there's a table for this calculation (fig. 6-7).

Actually, you can just about do this one by eye. The 25´ of additional declination in the example is just about half a degree, so if the altitude increases 35´ with a 1° change of declination, you should add about half of 35´, or 17´, to 29°36´. That makes the altitude at the AP 29°53´, just 2´ greater than your sight from the vicinity of the DR. Of course, to work to the normal precision of celestial you should multiply 35´ by 25/60, which is what the table in figure 6-7 does. I call this a crisscross table because it doesn't matter which way you enter it. Just find 25 on one edge and 35 on the other; where they intersect, 15, is the number of minutes to apply to the computed altitude you extract from the table. By this calculation, the final Hc for the AP is 29°51´, which means you are a bit closer to the GP of the sun than the eyeball interpolation had you and exactly on the LOP through the AP, since, for all practical purposes, your observed altitude and the computed altitude are the same.

The third number from the sight reduction table, 84°, is the one labeled Z in figure 6-1. Essentially this value tells the direction to the GP, but as it stands it is not a true bearing (termed Zn) because bearings are reckoned *clockwise* from north. If you look again at figure 6-1 and recall that while the GP is in the Gulf of Mexico you're in the Atlantic, you'll see that the bearing to the GP must be close to west; a true bearing of 84° is pretty much east. If you study the figure, you'll see that to get the bearing you have to subtract 84° from the direction the meridian runs (north, or 360°), so the true bearing is 276°, pretty much west, as common sense suggested.

Figure 6-8 is the work sheet completely filled out, and figure 6-9 is a sketch to help you visualize the results of all this labor. As you see, the LOP agrees quite well with the DR, something that makes all navigators everywhere smile and breathe easier.

The next chapter covers the third number from the sight reduction table in more detail, discusses what happens when the sun is to your

TABLE 5.—Correction to Tabulated Altitude for Minutes of Declination

| d / ′ | 1 | 2 | 3 | 4 | 5 | 6 | 7 | 8 | 9 | 10 | 11 | 12 | 13 | 14 | 15 | 16 | 17 | 18 | 19 | 20 | 21 | 22 | 23 | 24 | 25 | 26 | 27 | 28 | 29 | 30 | 31 | 32 | 33 | 34 | 35 | 36 | 37 | 38 | 39 | 40 | 41 | 42 | 43 | 44 | 45 | 46 | 47 | 48 | 49 | 50 | 51 | 52 | 53 | 54 | 55 | 56 | 57 | 58 | 59 | 60 | d / ′ |
|---|---|---|---|---|---|---|---|---|---|---|---|---|---|---|---|---|---|---|---|---|---|---|---|---|---|---|---|---|---|---|---|---|---|---|---|---|---|---|---|---|---|---|---|---|---|---|---|---|---|---|---|---|---|---|---|---|---|---|---|---|---|
| 0 | 0 | 0 | 0 | 0 | 0 | 0 | 0 | 0 | 0 | 0 | 0 | 0 | 0 | 0 | 0 | 0 | 0 | 0 | 0 | 0 | 0 | 0 | 0 | 0 | 0 | 0 | 0 | 0 | 0 | 0 | 0 | 0 | 0 | 0 | 0 | 0 | 0 | 0 | 0 | 0 | 0 | 0 | 0 | 0 | 0 | 0 | 0 | 0 | 0 | 0 | 0 | 0 | 0 | 0 | 0 | 0 | 0 | 0 | 0 | 0 | 0 |
| 1 | 0 | 0 | 0 | 0 | 0 | 0 | 0 | 0 | 0 | 0 | 0 | 0 | 0 | 0 | 0 | 0 | 0 | 0 | 0 | 0 | 0 | 0 | 0 | 0 | 0 | 0 | 0 | 0 | 0 | 0 | 1 | 1 | 1 | 1 | 1 | 1 | 1 | 1 | 1 | 1 | 1 | 1 | 1 | 1 | 1 | 1 | 1 | 1 | 1 | 1 | 1 | 1 | 1 | 1 | 1 | 1 | 1 | 1 | 1 | 1 | 1 |
| 2 | 0 | 0 | 0 | 0 | 0 | 0 | 0 | 0 | 0 | 0 | 0 | 0 | 0 | 0 | 0 | 1 | 1 | 1 | 1 | 1 | 1 | 1 | 1 | 1 | 1 | 1 | 1 | 1 | 1 | 1 | 1 | 1 | 1 | 1 | 1 | 1 | 1 | 1 | 1 | 1 | 1 | 1 | 1 | 1 | 2 | 2 | 2 | 2 | 2 | 2 | 2 | 2 | 2 | 2 | 2 | 2 | 2 | 2 | 2 | 2 | 2 |
| 3 | 0 | 0 | 0 | 0 | 0 | 0 | 0 | 0 | 0 | 0 | 1 | 1 | 1 | 1 | 1 | 1 | 1 | 1 | 1 | 1 | 1 | 1 | 1 | 1 | 1 | 1 | 1 | 1 | 1 | 2 | 2 | 2 | 2 | 2 | 2 | 2 | 2 | 2 | 2 | 2 | 2 | 2 | 2 | 2 | 2 | 2 | 2 | 2 | 2 | 2 | 3 | 3 | 3 | 3 | 3 | 3 | 3 | 3 | 3 | 3 | 3 |
| 4 | 0 | 0 | 0 | 0 | 0 | 0 | 0 | 1 | 1 | 1 | 1 | 1 | 1 | 1 | 1 | 1 | 1 | 1 | 1 | 1 | 1 | 1 | 2 | 2 | 2 | 2 | 2 | 2 | 2 | 2 | 2 | 2 | 2 | 2 | 2 | 2 | 2 | 3 | 3 | 3 | 3 | 3 | 3 | 3 | 3 | 3 | 3 | 3 | 3 | 3 | 3 | 3 | 4 | 4 | 4 | 4 | 4 | 4 | 4 | 4 | 4 |
| 5 | 0 | 0 | 0 | 0 | 0 | 0 | 1 | 1 | 1 | 1 | 1 | 1 | 1 | 1 | 1 | 1 | 1 | 2 | 2 | 2 | 2 | 2 | 2 | 2 | 2 | 2 | 2 | 2 | 2 | 2 | 3 | 3 | 3 | 3 | 3 | 3 | 3 | 3 | 3 | 3 | 3 | 4 | 4 | 4 | 4 | 4 | 4 | 4 | 4 | 4 | 4 | 4 | 4 | 4 | 5 | 5 | 5 | 5 | 5 | 5 | 5 |
| 6 | 0 | 0 | 0 | 0 | 0 | 1 | 1 | 1 | 1 | 1 | 1 | 1 | 1 | 1 | 2 | 2 | 2 | 2 | 2 | 2 | 2 | 2 | 2 | 2 | 2 | 3 | 3 | 3 | 3 | 3 | 3 | 3 | 3 | 3 | 4 | 4 | 4 | 4 | 4 | 4 | 4 | 4 | 4 | 4 | 4 | 5 | 5 | 5 | 5 | 5 | 5 | 5 | 5 | 5 | 6 | 6 | 6 | 6 | 6 | 6 | 6 |
| 7 | 0 | 0 | 0 | 0 | 1 | 1 | 1 | 1 | 1 | 1 | 1 | 1 | 2 | 2 | 2 | 2 | 2 | 2 | 2 | 2 | 2 | 3 | 3 | 3 | 3 | 3 | 3 | 3 | 3 | 4 | 4 | 4 | 4 | 4 | 4 | 4 | 4 | 4 | 5 | 5 | 5 | 5 | 5 | 5 | 5 | 5 | 5 | 6 | 6 | 6 | 6 | 6 | 6 | 6 | 6 | 7 | 7 | 7 | 7 | 7 | 7 |
| 8 | 0 | 0 | 0 | 1 | 1 | 1 | 1 | 1 | 1 | 1 | 1 | 2 | 2 | 2 | 2 | 2 | 2 | 2 | 3 | 3 | 3 | 3 | 3 | 3 | 3 | 3 | 4 | 4 | 4 | 4 | 4 | 4 | 4 | 5 | 5 | 5 | 5 | 5 | 5 | 5 | 5 | 6 | 6 | 6 | 6 | 6 | 6 | 6 | 7 | 7 | 7 | 7 | 7 | 7 | 7 | 7 | 8 | 8 | 8 | 8 | 8 |
| 9 | 0 | 0 | 0 | 1 | 1 | 1 | 1 | 1 | 1 | 2 | 2 | 2 | 2 | 2 | 2 | 2 | 3 | 3 | 3 | 3 | 3 | 3 | 3 | 4 | 4 | 4 | 4 | 4 | 4 | 4 | 5 | 5 | 5 | 5 | 5 | 5 | 6 | 6 | 6 | 6 | 6 | 6 | 6 | 7 | 7 | 7 | 7 | 7 | 7 | 8 | 8 | 8 | 8 | 8 | 8 | 8 | 9 | 9 | 9 | 9 | 9 |
| 10 | 0 | 0 | 0 | 1 | 1 | 1 | 1 | 1 | 2 | 2 | 2 | 2 | 2 | 2 | 2 | 3 | 3 | 3 | 3 | 3 | 4 | 4 | 4 | 4 | 4 | 4 | 4 | 5 | 5 | 5 | 5 | 5 | 6 | 6 | 6 | 6 | 6 | 6 | 6 | 7 | 7 | 7 | 7 | 7 | 8 | 8 | 8 | 8 | 8 | 8 | 8 | 9 | 9 | 9 | 9 | 9 | 10 | 10 | 10 | 10 | 10 |
| 11 | 0 | 0 | 1 | 1 | 1 | 1 | 1 | 1 | 2 | 2 | 2 | 2 | 2 | 3 | 3 | 3 | 3 | 3 | 3 | 4 | 4 | 4 | 4 | 4 | 5 | 5 | 5 | 5 | 5 | 6 | 6 | 6 | 6 | 6 | 6 | 7 | 7 | 7 | 7 | 7 | 8 | 8 | 8 | 8 | 8 | 8 | 9 | 9 | 9 | 9 | 9 | 10 | 10 | 10 | 10 | 10 | 10 | 11 | 11 | 11 | 11 |
| 12 | 0 | 0 | 1 | 1 | 1 | 1 | 1 | 2 | 2 | 2 | 2 | 2 | 3 | 3 | 3 | 3 | 3 | 4 | 4 | 4 | 4 | 4 | 5 | 5 | 5 | 5 | 5 | 6 | 6 | 6 | 6 | 6 | 7 | 7 | 7 | 7 | 7 | 8 | 8 | 8 | 8 | 8 | 9 | 9 | 9 | 9 | 9 | 10 | 10 | 10 | 10 | 10 | 11 | 11 | 11 | 11 | 11 | 12 | 12 | 12 | 12 |
| 13 | 0 | 0 | 1 | 1 | 1 | 1 | 2 | 2 | 2 | 2 | 2 | 3 | 3 | 3 | 3 | 3 | 4 | 4 | 4 | 4 | 5 | 5 | 5 | 5 | 5 | 6 | 6 | 6 | 6 | 6 | 7 | 7 | 7 | 7 | 8 | 8 | 8 | 8 | 8 | 9 | 9 | 9 | 9 | 10 | 10 | 10 | 10 | 10 | 11 | 11 | 11 | 11 | 11 | 12 | 12 | 12 | 12 | 13 | 13 | 13 | 13 |
| 14 | 0 | 0 | 1 | 1 | 1 | 1 | 2 | 2 | 2 | 2 | 3 | 3 | 3 | 3 | 4 | 4 | 4 | 4 | 4 | 5 | 5 | 5 | 5 | 6 | 6 | 6 | 6 | 7 | 7 | 7 | 7 | 7 | 8 | 8 | 8 | 8 | 9 | 9 | 9 | 9 | 10 | 10 | 10 | 10 | 10 | 11 | 11 | 11 | 11 | 12 | 12 | 12 | 12 | 13 | 13 | 13 | 13 | 14 | 14 | 14 | 14 |
| 15 | 0 | 0 | 1 | 1 | 1 | 2 | 2 | 2 | 2 | 2 | 3 | 3 | 3 | 4 | 4 | 4 | 4 | 4 | 5 | 5 | 5 | 6 | 6 | 6 | 6 | 6 | 7 | 7 | 7 | 8 | 8 | 8 | 8 | 8 | 9 | 9 | 9 | 10 | 10 | 10 | 10 | 10 | 11 | 11 | 11 | 12 | 12 | 12 | 12 | 12 | 13 | 13 | 13 | 14 | 14 | 14 | 14 | 14 | 15 | 15 | 15 |
| 16 | 0 | 1 | 1 | 1 | 1 | 2 | 2 | 2 | 2 | 3 | 3 | 3 | 3 | 4 | 4 | 4 | 5 | 5 | 5 | 5 | 6 | 6 | 6 | 6 | 7 | 7 | 7 | 7 | 8 | 8 | 8 | 9 | 9 | 9 | 9 | 10 | 10 | 10 | 10 | 11 | 11 | 11 | 11 | 12 | 12 | 12 | 13 | 13 | 13 | 13 | 14 | 14 | 14 | 14 | 15 | 15 | 15 | 15 | 16 | 16 | 16 |
| 17 | 0 | 1 | 1 | 1 | 1 | 2 | 2 | 2 | 3 | 3 | 3 | 3 | 4 | 4 | 4 | 5 | 5 | 5 | 5 | 6 | 6 | 6 | 7 | 7 | 7 | 7 | 8 | 8 | 8 | 8 | 9 | 9 | 9 | 10 | 10 | 10 | 10 | 11 | 11 | 11 | 12 | 12 | 12 | 12 | 13 | 13 | 13 | 14 | 14 | 14 | 14 | 15 | 15 | 15 | 16 | 16 | 16 | 16 | 17 | 17 | 17 |
| 18 | 0 | 1 | 1 | 1 | 2 | 2 | 2 | 2 | 3 | 3 | 3 | 4 | 4 | 4 | 4 | 5 | 5 | 5 | 6 | 6 | 6 | 7 | 7 | 7 | 8 | 8 | 8 | 8 | 9 | 9 | 9 | 10 | 10 | 10 | 10 | 11 | 11 | 11 | 12 | 12 | 12 | 13 | 13 | 13 | 14 | 14 | 14 | 14 | 15 | 15 | 15 | 16 | 16 | 16 | 16 | 17 | 17 | 17 | 18 | 18 | 18 |
| 19 | 0 | 1 | 1 | 1 | 2 | 2 | 2 | 3 | 3 | 3 | 3 | 4 | 4 | 4 | 5 | 5 | 5 | 6 | 6 | 6 | 7 | 7 | 7 | 8 | 8 | 8 | 9 | 9 | 9 | 10 | 10 | 10 | 10 | 11 | 11 | 11 | 12 | 12 | 12 | 13 | 13 | 13 | 14 | 14 | 14 | 15 | 15 | 15 | 16 | 16 | 16 | 16 | 17 | 17 | 17 | 18 | 18 | 18 | 19 | 19 | 19 |
| 20 | 0 | 1 | 1 | 1 | 2 | 2 | 2 | 3 | 3 | 3 | 4 | 4 | 4 | 5 | 5 | 5 | 6 | 6 | 6 | 7 | 7 | 7 | 8 | 8 | 8 | 9 | 9 | 9 | 10 | 10 | 10 | 11 | 11 | 11 | 12 | 12 | 12 | 13 | 13 | 13 | 14 | 14 | 14 | 15 | 15 | 15 | 16 | 16 | 16 | 17 | 17 | 17 | 18 | 18 | 18 | 19 | 19 | 19 | 20 | 20 | 20 |
| 21 | 0 | 1 | 1 | 1 | 2 | 2 | 2 | 3 | 3 | 4 | 4 | 4 | 5 | 5 | 5 | 6 | 6 | 6 | 7 | 7 | 7 | 8 | 8 | 8 | 9 | 9 | 9 | 10 | 10 | 10 | 11 | 11 | 12 | 12 | 12 | 13 | 13 | 13 | 14 | 14 | 14 | 15 | 15 | 15 | 16 | 16 | 16 | 17 | 17 | 18 | 18 | 18 | 19 | 19 | 19 | 20 | 20 | 20 | 21 | 21 | 21 |
| 22 | 0 | 1 | 1 | 1 | 2 | 2 | 3 | 3 | 3 | 4 | 4 | 4 | 5 | 5 | 6 | 6 | 6 | 7 | 7 | 7 | 8 | 8 | 8 | 9 | 9 | 10 | 10 | 10 | 11 | 11 | 11 | 12 | 12 | 12 | 13 | 13 | 14 | 14 | 14 | 15 | 15 | 15 | 16 | 16 | 16 | 17 | 17 | 18 | 18 | 18 | 19 | 19 | 19 | 20 | 20 | 21 | 21 | 21 | 22 | 22 | 22 |
| 23 | 0 | 1 | 1 | 2 | 2 | 2 | 3 | 3 | 3 | 4 | 4 | 5 | 5 | 5 | 6 | 6 | 7 | 7 | 7 | 8 | 8 | 8 | 9 | 9 | 10 | 10 | 10 | 11 | 11 | 12 | 12 | 12 | 13 | 13 | 13 | 14 | 14 | 15 | 15 | 15 | 16 | 16 | 16 | 17 | 17 | 18 | 18 | 18 | 19 | 19 | 20 | 20 | 20 | 21 | 21 | 21 | 22 | 22 | 23 | 23 | 23 |
| 24 | 0 | 1 | 1 | 2 | 2 | 2 | 3 | 3 | 4 | 4 | 4 | 5 | 5 | 6 | 6 | 6 | 7 | 7 | 8 | 8 | 8 | 9 | 9 | 10 | 10 | 10 | 11 | 11 | 12 | 12 | 12 | 13 | 13 | 14 | 14 | 14 | 15 | 15 | 16 | 16 | 16 | 17 | 17 | 18 | 18 | 18 | 19 | 19 | 20 | 20 | 20 | 21 | 21 | 22 | 22 | 22 | 23 | 23 | 24 | 24 | 24 |
| 25 | 0 | 1 | 1 | 2 | 2 | 2 | 3 | 3 | 4 | 4 | 5 | 5 | 5 | 6 | 6 | 7 | 7 | 8 | 8 | 8 | 9 | 9 | 10 | 10 | 10 | 11 | 11 | 12 | 12 | 12 | 13 | 13 | 14 | 14 | 15 | 15 | 15 | 16 | 16 | 17 | 17 | 18 | 18 | 18 | 19 | 19 | 20 | 20 | 20 | 21 | 21 | 22 | 22 | 22 | 23 | 23 | 24 | 24 | 25 | 25 | 25 |
| 26 | 0 | 1 | 1 | 2 | 2 | 3 | 3 | 3 | 4 | 4 | 5 | 5 | 6 | 6 | 6 | 7 | 7 | 8 | 8 | 9 | 9 | 10 | 10 | 10 | 11 | 11 | 12 | 12 | 13 | 13 | 13 | 14 | 14 | 15 | 15 | 16 | 16 | 16 | 17 | 17 | 18 | 18 | 19 | 19 | 20 | 20 | 20 | 21 | 21 | 22 | 22 | 23 | 23 | 23 | 24 | 24 | 25 | 25 | 26 | 26 | 26 |
| 27 | 0 | 1 | 1 | 2 | 2 | 3 | 3 | 4 | 4 | 4 | 5 | 5 | 6 | 6 | 7 | 7 | 8 | 8 | 9 | 9 | 9 | 10 | 10 | 11 | 11 | 12 | 12 | 13 | 13 | 14 | 14 | 14 | 15 | 15 | 16 | 16 | 17 | 17 | 18 | 18 | 18 | 19 | 19 | 20 | 20 | 21 | 21 | 22 | 22 | 22 | 23 | 23 | 24 | 24 | 25 | 25 | 26 | 26 | 27 | 27 | 27 |
| 28 | 0 | 1 | 1 | 2 | 2 | 3 | 3 | 4 | 4 | 5 | 5 | 6 | 6 | 7 | 7 | 7 | 8 | 8 | 9 | 9 | 10 | 10 | 11 | 11 | 12 | 12 | 13 | 13 | 14 | 14 | 14 | 15 | 15 | 16 | 16 | 17 | 17 | 18 | 18 | 19 | 19 | 20 | 20 | 21 | 21 | 21 | 22 | 22 | 23 | 23 | 24 | 24 | 25 | 25 | 26 | 26 | 27 | 27 | 28 | 28 | 28 |
| 29 | 0 | 1 | 1 | 2 | 2 | 3 | 3 | 4 | 4 | 5 | 5 | 6 | 6 | 7 | 7 | 8 | 8 | 9 | 9 | 10 | 10 | 11 | 11 | 12 | 12 | 13 | 13 | 14 | 14 | 14 | 15 | 15 | 16 | 16 | 17 | 17 | 18 | 18 | 19 | 19 | 20 | 20 | 21 | 21 | 22 | 22 | 23 | 23 | 24 | 24 | 25 | 25 | 26 | 26 | 27 | 27 | 28 | 28 | 29 | 29 | 29 |
| 30 | 0 | 1 | 2 | 2 | 2 | 3 | 4 | 4 | 4 | 5 | 6 | 6 | 6 | 7 | 8 | 8 | 8 | 9 | 10 | 10 | 10 | 11 | 12 | 12 | 12 | 13 | 14 | 14 | 14 | 15 | 16 | 16 | 16 | 17 | 18 | 18 | 18 | 19 | 20 | 20 | 20 | 21 | 22 | 22 | 22 | 23 | 24 | 24 | 24 | 25 | 26 | 26 | 26 | 27 | 28 | 28 | 28 | 29 | 30 | 30 | 30 |
| 31 | 1 | 1 | 2 | 2 | 3 | 3 | 4 | 4 | 5 | 5 | 6 | 6 | 7 | 7 | 8 | 8 | 9 | 9 | 10 | 10 | 11 | 11 | 12 | 12 | 13 | 13 | 14 | 14 | 15 | 16 | 16 | 17 | 17 | 18 | 18 | 19 | 19 | 20 | 20 | 21 | 21 | 22 | 22 | 23 | 23 | 24 | 24 | 25 | 25 | 26 | 26 | 27 | 27 | 28 | 28 | 29 | 29 | 30 | 30 | 31 | 31 |
| 32 | 1 | 1 | 2 | 2 | 3 | 3 | 4 | 4 | 5 | 5 | 6 | 6 | 7 | 7 | 8 | 9 | 9 | 10 | 10 | 11 | 11 | 12 | 12 | 13 | 13 | 14 | 14 | 15 | 15 | 16 | 17 | 17 | 18 | 18 | 19 | 19 | 20 | 20 | 21 | 21 | 22 | 22 | 23 | 23 | 24 | 25 | 25 | 26 | 26 | 27 | 27 | 28 | 28 | 29 | 29 | 30 | 30 | 31 | 31 | 32 | 32 |
| 33 | 1 | 1 | 2 | 2 | 3 | 3 | 4 | 4 | 5 | 6 | 6 | 7 | 7 | 8 | 8 | 9 | 9 | 10 | 10 | 11 | 12 | 12 | 13 | 13 | 14 | 14 | 15 | 15 | 16 | 16 | 17 | 18 | 18 | 19 | 19 | 20 | 20 | 21 | 21 | 22 | 23 | 23 | 24 | 24 | 25 | 25 | 26 | 26 | 27 | 28 | 28 | 29 | 29 | 30 | 30 | 31 | 31 | 32 | 32 | 33 | 33 |
| 34 | 1 | 1 | 2 | 2 | 3 | 3 | 4 | 5 | 5 | 6 | 6 | 7 | 7 | 8 | 8 | 9 | 10 | 10 | 11 | 11 | 12 | 12 | 13 | 14 | 14 | 15 | 15 | 16 | 16 | 17 | 18 | 18 | 19 | 19 | 20 | 20 | 21 | 22 | 22 | 23 | 23 | 24 | 24 | 25 | 26 | 26 | 27 | 27 | 28 | 28 | 29 | 29 | 30 | 31 | 31 | 32 | 32 | 33 | 33 | 34 | 34 |
| 35 | 1 | 1 | 2 | 2 | 3 | 4 | 4 | 5 | 5 | 6 | 6 | 7 | 8 | 8 | 9 | 9 | 10 | 10 | 11 | 12 | 12 | 13 | 13 | 14 | 15 | 15 | 16 | 16 | 17 | 18 | 18 | 19 | 19 | 20 | 20 | 21 | 22 | 22 | 23 | 23 | 24 | 24 | 25 | 26 | 26 | 27 | 27 | 28 | 29 | 29 | 30 | 30 | 31 | 32 | 32 | 33 | 33 | 34 | 34 | 35 | 35 |
| 36 | 1 | 1 | 2 | 2 | 3 | 4 | 4 | 5 | 5 | 6 | 7 | 7 | 8 | 8 | 9 | 10 | 10 | 11 | 11 | 12 | 13 | 13 | 14 | 14 | 15 | 16 | 16 | 17 | 17 | 18 | 19 | 19 | 20 | 20 | 21 | 22 | 22 | 23 | 23 | 24 | 25 | 25 | 26 | 26 | 27 | 28 | 28 | 29 | 29 | 30 | 31 | 31 | 32 | 32 | 33 | 34 | 34 | 35 | 35 | 36 | 36 |
| 37 | 1 | 1 | 2 | 2 | 3 | 4 | 4 | 5 | 6 | 6 | 7 | 7 | 8 | 9 | 9 | 10 | 10 | 11 | 12 | 12 | 13 | 14 | 14 | 15 | 15 | 16 | 17 | 17 | 18 | 18 | 19 | 20 | 20 | 21 | 22 | 22 | 23 | 23 | 24 | 25 | 25 | 26 | 27 | 27 | 28 | 28 | 29 | 30 | 30 | 31 | 31 | 32 | 33 | 33 | 34 | 35 | 35 | 36 | 36 | 37 | 37 |
| 38 | 1 | 1 | 2 | 3 | 3 | 4 | 4 | 5 | 6 | 6 | 7 | 8 | 8 | 9 | 10 | 10 | 11 | 11 | 12 | 13 | 13 | 14 | 15 | 15 | 16 | 16 | 17 | 18 | 18 | 19 | 20 | 20 | 21 | 22 | 22 | 23 | 23 | 24 | 25 | 25 | 26 | 27 | 27 | 28 | 28 | 29 | 30 | 30 | 31 | 32 | 32 | 33 | 34 | 34 | 35 | 35 | 36 | 37 | 37 | 38 | 38 |
| 39 | 1 | 1 | 2 | 3 | 3 | 4 | 5 | 5 | 6 | 6 | 7 | 8 | 8 | 9 | 10 | 10 | 11 | 12 | 12 | 13 | 14 | 14 | 15 | 16 | 16 | 17 | 18 | 18 | 19 | 20 | 20 | 21 | 21 | 22 | 23 | 23 | 24 | 25 | 25 | 26 | 27 | 27 | 28 | 29 | 29 | 30 | 31 | 31 | 32 | 32 | 33 | 34 | 34 | 35 | 36 | 36 | 37 | 38 | 38 | 39 | 39 |
| 40 | 1 | 1 | 2 | 3 | 3 | 4 | 5 | 5 | 6 | 7 | 7 | 8 | 9 | 9 | 10 | 11 | 11 | 12 | 13 | 13 | 14 | 15 | 15 | 16 | 17 | 17 | 18 | 19 | 19 | 20 | 21 | 21 | 22 | 23 | 23 | 24 | 25 | 25 | 26 | 27 | 27 | 28 | 29 | 29 | 30 | 31 | 31 | 32 | 33 | 33 | 34 | 35 | 35 | 36 | 37 | 37 | 38 | 39 | 39 | 40 | 40 |
| 41 | 1 | 1 | 2 | 3 | 3 | 4 | 5 | 5 | 6 | 7 | 8 | 8 | 9 | 10 | 10 | 11 | 12 | 12 | 13 | 14 | 14 | 15 | 16 | 16 | 17 | 18 | 18 | 19 | 20 | 20 | 21 | 22 | 23 | 23 | 24 | 25 | 25 | 26 | 27 | 27 | 28 | 29 | 29 | 30 | 31 | 31 | 32 | 33 | 33 | 34 | 35 | 36 | 36 | 37 | 38 | 38 | 39 | 40 | 40 | 41 | 41 |
| 42 | 1 | 1 | 2 | 3 | 4 | 4 | 5 | 6 | 6 | 7 | 8 | 8 | 9 | 10 | 10 | 11 | 12 | 13 | 13 | 14 | 15 | 15 | 16 | 17 | 18 | 18 | 19 | 20 | 20 | 21 | 22 | 22 | 23 | 24 | 24 | 25 | 26 | 27 | 27 | 28 | 29 | 29 | 30 | 31 | 32 | 32 | 33 | 34 | 34 | 35 | 36 | 36 | 37 | 38 | 38 | 39 | 40 | 41 | 41 | 42 | 42 |
| 43 | 1 | 1 | 2 | 3 | 4 | 4 | 5 | 6 | 6 | 7 | 8 | 9 | 9 | 10 | 11 | 11 | 12 | 13 | 14 | 14 | 15 | 16 | 16 | 17 | 18 | 19 | 19 | 20 | 21 | 22 | 22 | 23 | 24 | 24 | 25 | 26 | 27 | 27 | 28 | 29 | 29 | 30 | 31 | 32 | 32 | 33 | 34 | 34 | 35 | 36 | 37 | 37 | 38 | 39 | 39 | 40 | 41 | 42 | 42 | 43 | 43 |
| 44 | 1 | 1 | 2 | 3 | 4 | 4 | 5 | 6 | 7 | 7 | 8 | 9 | 10 | 10 | 11 | 12 | 12 | 13 | 14 | 15 | 15 | 16 | 17 | 18 | 18 | 19 | 20 | 21 | 21 | 22 | 23 | 23 | 24 | 25 | 26 | 26 | 27 | 28 | 29 | 29 | 30 | 31 | 32 | 32 | 33 | 34 | 34 | 35 | 36 | 37 | 37 | 38 | 39 | 40 | 40 | 41 | 42 | 43 | 43 | 44 | 44 |
| 45 | 1 | 2 | 2 | 3 | 4 | 4 | 5 | 6 | 7 | 8 | 8 | 9 | 10 | 10 | 11 | 12 | 13 | 14 | 14 | 15 | 16 | 16 | 17 | 18 | 19 | 20 | 20 | 21 | 22 | 22 | 23 | 24 | 25 | 26 | 26 | 27 | 28 | 28 | 29 | 30 | 31 | 32 | 32 | 33 | 34 | 34 | 35 | 36 | 37 | 38 | 38 | 39 | 40 | 40 | 41 | 42 | 43 | 44 | 44 | 45 | 45 |
| 46 | 1 | 2 | 2 | 3 | 4 | 5 | 5 | 6 | 7 | 8 | 8 | 9 | 10 | 11 | 12 | 12 | 13 | 14 | 15 | 15 | 16 | 17 | 18 | 18 | 19 | 20 | 21 | 21 | 22 | 23 | 24 | 25 | 25 | 26 | 27 | 28 | 28 | 29 | 30 | 31 | 31 | 32 | 33 | 34 | 34 | 35 | 36 | 37 | 38 | 38 | 39 | 40 | 41 | 41 | 42 | 43 | 44 | 44 | 45 | 46 | 46 |
| 47 | 1 | 2 | 2 | 3 | 4 | 5 | 5 | 6 | 7 | 8 | 9 | 9 | 10 | 11 | 12 | 13 | 13 | 14 | 15 | 16 | 16 | 17 | 18 | 19 | 20 | 20 | 21 | 22 | 23 | 24 | 24 | 25 | 26 | 27 | 27 | 28 | 29 | 30 | 31 | 31 | 32 | 33 | 34 | 34 | 35 | 36 | 37 | 38 | 38 | 39 | 40 | 41 | 42 | 42 | 43 | 44 | 45 | 45 | 46 | 47 | 47 |
| 48 | 1 | 2 | 2 | 3 | 4 | 5 | 6 | 6 | 7 | 8 | 9 | 10 | 10 | 11 | 12 | 13 | 14 | 14 | 15 | 16 | 17 | 18 | 18 | 19 | 20 | 21 | 22 | 22 | 23 | 24 | 25 | 26 | 26 | 27 | 28 | 29 | 30 | 30 | 31 | 32 | 33 | 34 | 34 | 35 | 36 | 37 | 38 | 38 | 39 | 40 | 41 | 42 | 42 | 43 | 44 | 45 | 46 | 46 | 47 | 48 | 48 |
| 49 | 1 | 2 | 2 | 3 | 4 | 5 | 6 | 7 | 7 | 8 | 9 | 10 | 11 | 11 | 12 | 13 | 14 | 15 | 16 | 16 | 17 | 18 | 19 | 20 | 20 | 21 | 22 | 23 | 24 | 24 | 25 | 26 | 27 | 28 | 29 | 29 | 30 | 31 | 32 | 33 | 33 | 34 | 35 | 36 | 37 | 38 | 38 | 39 | 40 | 41 | 42 | 42 | 43 | 44 | 45 | 46 | 47 | 47 | 48 | 49 | 49 |
| 50 | 1 | 2 | 2 | 3 | 4 | 5 | 6 | 7 | 8 | 8 | 9 | 10 | 11 | 12 | 12 | 13 | 14 | 15 | 16 | 17 | 18 | 18 | 19 | 20 | 21 | 22 | 22 | 23 | 24 | 25 | 26 | 27 | 28 | 28 | 29 | 30 | 31 | 32 | 32 | 33 | 34 | 35 | 36 | 37 | 38 | 38 | 39 | 40 | 41 | 42 | 42 | 43 | 44 | 45 | 46 | 47 | 48 | 48 | 49 | 50 | 50 |
| 51 | 1 | 2 | 3 | 3 | 4 | 5 | 6 | 7 | 8 | 8 | 9 | 10 | 11 | 12 | 13 | 14 | 14 | 15 | 16 | 17 | 18 | 19 | 20 | 20 | 21 | 22 | 23 | 24 | 25 | 26 | 26 | 27 | 28 | 29 | 30 | 31 | 31 | 32 | 33 | 34 | 35 | 36 | 37 | 37 | 38 | 39 | 40 | 41 | 42 | 42 | 43 | 44 | 45 | 46 | 47 | 48 | 48 | 49 | 50 | 51 | 51 |
| 52 | 1 | 2 | 3 | 3 | 4 | 5 | 6 | 7 | 8 | 9 | 10 | 10 | 11 | 12 | 13 | 14 | 15 | 16 | 16 | 17 | 18 | 19 | 20 | 21 | 22 | 23 | 23 | 24 | 25 | 26 | 27 | 28 | 29 | 29 | 30 | 31 | 32 | 33 | 34 | 35 | 36 | 36 | 37 | 38 | 39 | 40 | 41 | 42 | 42 | 43 | 44 | 45 | 46 | 47 | 48 | 49 | 49 | 50 | 51 | 52 | 52 |
| 53 | 1 | 2 | 3 | 4 | 4 | 5 | 6 | 7 | 8 | 9 | 10 | 11 | 11 | 12 | 13 | 14 | 15 | 16 | 17 | 18 | 19 | 19 | 20 | 21 | 22 | 23 | 24 | 25 | 26 | 26 | 27 | 28 | 29 | 30 | 31 | 32 | 33 | 34 | 34 | 35 | 36 | 37 | 38 | 39 | 40 | 41 | 42 | 42 | 43 | 44 | 45 | 46 | 47 | 48 | 49 | 49 | 50 | 51 | 52 | 53 | 53 |
| 54 | 1 | 2 | 3 | 4 | 4 | 5 | 6 | 7 | 8 | 9 | 10 | 11 | 12 | 13 | 14 | 14 | 15 | 16 | 17 | 18 | 19 | 20 | 21 | 22 | 22 | 23 | 24 | 25 | 26 | 27 | 28 | 29 | 30 | 31 | 32 | 32 | 33 | 34 | 35 | 36 | 37 | 38 | 39 | 40 | 40 | 41 | 42 | 43 | 44 | 45 | 46 | 47 | 48 | 49 | 50 | 50 | 51 | 52 | 53 | 54 | 54 |
| 55 | 1 | 2 | 3 | 4 | 5 | 6 | 6 | 7 | 8 | 9 | 10 | 11 | 12 | 13 | 14 | 15 | 16 | 16 | 17 | 18 | 19 | 20 | 21 | 22 | 23 | 24 | 25 | 26 | 27 | 28 | 28 | 29 | 30 | 31 | 32 | 33 | 34 | 35 | 36 | 37 | 38 | 38 | 39 | 40 | 41 | 42 | 43 | 44 | 45 | 46 | 47 | 48 | 49 | 50 | 50 | 51 | 52 | 53 | 54 | 55 | 55 |
| 56 | 1 | 2 | 3 | 4 | 5 | 6 | 7 | 7 | 8 | 9 | 10 | 11 | 12 | 13 | 14 | 15 | 16 | 17 | 18 | 19 | 20 | 21 | 21 | 22 | 23 | 24 | 25 | 26 | 27 | 28 | 29 | 30 | 31 | 32 | 33 | 34 | 35 | 35 | 36 | 37 | 38 | 39 | 40 | 41 | 42 | 43 | 44 | 45 | 46 | 47 | 48 | 49 | 49 | 50 | 51 | 52 | 53 | 54 | 55 | 56 | 56 |
| 57 | 1 | 2 | 3 | 4 | 5 | 6 | 7 | 8 | 9 | 10 | 10 | 11 | 12 | 13 | 14 | 15 | 16 | 17 | 18 | 19 | 20 | 21 | 22 | 23 | 24 | 25 | 26 | 27 | 28 | 28 | 29 | 30 | 31 | 32 | 33 | 34 | 35 | 36 | 37 | 38 | 39 | 40 | 41 | 42 | 43 | 44 | 45 | 46 | 47 | 48 | 48 | 49 | 50 | 51 | 52 | 53 | 54 | 55 | 56 | 57 | 57 |
| 58 | 1 | 2 | 3 | 4 | 5 | 6 | 7 | 8 | 9 | 10 | 11 | 12 | 13 | 14 | 14 | 15 | 16 | 17 | 18 | 19 | 20 | 21 | 22 | 23 | 24 | 25 | 26 | 27 | 28 | 29 | 30 | 31 | 32 | 33 | 34 | 35 | 36 | 37 | 38 | 39 | 40 | 41 | 42 | 43 | 44 | 44 | 45 | 46 | 47 | 48 | 49 | 50 | 51 | 52 | 53 | 54 | 55 | 56 | 57 | 58 | 58 |
| 59 | 1 | 2 | 3 | 4 | 5 | 6 | 7 | 8 | 9 | 10 | 11 | 12 | 13 | 14 | 15 | 16 | 17 | 18 | 19 | 20 | 21 | 22 | 23 | 24 | 25 | 26 | 27 | 28 | 29 | 30 | 30 | 31 | 32 | 33 | 34 | 35 | 36 | 37 | 38 | 39 | 40 | 41 | 42 | 43 | 44 | 45 | 46 | 47 | 48 | 49 | 50 | 51 | 52 | 53 | 54 | 55 | 56 | 57 | 58 | 59 | 59 |

*Figure 6–7.* Interpolation table for minutes of declination, from *HO 249*

Date: 6-19-99                    DR:     41°12′ N
                                         28°42′ W

Sextant reads      [Hs]          _____29°36′_____
Index corr.        [IC]          _____ + 04′_____
Dip corr.          [D]           _____ − 03′_____
Apparent alt.      [Ha]          _____29°37′_____
Ref/SD                           _____ + 14.3′_____
Observed alt.      [Ho]          _____29°51.3′_____


GHA  1800 UT    __89°40.5′__    Dec.    __N 23°25.4′__
+ 36m, 49s        9°12.3′
GHA  18-36-49    98°52.8′       Dec.    N 23°25.4′


GHA  18-36-49    __98°53′__     Dec.    __N 23°25′__
    AP longitude  − 28°53′ W    AP latitude = 41° N
LHA              70°00′

Data for HO 249:  lat. = 41° (Same/Contr)  | LHA = 70°  Dec. = 23°

Data from HO 249: Hc = 29°36′  d = ⊕35′ | Z = 84°

Hc      29°36′                     Dec. increment = __ + 35′__
Corr    ⊕15′
Hc      29°51′
Ho      29°51′
        00′  Toward            Zn = 276°
             Away

*Figure 6–8.* Work sheet for finding the AP's computed altitude (Hc) and true bearing (Zn) to the GP

east and across the equator, and explains how to put a line of position on a blank chart, or *plotting sheet.*

Meanwhile, remember that the practice of celestial navigation involves these steps: taking a sight; establishing a benchmark, which must be an AP if you are using a sight reduction table; looking up in the table a sight precomputed for that AP; comparing the sights; and using the difference—the intercept—to plot an LOP.

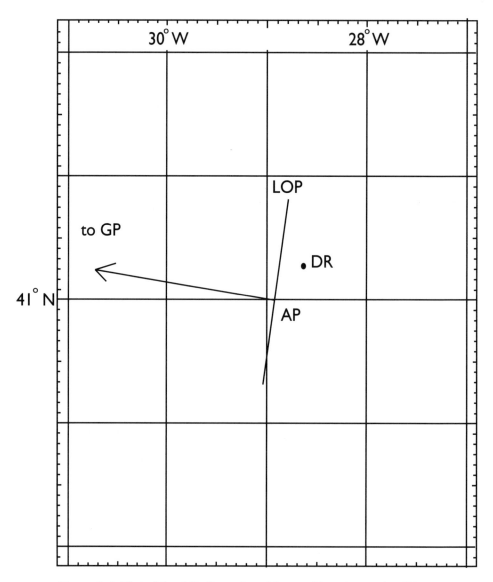

*Figure 6–9.* Plot of the AP's line of position and bearing to the GP

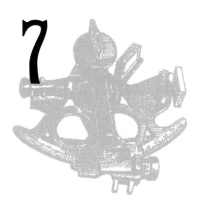

# 7

# Plot, Counterplot

One sight produces one line, the line of position; theoretically you can be at any one of the many points that make up that line. The odds are very high that you are in the immediate vicinity of the point on the LOP closest to your DR, but to produce a fix by celestial navigation you need to take another sight, produce another line, and cross the two.

As you know by now, getting an LOP on paper means putting down a fair number of lines and points that serve as a kind of scaffolding for the LOP's construction. These ancillary lines and points tend to clutter a chart pretty quickly, so navigators do not usually plot LOPs on a passage chart. Instead, they use a blank chart called a plotting sheet. Once two or more LOPs have been crossed to form a fix, the fix is then posted on the passage chart, and a new DR track started from it. That way the passage chart always shows a clean picture of the boat's track and position vis-à-vis the destination.

One widely used plotting sheet is produced by the Defense Mapping Agency. Printed in green ink and available in pads of 50 sheets, the "Universal Plotting Sheet VP-OS" is shown here as figure 7-1. Each sheet measures about 14 by 11 inches, which fits comfortably on most nav tables and a high proportion of the icebox lids in small boats.

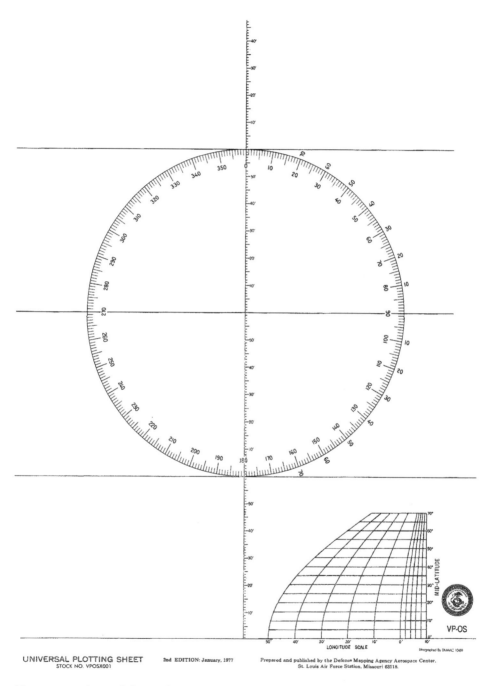

*Figure 7–1.* The widely used "Universal Plotting Sheet VP-OS," printed by the Defense Mapping Agency

Notice that there are no longitude lines, which tends to give people fits at first sight. That's because the plotting sheet is "universal"; it is intended to be used no matter where you are on the globe, and longitude lines become closer the farther you are from the equator. Thus, you, the navigator, have to put in the longitude lines yourself. How far apart you place them depends on your latitude.

The basic scale of this blank chart is given by the five preprinted latitude lines. The space between them is conveniently divided into sixty increments, which are ticked off along the central longitude meridian. Each of those sixty little spaces represents, of course, 1´ of latitude, or 1 nautical mile.

The first step in placing the longitude lines is to decide what to label the middle latitude line. For a quick example, assume you are on a passage to Iceland, and your DR has you at about 60° N. Look at the northeast quadrant of the true compass rose, or bearing ring, in the center of the plotting sheet. Along the outside of the quadrant, 1° steps are marked off at 10° intervals, beginning at the mid-latitude line and increasing as you move toward the top of the sheet: 10°, 20°, 30°, and so on, to 70°. The southeast quadrant is similarly marked, except that the numbers increase from 10° to 70° as you move toward the bottom. These numbers represent latitudes. Put your pencil point on any one of them; the distance from your pencil point to the vertical central meridian represents 1° of longitude at that latitude.

For instance, if you make pencil marks at 60° on the upper and lower quadrants and draw a vertical line between them, you have a longitude line parallel to the central one and correctly spaced for a latitude of 60° N or 60° S. That is what you then label the horizontal latitude line in the middle of the plotting sheet, the so-called mid-latitude (fig. 7-2).

An interesting side note here is that at 60° latitude the space between the longitude lines is exactly half that between latitudes—that is, 1´ of longitude is 0.5 nautical mile. And that raises the question of a scale for minutes of longitude, which you obviously need in order to put down DRs and APs on the plotting sheet and to take off the coordinates of fixes to transfer to your passage chart.

Did you notice the device in the lower right corner of the plotting sheet? The thingamajig that looks like a fishing net hung out to dry? That's the longitude scale. The bottom of this netlike grid is divided into six 10´ intervals, the last group of which is subdivided into 2´

intervals. The distance along that bottom line from one side of the net to the other is 1° of longitude at the equator. The distance along the top line is 1° of longitude at 70° latitude, N or S, and the spans of the other horizontal lines are 60′ of longitude at the latitudes between the equator and 70°. There are lines for every 5° of latitude, which are numbered in 10° steps. (If you like, for practice, take a pair of dividers and use the grid to check my statement that at 60° latitude 1° of longitude equals 30′ of latitude.)

The usual practice in celestial navigation is to make the middle latitude line the latitude of the AP. There's no need to fill up the page with longitudes; one on each side of the middle meridian is usually enough. When you are finished, you have a blank chart of the patch of ocean around you within a radius of about 120 nautical miles—on average, about one day's sailing distance in a forty-footer.

Remember, it's natural to want to pick the longitudes off the vertical central scale, which is only for latitude and nautical miles. For longitudes use the netlike grid. It helps to draw a line across the grid at the proper latitude, as I did in figure 7-2.

As you may well realize by now, celestial navigation has the flavor of a Rube Goldberg contraption. It is a melange of compromises and approximations, uses quite basic tools, and is usually practiced under less than ideal conditions. It works, but if you are depending only on celestial to find a low island or to keep you clear of a charted danger, remember the first rule of seafaring: Keep a good lookout. Get up from the chart table, go on deck, and look around. (This caution applies, of course, whenever you rely solely on a single navigation method, whatever it is.)

What teaches you best the kind of accuracy you personally can expect from celestial are the results of your practice ashore. There is nothing about celestial that can't be figured out on land, and that's where the best learning occurs. Whatever accuracy you achieve ashore, it's not going to get better at sea. And it's prudent to have some inkling of the best you can do under stable conditions before you get on a boat.

All this sounds somewhat somber, but in fact, celestial navigation is mostly a delight. Because you mix into it so directly by making the observations, thumbing through the books, and laying out the plotting sheet, celestial fosters and sustains a sense of self-reliance and self-sufficiency. Also, you are generally not aiming for something low or dangerous; that's not being a smart navigator. You are aiming at a

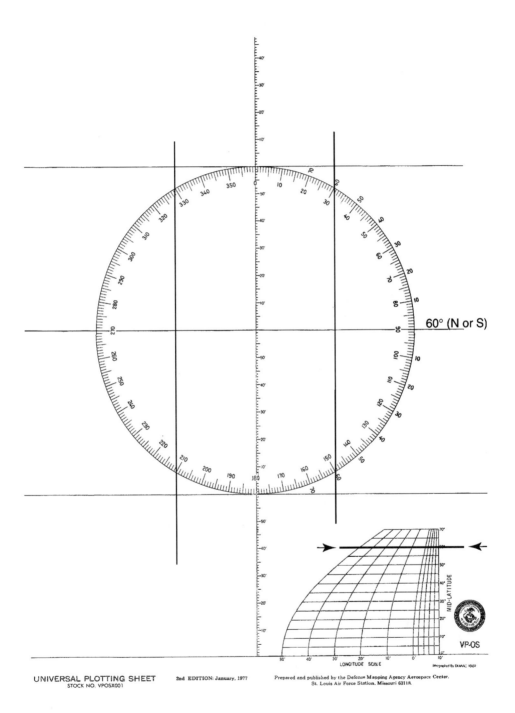

*Figure 7–2.* Marking the plotting sheet with the mid-latitude and longitude lines

high target that can be seen from many, many miles at sea. No matter what, when that looked-for land nicks the horizon or you see the first sparkle of an anticipated lighthouse, it's magic. No one is going to stop then to figure out whether the boat is 6 miles to the left or right of where the navigator said it would be. Everybody is just going to stand in awe (especially the navigator).

So, return now to the work that makes the magic happen.

As mentioned at the outset of this chapter, a single LOP that runs close to the DR confirms the DR. While you are most likely at the point on the LOP closest to the DR, you could be anywhere on the line. To be more precise, you need another LOP to cross with the first. For that you have to wait a while between sights, until the sun's bearing has changed enough to ensure that the LOPs cross at an angle of 30° or more. The normal procedure at sea is to take one sight of the sun in the morning, another in the afternoon, and then cross the LOPs for a fix at the time of the afternoon sight.

Assume it is October 11, 1999. You are thirty-three days out on a passage from the Canaries and approaching the Bahamas. It's not the best time of the year to be making this passage, but there have been no hurricanes as yet. If anything, the winds have been on the light side, although today they are pretty brisk. Still, you'll be glad to arrive.

Your DR is 25°19′ N, 72°48′ W. Late in the morning, you take five shots of the sun and find their average is a sight of 46°49′ at a GMT of 14-42-13.

Two factors here are different from the example in the previous chapter. First, it is October, which means the sun is over the southern hemisphere. You must find the correct page in the sight reduction table under the heading "Declination Contrary Name" because the GP is on the other side of the equator from the AP.

Second, because it is morning, the sun is to your east, which makes a difference in how local hour angle (LHA) is reckoned. Unlike GHA, which is always measured westward from the Greenwich meridian, LHA is always measured westward from the AP, so LHA is not always the angle at the apex of the navigational spherical triangle.

Figure 7-3 is a sketch illustrating these two concepts. When the sun is to your east, LHA is greater than 180°. When the sun is across the equator, you get a distinctly different spherical triangle.

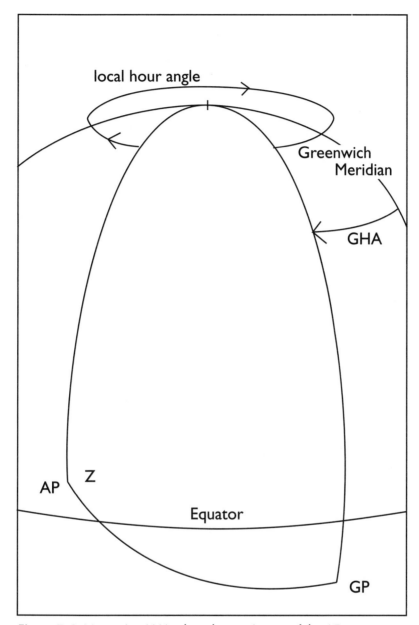

*Figure 7–3.* Measuring LHA when the sun is east of the AP

Figure 7-4 is the sun data column for October 11, 1999, from the *Nautical Almanac.* Figure 7-5 is the correct page for this example from the sight reduction table. Notice that the LHAs greater than 180°—when the sun is in the east—are on the right-hand side of the page. Figure 7-6 is the work sheet filled out for the morning sight.

The calculations in two places on this work sheet are a little different from the example in the previous chapter and therefore need

## 1999 OCTOBER 10, 11, 12 (SUN., MON., TUES.)

| UT | SUN GHA | SUN Dec | MOON GHA | MOON v | MOON Dec | MOON d | MOON HP |
|---|---|---|---|---|---|---|---|
| **10 00** | 183 11.5 | S 6 23.2 | 175 49.5 | 14.1 | S 4 12.9 | 10.6 | 55.3 |
| 01 | 198 11.6 | 24.2 | 190 22.6 | 14.2 | 4 23.5 | 10.7 | 55.3 |
| 02 | 213 11.8 | 25.1 | 204 55.8 | 14.2 | 4 34.2 | 10.6 | 55.3 |
| 03 | 228 12.0 | .. 26.1 | 219 29.0 | 14.1 | 4 44.8 | 10.6 | 55.3 |
| 04 | 243 12.2 | 27.0 | 234 02.1 | 14.2 | 4 55.4 | 10.5 | 55.3 |
| 05 | 258 12.3 | 28.0 | 248 35.3 | 14.2 | 5 05.9 | 10.5 | 55.2 |
| 06 | 273 12.5 | S 6 28.9 | 263 08.5 | 14.2 | S 5 16.4 | 10.5 | 55.2 |
| 07 | 288 12.7 | 29.9 | 277 41.7 | 14.2 | 5 26.9 | 10.5 | 55.2 |
| 08 | 303 12.8 | 30.8 | 292 14.9 | 14.2 | 5 37.4 | 10.4 | 55.2 |
| **S** 09 | 318 13.0 | .. 31.8 | 306 48.1 | 14.2 | 5 47.8 | 10.4 | 55.2 |
| **U** 10 | 333 13.2 | 32.7 | 321 21.3 | 14.2 | 5 58.2 | 10.4 | 55.1 |
| **N** 11 | 348 13.3 | 33.7 | 335 54.5 | 14.2 | 6 08.6 | 10.4 | 55.1 |
| **D** 12 | 3 13.5 | S 6 34.6 | 350 27.7 | 14.2 | S 6 19.0 | 10.3 | 55.1 |
| **A** 13 | 18 13.7 | 35.6 | 5 00.9 | 14.2 | 6 29.3 | 10.2 | 55.1 |
| **Y** 14 | 33 13.8 | 36.5 | 19 34.1 | 14.2 | 6 39.5 | 10.3 | 55.1 |
| 15 | 48 14.0 | .. 37.5 | 34 07.3 | 14.2 | 6 49.8 | 10.2 | 55.1 |
| 16 | 63 14.2 | 38.4 | 48 40.5 | 14.2 | 7 00.0 | 10.1 | 55.0 |
| 17 | 78 14.3 | 39.4 | 63 13.7 | 14.2 | 7 10.1 | 10.2 | 55.0 |
| 18 | 93 14.5 | S 6 40.3 | 77 46.9 | 14.2 | S 7 20.3 | 10.0 | 55.0 |
| 19 | 108 14.6 | 41.3 | 92 20.1 | 14.2 | 7 30.3 | 10.1 | 55.0 |
| 20 | 123 14.8 | 42.2 | 106 53.3 | 14.2 | 7 40.4 | 10.0 | 55.0 |
| 21 | 138 15.0 | .. 43.2 | 121 26.5 | 14.1 | 7 50.4 | 10.0 | 55.0 |
| 22 | 153 15.1 | 44.1 | 135 59.6 | 14.2 | 8 00.4 | 9.9 | 54.9 |
| 23 | 168 15.3 | 45.0 | 150 32.8 | 14.2 | 8 10.3 | 9.9 | 54.9 |
| **11 00** | 183 15.5 | S 6 46.0 | 165 06.0 | 14.2 | S 8 20.2 | 9.8 | 54.9 |
| 01 | 198 15.6 | 46.9 | 179 39.2 | 14.1 | 8 30.0 | 9.8 | 54.9 |
| 02 | 213 15.8 | 47.9 | 194 12.3 | 14.2 | 8 39.8 | 9.8 | 54.9 |
| 03 | 228 16.0 | .. 48.8 | 208 45.5 | 14.1 | 8 49.6 | 9.7 | 54.9 |
| 04 | 243 16.1 | 49.8 | 223 18.6 | 14.2 | 8 59.3 | 9.7 | 54.8 |
| 05 | 258 16.3 | 50.7 | 237 51.8 | 14.1 | 9 09.0 | 9.6 | 54.8 |
| 06 | 273 16.4 | S 6 51.7 | 252 24.9 | 14.1 | S 9 18.6 | 9.6 | 54.8 |
| 07 | 288 16.6 | 52.6 | 266 58.0 | 14.1 | 9 28.2 | 9.5 | 54.8 |
| 08 | 303 16.8 | 53.6 | 281 31.1 | 14.2 | 9 37.7 | 9.5 | 54.8 |
| **M** 09 | 318 16.9 | .. 54.5 | 296 04.3 | 14.1 | 9 47.2 | 9.5 | 54.8 |
| **O** 10 | 333 17.1 | 55.4 | 310 37.4 | 14.0 | 9 56.7 | 9.4 | 54.7 |
| **N** 11 | 348 17.3 | 56.4 | 325 10.4 | 14.1 | 10 06.1 | 9.3 | 54.7 |
| **D** 12 | 3 17.4 | S 6 57.3 | 339 43.5 | 14.1 | S10 15.4 | 9.3 | 54.7 |
| **A** 13 | 18 17.6 | 58.2 | 354 16.6 | 14.0 | 10 24.7 | 9.3 | 54.7 |
| **Y** 14 | 33 17.7 | 6 59.2 | 8 49.6 | 14.1 | 10 34.0 | 9.1 | 54.7 |
| 15 | 48 17.9 | 7 00.2 | 23 22.7 | 14.0 | 10 43.1 | 9.2 | 54.7 |
| 16 | 63 18.1 | 01.1 | 37 55.7 | 14.0 | 10 52.3 | 9.1 | 54.7 |
| 17 | 78 18.2 | 02.0 | 52 28.7 | 14.0 | 11 01.4 | 9.0 | 54.6 |
| 18 | 93 18.4 | S 7 03.0 | 67 01.7 | 14.0 | S11 10.4 | 9.0 | 54.6 |
| 19 | 108 18.5 | 03.9 | 81 34.7 | 14.0 | 11 19.4 | 8.9 | 54.6 |
| 20 | 123 18.7 | 04.9 | 96 07.7 | 14.0 | 11 28.3 | 8.9 | 54.6 |
| 21 | 138 18.9 | .. 05.8 | 110 40.7 | 13.9 | 11 37.2 | 8.8 | 54.6 |
| 22 | 153 19.0 | 06.8 | 125 13.6 | 14.0 | 11 46.0 | 8.8 | 54.6 |
| 23 | 168 19.2 | 07.7 | 139 46.6 | 13.9 | 11 54.8 | 8.7 | 54.6 |
| **12 00** | 183 19.3 | S 7 08.6 | 154 19.5 | 13.9 | S12 03.5 | 8.7 | 54.5 |
| 01 | 198 19.5 | 09.6 | 168 52.4 | 13.9 | 12 12.2 | 8.6 | 54.5 |
| 02 | 213 19.7 | 10.5 | 183 25.3 | 13.9 | 12 20.8 | 8.5 | 54.5 |
| 03 | 228 19.8 | .. 11.5 | 197 58.2 | 13.8 | 12 29.3 | 8.5 | 54.5 |
| 04 | 243 20.0 | 12.4 | 212 31.0 | 13.9 | 12 37.8 | 8.4 | 54.5 |
| 05 | 258 20.1 | 13.3 | 227 03.9 | 13.8 | 12 46.2 | 8.4 | 54.5 |
| 06 | 273 20.3 | S 7 14.3 | 241 36.7 | 13.8 | S12 54.6 | 8.3 | 54.5 |
| 07 | 288 20.4 | 15.2 | 256 09.5 | 13.8 | 13 02.9 | 8.3 | 54.5 |
| **T** 08 | 303 20.6 | 16.2 | 270 42.3 | 13.8 | 13 11.2 | 8.1 | 54.4 |
| **U** 09 | 318 20.8 | .. 17.1 | 285 15.1 | 13.8 | 13 19.3 | 8.2 | 54.4 |
| **E** 10 | 333 20.9 | 18.1 | 299 47.9 | 13.7 | 13 27.5 | 8.0 | 54.4 |
| **S** 11 | 348 21.1 | 19.0 | 314 20.6 | 13.7 | 13 35.5 | 8.0 | 54.4 |
| **D** 12 | 3 21.2 | S 7 19.9 | 328 53.3 | 13.7 | S13 43.5 | 8.0 | 54.4 |
| **A** 13 | 18 21.4 | 20.9 | 343 26.0 | 13.7 | 13 51.5 | 7.8 | 54.4 |
| **Y** 14 | 33 21.6 | 21.8 | 357 58.7 | 13.7 | 13 59.3 | 7.9 | 54.4 |
| 15 | 48 21.7 | .. 22.7 | 12 31.4 | 13.6 | 14 07.2 | 7.7 | 54.4 |
| 16 | 63 21.9 | 23.7 | 27 04.0 | 13.6 | 14 14.9 | 7.7 | 54.4 |
| 17 | 78 22.0 | 24.6 | 41 36.6 | 13.6 | 14 22.6 | 7.6 | 54.3 |
| 18 | 93 22.2 | S 7 25.6 | 56 09.2 | 13.6 | S14 30.2 | 7.5 | 54.3 |
| 19 | 108 22.3 | 26.5 | 70 41.8 | 13.6 | 14 37.7 | 7.5 | 54.3 |
| 20 | 123 22.5 | 27.4 | 85 14.4 | 13.5 | 14 45.2 | 7.4 | 54.3 |
| 21 | 138 22.6 | .. 28.4 | 99 46.9 | 13.5 | 14 52.6 | 7.4 | 54.3 |
| 22 | 153 22.8 | 29.3 | 114 19.4 | 13.5 | 15 00.0 | 7.3 | 54.3 |
| 23 | 168 22.9 | 30.3 | 128 51.9 | 13.5 | S15 07.3 | 7.2 | 54.3 |
| | SD 16.0 | d 0.9 | SD 15.0 | 14.9 | | | 14.8 |

### Twilight / Sunrise / Moonrise

| Lat. | Naut. | Civil | Sunrise | Moonrise 10 | 11 | 12 | 13 |
|---|---|---|---|---|---|---|---|
| N 72 | 04 35 | 05 54 | 07 02 | 07 42 | 09 27 | 11 18 | 13 26 |
| N 70 | 04 41 | 05 52 | 06 54 | 07 33 | 09 11 | 10 50 | 12 32 |
| 68 | 04 46 | 05 51 | 06 47 | 07 27 | 08 58 | 10 29 | 12 00 |
| 66 | 04 50 | 05 49 | 06 41 | 07 21 | 08 47 | 10 13 | 11 37 |
| 64 | 04 53 | 05 48 | 06 36 | 07 16 | 08 38 | 09 59 | 11 18 |
| 62 | 04 56 | 05 47 | 06 32 | 07 12 | 08 31 | 09 48 | 11 03 |
| 60 | 04 58 | 05 46 | 06 28 | 07 09 | 08 24 | 09 39 | 10 50 |
| N 58 | 05 00 | 05 45 | 06 25 | 07 05 | 08 19 | 09 30 | 10 40 |
| 56 | 05 02 | 05 45 | 06 22 | 07 03 | 08 14 | 09 23 | 10 30 |
| 54 | 05 03 | 05 44 | 06 19 | 07 00 | 08 09 | 09 17 | 10 22 |
| 52 | 05 04 | 05 43 | 06 17 | 06 58 | 08 05 | 09 11 | 10 14 |
| 50 | 05 05 | 05 42 | 06 15 | 06 56 | 08 01 | 09 05 | 10 08 |
| 45 | 05 06 | 05 40 | 06 10 | 06 51 | 07 53 | 08 54 | 09 53 |
| N 40 | 05 07 | 05 39 | 06 06 | 06 48 | 07 47 | 08 45 | 09 42 |
| 35 | 05 07 | 05 37 | 06 02 | 06 44 | 07 41 | 08 37 | 09 32 |
| 30 | 05 07 | 05 35 | 05 59 | 06 42 | 07 36 | 08 30 | 09 23 |
| 20 | 05 06 | 05 31 | 05 53 | 06 37 | 07 27 | 08 18 | 09 08 |
| N 10 | 05 03 | 05 27 | 05 48 | 06 33 | 07 20 | 08 07 | 08 55 |
| 0 | 04 59 | 05 23 | 05 44 | 06 29 | 07 13 | 07 57 | 08 43 |
| S 10 | 04 53 | 05 17 | 05 39 | 06 25 | 07 06 | 07 48 | 08 31 |
| 20 | 04 45 | 05 11 | 05 33 | 06 21 | 06 59 | 07 37 | 08 18 |
| 30 | 04 34 | 05 03 | 05 27 | 06 16 | 06 50 | 07 26 | 08 03 |
| 35 | 04 28 | 04 58 | 05 23 | 06 13 | 06 45 | 07 19 | 07 55 |
| 40 | 04 19 | 04 52 | 05 19 | 06 10 | 06 40 | 07 11 | 07 45 |
| 45 | 04 09 | 04 45 | 05 15 | 06 07 | 06 34 | 07 02 | 07 34 |
| S 50 | 03 55 | 04 35 | 05 09 | 06 03 | 06 26 | 06 52 | 07 20 |
| 52 | 03 49 | 04 31 | 05 06 | 06 01 | 06 23 | 06 47 | 07 14 |
| 54 | 03 41 | 04 26 | 05 03 | 05 59 | 06 19 | 06 41 | 07 07 |
| 56 | 03 33 | 04 21 | 05 00 | 05 57 | 06 15 | 06 35 | 06 59 |
| 58 | 03 23 | 04 15 | 04 56 | 05 54 | 06 10 | 06 29 | 06 50 |
| S 60 | 03 12 | 04 08 | 04 52 | 05 51 | 06 05 | 06 21 | 06 40 |

### Sunset / Twilight / Moonset

| Lat. | Sunset | Civil | Naut. | Moonset 10 | 11 | 12 | 13 |
|---|---|---|---|---|---|---|---|
| N 72 | 16 29 | 17 38 | 18 56 | 17 14 | 17 01 | 16 43 | 16 11 |
| N 70 | 16 38 | 17 40 | 18 50 | 17 25 | 17 19 | 17 13 | 17 05 |
| 68 | 16 45 | 17 41 | 18 45 | 17 33 | 17 34 | 17 35 | 17 38 |
| 66 | 16 51 | 17 43 | 18 42 | 17 41 | 17 45 | 17 52 | 18 02 |
| 64 | 16 56 | 17 44 | 18 39 | 17 47 | 17 55 | 18 06 | 18 21 |
| 62 | 17 00 | 17 45 | 18 36 | 17 52 | 18 04 | 18 18 | 18 37 |
| 60 | 17 04 | 17 46 | 18 34 | 17 56 | 18 11 | 18 28 | 18 50 |
| N 58 | 17 08 | 17 47 | 18 32 | 18 01 | 18 18 | 18 37 | 19 01 |
| 56 | 17 11 | 17 48 | 18 31 | 18 04 | 18 23 | 18 45 | 19 11 |
| 54 | 17 13 | 17 49 | 18 30 | 18 07 | 18 29 | 18 52 | 19 20 |
| 52 | 17 16 | 17 50 | 18 29 | 18 10 | 18 33 | 18 58 | 19 27 |
| 50 | 17 18 | 17 51 | 18 28 | 18 13 | 18 37 | 19 04 | 19 35 |
| 45 | 17 23 | 17 53 | 18 27 | 18 19 | 18 47 | 19 16 | 19 50 |
| N 40 | 17 27 | 17 55 | 18 26 | 18 24 | 18 54 | 19 27 | 20 02 |
| 35 | 17 31 | 17 56 | 18 26 | 18 28 | 19 01 | 19 35 | 20 13 |
| 30 | 17 34 | 17 58 | 18 26 | 18 32 | 19 07 | 19 43 | 20 22 |
| 20 | 17 40 | 18 02 | 18 28 | 18 39 | 19 17 | 19 57 | 20 38 |
| N 10 | 17 45 | 18 06 | 18 31 | 18 44 | 19 26 | 20 08 | 20 52 |
| 0 | 17 50 | 18 11 | 18 35 | 18 50 | 19 34 | 20 19 | 21 05 |
| S 10 | 17 55 | 18 16 | 18 41 | 18 55 | 19 43 | 20 30 | 21 18 |
| 20 | 18 01 | 18 23 | 18 49 | 19 01 | 19 52 | 20 42 | 21 32 |
| 30 | 18 07 | 18 31 | 19 00 | 19 08 | 20 02 | 20 56 | 21 48 |
| 35 | 18 11 | 18 37 | 19 07 | 19 12 | 20 08 | 21 03 | 21 58 |
| 40 | 18 15 | 18 43 | 19 15 | 19 16 | 20 15 | 21 12 | 22 09 |
| 45 | 18 20 | 18 50 | 19 26 | 19 21 | 20 23 | 21 23 | 22 21 |
| S 50 | 18 26 | 18 59 | 19 40 | 19 27 | 20 32 | 21 36 | 22 37 |
| 52 | 18 29 | 19 04 | 19 47 | 19 30 | 20 37 | 21 41 | 22 44 |
| 54 | 18 32 | 19 09 | 19 54 | 19 33 | 20 42 | 21 48 | 22 52 |
| 56 | 18 35 | 19 14 | 20 03 | 19 37 | 20 47 | 21 55 | 23 01 |
| 58 | 18 39 | 19 20 | 20 13 | 19 41 | 20 53 | 22 04 | 23 11 |
| S 60 | 18 43 | 19 28 | 20 24 | 19 45 | 21 00 | 22 13 | 23 23 |

### SUN / MOON

| Day | Eqn. of Time 00h | 12h | Mer. Pass. | Mer. Pass. Upper | Lower | Age | Phase |
|---|---|---|---|---|---|---|---|
| 10 | 12 46 | 12 54 | 11 47 | 12 39 | 00 17 | 01 | 1 |
| 11 | 13 02 | 13 09 | 11 47 | 13 24 | 01 01 | 02 | 4 |
| 12 | 13 17 | 13 25 | 11 47 | 14 08 | 01 46 | 03 | 9 |

*Figure 7–4.* Extract of GP data for the sun on October 11, 1999, from the *Nautical Almanac*

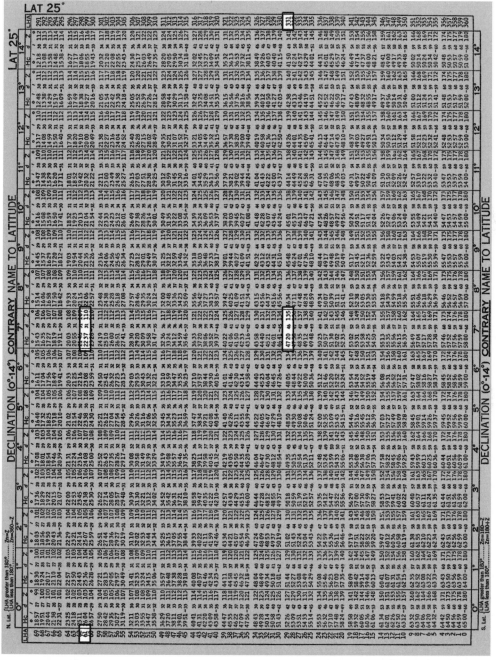

Figure 7–5. Sight reduction page for latitude 25°, declination contrary name, from *HO 249*

| Date: 10-11-99 | | DR: | 25°19′ N |
| --- | --- | --- | --- |
| | | | 72°48′ W |

| Sextant reads | [Hs] | 46°49′ |
| --- | --- | --- |
| Index corr. | [IC] | + 02′ |
| Dip corr. | [D] | − 03′ |
| Apparent alt. | [Ha] | 46°48′ |
| Ref/SD | | + 15′ |
| Observed alt. | [Ho] | 47°03′ |

| GHA 1400 UT | 33°17.7′ | Dec. | S 6°59.2′ |
| --- | --- | --- | --- |
| + 42m, 13s | 10°33.2′ | | + 0.7′ |
| **GHA** | 43°50.9′ | Dec. | S 6°59.9′ |
| **GHA** | 43°51′ | Dec. | S 7°00′ |
| (+ 360°?) | 360°00′ | | |
| **AP longitude** −W +E | 72°51′ W | **AP latitude = 25° N** | |
| (− 360°?) | | | |
| **LHA** | 331°00′ | | |

Data for HO 249: lat. = 25° Same ⟨Contr⟩ | LHA = 331°  Dec. = 7°

Data from HO 249: Hc = 47°20′  d = ⁺₋ 46′ | Z = 135°

| **Hc** | 47°20′ | | Dec. increment = 00′ |
| --- | --- | --- | --- |
| Corr | ± 00′ | | |
| **Hc** | 47°20′ | | |
| **Ho** | 47°03′ | | |
| | 17′ Toward ⟨Away⟩ | | **Zn = 135°** |

*Figure 7–6.* Work sheet for finding the AP's computed altitude (Hc) and true bearing (Zn) to the GP when the sun is east of the AP and the GP is in the opposite hemisphere

particular attention: where LHA is figured and where the adjustment for the extra minutes of declination is determined.

In west longitudes LHA is found by subtracting the longitude of the AP from GHA. In the morning, though, you are farther west of Greenwich than the sun is, which means that GHA is numerically smaller than the longitude of the AP, so subtracting gives you a negative number, which the reduction table is not arranged to handle. Therefore, you must *add* 360° to GHA (which changes nothing as far as trigonometry is concerned). Now you have a number larger than your assumed longitude from which to subtract, so you avoid coming up with a negative LHA. That's the case in this example and the reason for the notation "+360°?" on the work sheet in parentheses below GHA.

This is a good place to mention what happens when the AP is in an east longitude. As you might expect, there being a symmetry to mathematics, because you subtract west longitudes and add 360° when you can't, you add east longitudes and subtract 360° when you come up with a number greater than 360°.

Adding longitude to GHA when an AP is in an east longitude also means that you must pick the trailing minutes of the AP's longitude so that when you *add* them to GHA, you have a total of 60′. You can't eliminate the extra minutes of GHA by subtracting as you do in west longitudes, so you add to them to make another integral degree. For instance, if you are in the Mediterranean on October 11 at longitude 20°21′ E and take a sight at the same time of 14-42-13 GMT, GHA is the same 43°51′. With the sun 43°51′ west of Greenwich and you 20°21′ east, you arrive at LHA by picking a longitude of the AP of 20°09′ and adding it to the GHA of 43°51′. The result is an LHA of 63°60′, which is 64°00′.

Since it is hard to keep constantly visualizing these relationships, it's a good idea to jot down reminders on the work sheet. That's what I've done with the notes "(–W, +E)" alongside the line labeled AP longitude.

Now return to the situation that occurs when the declination is across the equator from the AP (declination and AP *contrary* name). As declination increases—that is, as you go from one declination column to the other in the sight reduction table—the computed altitude (Hc) decreases. You can see it quite plainly in figure 7-5 by looking from the 7° to the 8° column. As you scan up or down the column, you see also that *d* (the amount the computed altitude changes for a 1° change in declination) is tagged with a minus sign. You can also see what's happening by looking at figure 7-3 again. As the GP moves south, the declination increases, so the GP side of the triangle gets longer and the distance between the AP and GP increases; therefore, the altitude observed from the AP is less.

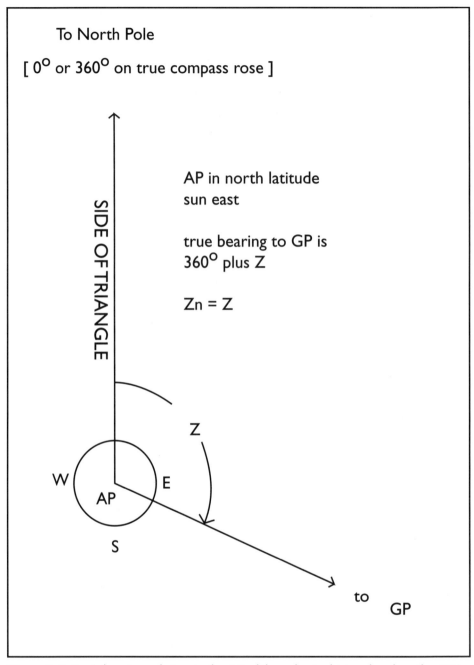

To North Pole

[ 0° or 360° on true compass rose ]

SIDE OF TRIANGLE

AP in north latitude
sun east

true bearing to GP is
360° plus Z

Zn = Z

Z

W
AP
E

S

to
GP

*Figure 7–7.* Sun's bearing relative to the AP of the spherical triangle when the AP is in the northern hemisphere and the sun is east of the AP

Finally, there is the question of Z, the angle by point AP in the spherical navigational triangle, versus the true bearing, or Zn, which is what you need to lay down the GP–AP line.

Figures 7-7 through 7-10 show the four possible ways the sun can bear from the AP points of navigational triangles. None of these

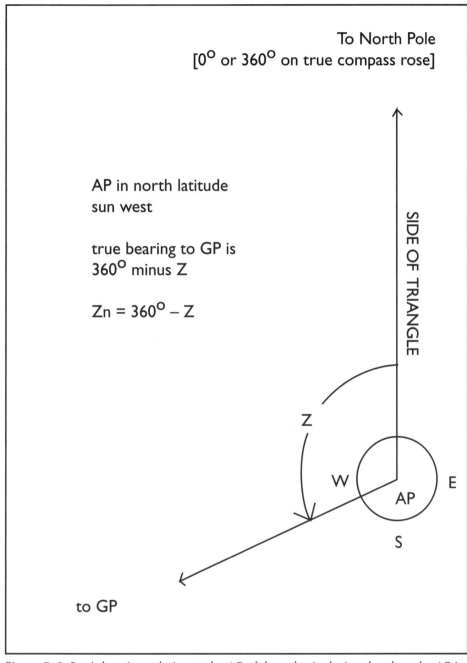

*Figure 7–8.* Sun's bearing relative to the AP of the spherical triangle when the AP is in the northern hemisphere and the sun is west of the AP

points can ever have an angle greater than 180°, because at 180° the triangle becomes a straight line, a line of longitude, in fact.

By mathematical convention, the azimuth angle, Z, is reckoned from the apex of the navigational triangle toward the GP of the body. When the apex is the North Pole, the measurement is clockwise

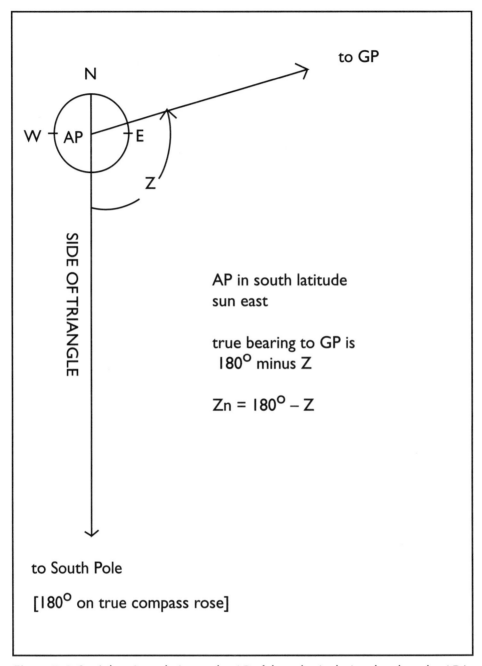

*Figure 7–9.* Sun's bearing relative to the AP of the spherical triangle when the AP is in the southern hemisphere and the sun is east of the AP

through 180° when the sun is east. When the sun is west, Z is measured counterclockwise, or *widdershins,* as some folks say. When the AP is south of the equator, the triangle is on its head (apex at the South Pole), and Z is reckoned counterclockwise when the sun is east and clockwise when it is west.

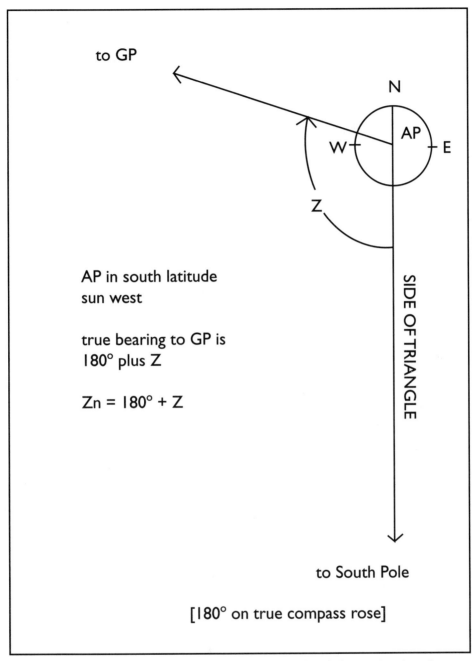

to GP

N

AP

W

E

Z

AP in south latitude
sun west

true bearing to GP is
180° plus Z

Zn = 180° + Z

SIDE OF TRIANGLE

to South Pole

[180° on true compass rose]

*Figure 7–10.* Sun's bearing relative to the AP of the spherical triangle when the AP
is in the southern hemisphere and the sun is west of the AP

Figure 7-7 is like the current example: AP in a north latitude and
sun east. Here Z obviously lines up with the true compass rose,
which is based on north and always reckons angles clockwise
through 360°, so Zn equals Z. When the sun is to the west, the situation is like the example in the previous chapter; Z is reckoned

counterclockwise, against the conventional compass reckoning, so Zn
equals 360° minus Z (fig. 7-8).

When the AP is in south latitudes, the apex of the spherical triangle is at
the South Pole, so angle Z has to be applied to 180° (true south) to get Zn.
Figure 7-9 shows the AP angle of such a triangle when the sun is to the east.
Here Z is reckoned counterclockwise from south, or 180° true, so Zn is 180°
minus Z. Figure 7-10 shows the situation when the sun is west; Z is reckoned clockwise, so Zn equals 180° plus Z.

Again, it's hard to visualize all this every time you sit down to a plotting
sheet, so mnemonics are printed in the left-hand corners of every page of
the sight reduction table, at the top of the page for APs north of the equator,
at the bottom for APs south. The key to their use is LHA, which tells whether
the sun is east or west, and is the main reason the LHA convention exists.

Return now to your passage from the Canaries to the Bahamas. Figure
7-11 is a plot of the morning sight; the LOP passes quite close to the DR.
Here's how you go about setting up and using a plotting sheet.

The coordinates of the DR are 25°19′ N, 72°48′ W; of the AP, 25°00′ N,
72°51′ W.

Using dividers and a parallel ruler, put in a couple of longitude lines for
a mid-latitude of 25°, and mark the DR and AP positions on the plotting
sheet. Remember to pick the longitude off the netlike grid in the lower right-
hand corner, not off the vertical central scale, which is only for latitude and
nautical miles (again, if you make it a habit to mark the longitude on the
grid first, you're less likely to err).

Now it's time to plot the LOP. According to the sight reduction table, the
true bearing to the sun from the AP is 135°, so use the true rose and a parallel ruler to lay off a line in that direction through the AP. (Use the parallel
ruler. Don't simply draw a line from the AP to 135° on the bearing ring. That
gives you instead a bearing of about 141°.) Put a chevron on the end of the
line to make it an arrow that points toward the GP. Label the arrow "to sun,"
or sketch a little sun near the arrow's end.

The next step is to lay down the LOP. The difference between your
observed altitude and the altitude computed for the AP is 17′. Since the
observed altitude is less than the computed, the LOP you are on has to be
17 nautical miles farther from the GP than the one through AP. There is no
need to draw that line, however, so use the vertical scale and your dividers
to pick off 17 nautical miles, and simply make a dot that distance from the
AP on the AP–GP line. Through the dot, draw a line perpendicular to the
AP–GP line (an ordinary grade-school protractor is handy for drawing per-
pendiculars, by the way).

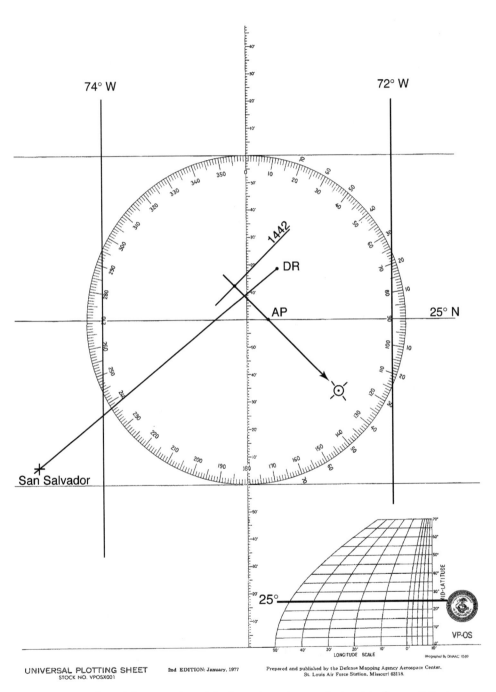

*Figure 7–11.* Plot of the morning sight found on the work sheet in figure 7-6

The perpendicular line is your LOP and is usually labeled with the time of the sight, GMT or ship's, your choice. There is no need to include the seconds when you label the LOP. The time of the sight was 1442 GMT, so that's the way it's tagged in the example.

What you now have before you is the final result of one sight. The LOP runs about 6 miles from the DR, which is a more or less average result for small boats. The gap between DR and LOP is rarely smaller than five percent of the distance run between sights and rarely larger than ten percent.

Again, unless the observed and computed altitudes happen to come out the same, as they did in the previous chapter, no LOP is drawn through the AP; it would just add clutter. The difference between the two altitudes, the *intercept,* is simply marked off toward or away from the AP along the AP–GP line, and the LOP is drawn through that point.

This particular LOP is interesting because it runs more or less parallel to the course of 230° true. Getting a fix is the goal of course, but a line like this is almost as useful, because it shows you close to the track to the Bahamian island of San Salvador. In fact, if you extend the LOP you see that it runs just a little south of the island, so even if the skies cloud over, you can simply alter course to port a few degrees and sail the LOP to make your destination.

But the weather stays clear and you are coming up on a landfall; you really do want a fix before sunset. In the late afternoon you again take five careful shots of the sun and average them. It is now 20-46-10 GMT, and the sextant reads 22°06′. Looking at the log, you see you have run 41 miles since your morning sight, which, plotted, gives you a DR of 24°53′ N, 73°24′ W.

The work sheet for this sight is shown in figure 7-12, and the resulting LOP is plotted in figure 7-13 on the same sheet as the morning sight. Again you have come up with a particularly useful LOP. It runs athwart your course and thus is a good check of the distance run and your offing from the island. It appears you are a little farther along than you thought, but you are reaching in a breeze through the southern part of the North Atlantic gyre, which, according to the Pilot Chart, tends westerly by about a half-knot. All in all, things add up pretty well, but you would like to have a fix; to get one, you need to advance the morning LOP to the time of the afternoon sight. Where the two LOPs cross is your fix—your *running fix,* strictly speaking.

| Date: 10-11-99 | | DR: | 25°53′ N |
|---|---|---|---|
| | | | 73°24′ W |

| Sextant reads | [Hs] | 22°06′ |
|---|---|---|
| Index corr. | [IC] | + 02′ |
| Dip corr. | [D] | – 03′ |
| Apparent alt. | [Ha] | 22°05′ |
| Ref/SD | | + 14′ |
| Observed alt. | [Ho] | 22°19′ |

| GHA  2000 UT | 123°18.7′ | Dec. | S 7°04.9′ |
|---|---|---|---|
| + 46m, 10s | 11°32.5′ | | + 0.6′ |
| **GHA** | 134°51.2′ | Dec. | S 7°05.5′ |
| **GHA** | 134°51′ | Dec. | S 7°06′ |

(+ 360°?)

**AP longitude** $_{+E}^{-W}$ – 73°51′ W      **AP latitude** = 25° N

(– 360°?)

**LHA**           61°00′

Data for HO 249: lat. = 25°  ⟨Same/Contr⟩ | LHA = 61°  Dec. = 7°

Data from HO 249: Hc = 22°37′ d = $^{+}_{⊖}$31′ | Z = 110°

| **Hc** | 22°37′ | | Dec. increment = 06′ |
|---|---|---|---|
| Corr | ± 03′ | | |
| **Hc** | 22°34′ | | |
| **Ho** | 22°19′ | | |
| | 17′ ⟨Toward/Away⟩ | | **Zn** = 250° |

*Figure 7–12.* Work sheet for finding the AP's computed altitude (Hc) and true bearing (Zn) to the GP when the sun is west of the AP and the GP is in the opposite hemisphere

There are many ways to advance a line of position. The one I always like is to take the point on the morning LOP closest to the DR—the so-called most probable position (MPP)—move that point the distance and direction traveled between sights (that is, the distance between the two DRs), and then use a parallel ruler to move the morning LOP to it. After all, you can be at any point on an LOP,

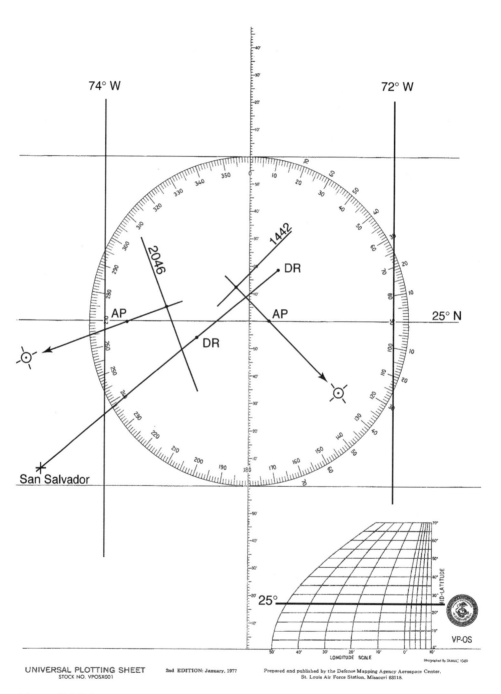

Figure 7–13. Plots of the morning sight found in figure 7-6 and the afternoon sight found in figure 7-12

so you might just as well move the one that most likely represents where you were.

Another reason I like this method is that it is easy to check; the morning MPP has to end up in the same relative position to the afternoon DR that it was to the morning DR. This situation holds in figure 7-14, the completed plot. The moved MPP is the little dot northwest of the afternoon DR. The dashed line is the advanced morning LOP; the point where the two LOPs cross is circled and is the running fix, 24°56′ N, 73°32′ W. It agrees well with the DR, placing you about 5 miles farther along, a little north of the course, and about 70 miles northeast of San Salvador.

The lighthouse on San Salvador is visible from about 20 miles out (shown by the circle around the island), so at your present rate of sailing, you should be inside its range in another seven hours—at about two in the morning, October 12. You figure you'll take the watch at midnight. With land in the offing, no navigator sleeps.

In addition to ordinary navigator's nerves, common sense, and good seamanship, there is another reason you might want to be on deck for this particular landfall. A long time ago someone else was in this same patch of sea at night in mid-October, searching for shore. He too found it in the early hours of the morning, and he left a note about it in his log: "October 12, 1492—At two hours after midnight appeared the land."

As I said, this stuff is soul-satisfying.

And do you wonder that Christopher Columbus called the island San Salvador (Holy Savior)? Those might be the very words he uttered that amazing night.

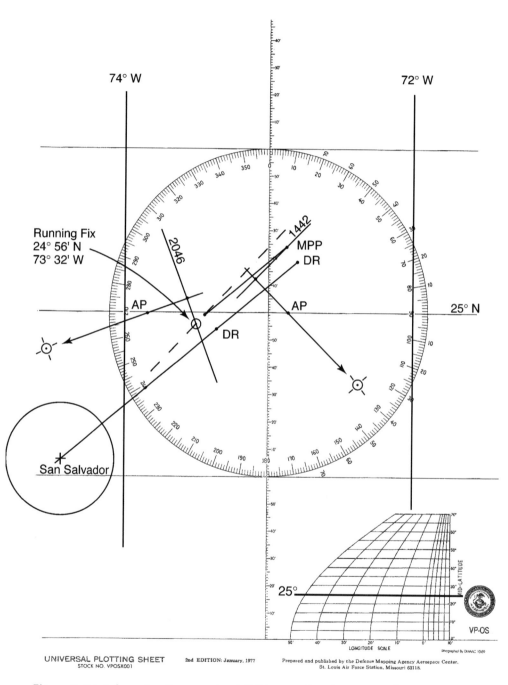

*Figure 7–14.* Advancing the morning LOP by moving the MPP to find a running fix, using sights found in figures 7-6 and 7-12

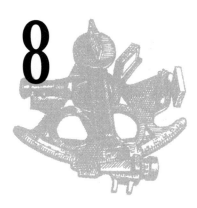

# 8

# Noon Sight for Latitude

Noon is literally the high point of the day—for the sun, at any rate. Sunlight is strong and shadows are short. As you watch the sun move through the sky on any given day, noon is the moment you see it reaching its greatest altitude above the horizon. At that moment, the sun is on your meridian, so it is either directly to your north or to your south.

To find noon, you get your sextant on the sun in the late morning and follow it until the sextant reading reaches a maximum. You apply the usual corrections, subtract the altitude from 90°, and use the *zenith distance* to find your latitude directly. No sight reduction tables are necessary because the navigational triangle has collapsed and is now a line of longitude, *your* line of longitude.

Accurate time is not required for this sight either, because the only component of the sun's GP used to find your latitude is declination. That doesn't change very fast—1′ per hour around the time of the equinoxes is the maximum amount. Time to the nearest hour is plenty good enough.

Here's an example:

It is July 23, 1999. Your DR is 40°08′ N, 60°35′ W. About four hours after your morning sun sight you notice the sun getting very high in the sky and approaching a true bearing of south. You get out your sextant and start taking sights.

The first sight you get is 69°27′. You don't write down the time because you are not going to use this sight in the ordinary way. It's just the initial step in following the sun to its maximum altitude.

A few minutes later, you put the sextant to your eye again and notice quite a gap has opened between the sun and the horizon. You close the gap by turning the micrometer drum and swing the arc. With the sun this high, it seems to skim along the horizon a long way before it rises clear. Your sextant reads 69°34′.

The next time you raise the sextant the gap between sun and horizon is not as great. You close it, swing the arc, and see you have an altitude of 69°36′.

Now you have to keep your sextant on the sun constantly, closing the gap and swinging the arc as an ever-tinier gap opens. Finally there is a period when nothing seems to change. You swing the arc and the sun just skims along the horizon. No gap opens.

After a couple of minutes, you suddenly notice that the lower edge of the sun is *biting into* the horizon. The moment of noon has passed. The sun is on its way down. You *don't move the drum* to put the sun back on the horizon. The sun reached its maximum altitude during the interval when you could detect no motion, and that reading is what you want.

You look at your sextant. It reads 69°37′. You glance at your watch/chronometer; GMT is 1615.

Turning to the almanac, you see that, for all practical purposes, the declination of the sun between 1600 and 1700 is 20°04′ N (fig. 8-1).

Figure 8-2 is a work sheet for this sight. You write down the maximum sextant reading of 69°37′ and apply index, dip, and refraction and semidiameter corrections from the tables on the inside front cover of the almanac (fig. 4-3) to get the true observed altitude of 69°53′.

Subtracting 69°53′ from 90° gives the zenith distance—the length of the arc between the sun's GP and you—as 20°07′. The little sketch on the work sheet illustrates this relationship. You are 20°07′ north of the GP of the sun, and since you and the GP are on the same line of longitude, finding your latitude is simply a matter of adding the number of degrees of latitude between you and the sun

## 1999 JULY 21, 22, 23 (WED., THURS., FRI.)

### SUN and MOON

| UT | SUN GHA | SUN Dec | MOON GHA | v | MOON Dec | d | HP |
|---|---|---|---|---|---|---|---|
| **21 00** | 178 24.6 | N20 35.7 | 84 03.5 | 14.8 | S 8 11.9 | 9.4 | 54.6 |
| 01 | 193 24.6 | 35.3 | 98 37.3 | 14.8 | 8 21.3 | 9.5 | 54.5 |
| 02 | 208 24.5 | 34.8 | 113 11.1 | 14.7 | 8 30.8 | 9.4 | 54.5 |
| 03 | 223 24.5 | .. 34.3 | 127 44.8 | 14.8 | 8 40.2 | 9.4 | 54.5 |
| 04 | 238 24.5 | 33.8 | 142 18.6 | 14.7 | 8 49.6 | 9.3 | 54.5 |
| 05 | 253 24.4 | 33.4 | 156 52.3 | 14.8 | 8 58.9 | 9.3 | 54.5 |
| **W 06** | 268 24.4 | N20 32.9 | 171 26.1 | 14.7 | S 9 08.2 | 9.2 | 54.5 |
| E 07 | 283 24.4 | 32.4 | 185 59.8 | 14.7 | 9 17.4 | 9.2 | 54.5 |
| D 08 | 298 24.3 | 31.9 | 200 33.5 | 14.7 | 9 26.6 | 9.2 | 54.4 |
| N 09 | 313 24.3 | .. 31.5 | 215 07.2 | 14.7 | 9 35.8 | 9.1 | 54.4 |
| E 10 | 328 24.3 | 31.0 | 229 40.9 | 14.7 | 9 44.9 | 9.0 | 54.4 |
| S 11 | 343 24.2 | 30.5 | 244 14.6 | 14.6 | 9 53.9 | 9.1 | 54.4 |
| D 12 | 358 24.2 | N20 30.0 | 258 48.2 | 14.7 | S10 03.0 | 9.0 | 54.4 |
| A 13 | 13 24.2 | 29.5 | 273 21.9 | 14.6 | 10 12.0 | 8.9 | 54.4 |
| Y 14 | 28 24.2 | 29.1 | 287 55.5 | 14.6 | 10 20.9 | 8.9 | 54.4 |
| 15 | 43 24.1 | .. 28.6 | 302 29.1 | 14.6 | 10 29.8 | 8.8 | 54.4 |
| 16 | 58 24.1 | 28.1 | 317 02.7 | 14.6 | 10 38.6 | 8.8 | 54.3 |
| 17 | 73 24.1 | 27.6 | 331 36.3 | 14.5 | 10 47.4 | 8.8 | 54.3 |
| 18 | 88 24.0 | N20 27.1 | 346 09.8 | 14.6 | S10 56.2 | 8.7 | 54.3 |
| 19 | 103 24.0 | 26.6 | 0 43.4 | 14.5 | 11 04.9 | 8.6 | 54.3 |
| 20 | 118 24.0 | 26.2 | 15 16.9 | 14.5 | 11 13.5 | 8.6 | 54.3 |
| 21 | 133 23.9 | .. 25.7 | 29 50.4 | 14.5 | 11 22.1 | 8.6 | 54.3 |
| 22 | 148 23.9 | 25.2 | 44 23.9 | 14.4 | 11 30.7 | 8.5 | 54.3 |
| 23 | 163 23.9 | 24.7 | 58 57.3 | 14.5 | 11 39.2 | 8.4 | 54.3 |
| **22 00** | 178 23.9 | N20 24.2 | 73 30.8 | 14.4 | S11 47.6 | 8.4 | 54.3 |
| 01 | 193 23.8 | 23.7 | 88 04.2 | 14.4 | 11 56.0 | 8.4 | 54.3 |
| 02 | 208 23.8 | 23.2 | 102 37.6 | 14.3 | 12 04.4 | 8.2 | 54.3 |
| 03 | 223 23.8 | .. 22.7 | 117 10.9 | 14.4 | 12 12.6 | 8.3 | 54.2 |
| 04 | 238 23.8 | 22.3 | 131 44.3 | 14.3 | 12 20.9 | 8.2 | 54.2 |
| 05 | 253 23.7 | 21.8 | 146 17.6 | 14.3 | 12 29.1 | 8.1 | 54.2 |
| **T 06** | 268 23.7 | N20 21.3 | 160 50.9 | 14.2 | S12 37.2 | 8.1 | 54.2 |
| H 07 | 283 23.7 | 20.8 | 175 24.1 | 14.3 | 12 45.3 | 8.0 | 54.2 |
| U 08 | 298 23.6 | 20.3 | 189 57.4 | 14.2 | 12 53.3 | 8.0 | 54.2 |
| R 09 | 313 23.6 | .. 19.8 | 204 30.6 | 14.2 | 13 01.3 | 7.9 | 54.2 |
| S 10 | 328 23.6 | 19.3 | 219 03.8 | 14.2 | 13 09.2 | 7.9 | 54.2 |
| D 11 | 343 23.6 | 18.8 | 233 37.0 | 14.1 | 13 17.1 | 7.8 | 54.2 |
| A 12 | 358 23.5 | N20 18.3 | 248 10.1 | 14.1 | S13 24.9 | 7.7 | 54.2 |
| Y 13 | 13 23.5 | 17.8 | 262 43.2 | 14.1 | 13 32.6 | 7.7 | 54.2 |
| 14 | 28 23.5 | 17.3 | 277 16.3 | 14.0 | 13 40.3 | 7.6 | 54.2 |
| 15 | 43 23.5 | .. 16.8 | 291 49.3 | 14.0 | 13 47.9 | 7.6 | 54.2 |
| 16 | 58 23.4 | 16.3 | 306 22.3 | 14.0 | 13 55.5 | 7.5 | 54.2 |
| 17 | 73 23.4 | 15.8 | 320 55.3 | 14.0 | 14 03.0 | 7.5 | 54.2 |
| 18 | 88 23.4 | N20 15.3 | 335 28.3 | 13.9 | S14 10.5 | 7.3 | 54.2 |
| 19 | 103 23.4 | 14.8 | 350 01.2 | 13.9 | 14 17.8 | 7.4 | 54.2 |
| 20 | 118 23.4 | 14.3 | 4 34.1 | 13.9 | 14 25.2 | 7.2 | 54.2 |
| 21 | 133 23.3 | .. 13.8 | 19 07.0 | 13.8 | 14 32.4 | 7.2 | 54.2 |
| 22 | 148 23.3 | 13.3 | 33 39.8 | 13.8 | 14 39.6 | 7.2 | 54.2 |
| 23 | 163 23.3 | 12.8 | 48 12.6 | 13.8 | 14 46.8 | 7.1 | 54.2 |
| **23 00** | 178 23.3 | N20 12.3 | 62 45.4 | 13.7 | S14 53.9 | 7.0 | 54.2 |
| 01 | 193 23.2 | 11.8 | 77 18.1 | 13.7 | 15 00.9 | 6.9 | 54.2 |
| 02 | 208 23.2 | 11.3 | 91 50.8 | 13.7 | 15 07.8 | 6.9 | 54.2 |
| 03 | 223 23.2 | .. 10.8 | 106 23.5 | 13.6 | 15 14.7 | 6.8 | 54.2 |
| 04 | 238 23.2 | 10.3 | 120 56.1 | 13.6 | 15 21.5 | 6.8 | 54.2 |
| 05 | 253 23.2 | 09.8 | 135 28.7 | 13.6 | 15 28.3 | 6.7 | 54.2 |
| **F 06** | 268 23.1 | N20 09.3 | 150 01.3 | 13.5 | S15 35.0 | 6.6 | 54.2 |
| R 07 | 283 23.1 | 08.8 | 164 33.8 | 13.5 | 15 41.6 | 6.6 | 54.2 |
| I 08 | 298 23.1 | 08.3 | 179 06.3 | 13.4 | 15 48.2 | 6.5 | 54.2 |
| D 09 | 313 23.1 | .. 07.8 | 193 38.7 | 13.5 | 15 54.7 | 6.4 | 54.2 |
| A 10 | 328 23.1 | 07.3 | 208 11.2 | 13.4 | 16 01.1 | 6.3 | 54.2 |
| Y 11 | 343 23.0 | 06.8 | 222 43.6 | 13.3 | 16 07.4 | 6.3 | 54.2 |
| 12 | 358 23.0 | N20 06.3 | 237 15.9 | 13.3 | S16 13.7 | 6.2 | 54.2 |
| 13 | 13 23.0 | 05.8 | 251 48.2 | 13.3 | 16 19.9 | 6.2 | 54.2 |
| 14 | 28 23.0 | 05.3 | 266 20.5 | 13.3 | 16 26.1 | 6.0 | 54.2 |
| 15 | 43 23.0 | 04.7 | 280 52.8 | 13.2 | 16 32.1 | 6.0 | 54.2 |
| 16 | 58 22.9 | 04.2 | 295 25.0 | 13.1 | 16 38.1 | 5.9 | 54.2 |
| 17 | 73 22.9 | 03.7 | 309 57.1 | 13.2 | 16 44.0 | 5.9 | 54.2 |
| 18 | 88 22.9 | N20 03.2 | 324 29.3 | 13.1 | S16 49.9 | 5.8 | 54.2 |
| 19 | 103 22.9 | 02.7 | 339 01.4 | 13.0 | 16 55.7 | 5.7 | 54.2 |
| 20 | 118 22.9 | 02.2 | 353 33.4 | 13.1 | 17 01.4 | 5.6 | 54.2 |
| 21 | 133 22.9 | .. 01.7 | 8 05.5 | 12.9 | 17 07.0 | 5.6 | 54.2 |
| 22 | 148 22.8 | 01.2 | 22 37.4 | 13.0 | 17 12.6 | 5.5 | 54.2 |
| 23 | 163 22.8 | 00.6 | 37 09.4 | 12.9 | S17 18.1 | 5.4 | 54.2 |
| | SD 15.8 | d 0.5 | SD 14.8 | | 14.8 | | 14.8 |

### Twilight, Sunrise and Moonrise

| Lat. | Naut. | Civil | Sunrise | Moonrise 21 | 22 | 23 | 24 |
|---|---|---|---|---|---|---|---|
| N 72 | ☐ | ☐ | ☐ | 15 11 | 17 00 | 19 06 | ■ |
| N 70 | ☐ | ☐ | ☐ | 14 53 | 16 30 | 18 10 | 19 56 |
| 68 | //// | //// | 01 10 | 14 39 | 16 08 | 17 36 | 19 02 |
| 66 | //// | //// | 02 03 | 14 28 | 15 50 | 17 12 | 18 30 |
| 64 | //// | //// | 02 35 | 14 18 | 15 37 | 16 53 | 18 06 |
| 62 | //// | 01 28 | 02 58 | 14 10 | 15 25 | 16 38 | 17 47 |
| 60 | //// | 02 06 | 03 17 | 14 03 | 15 15 | 16 25 | 17 32 |
| N 58 | //// | 02 32 | 03 32 | 13 57 | 15 06 | 16 14 | 17 18 |
| 56 | 01 21 | 02 52 | 03 45 | 13 51 | 14 59 | 16 04 | 17 07 |
| 54 | 01 55 | 03 08 | 03 56 | 13 47 | 14 52 | 15 56 | 16 57 |
| 52 | 02 20 | 03 22 | 04 06 | 13 42 | 14 46 | 15 48 | 16 49 |
| 50 | 02 38 | 03 34 | 04 15 | 13 38 | 14 41 | 15 42 | 16 41 |
| 45 | 03 13 | 03 59 | 04 34 | 13 30 | 14 29 | 15 27 | 16 24 |
| N 40 | 03 39 | 04 18 | 04 49 | 13 23 | 14 19 | 15 15 | 16 10 |
| 35 | 03 58 | 04 33 | 05 02 | 13 17 | 14 11 | 15 05 | 15 59 |
| 30 | 04 14 | 04 46 | 05 13 | 13 11 | 14 04 | 14 56 | 15 49 |
| 20 | 04 39 | 05 08 | 05 32 | 13 02 | 13 51 | 14 41 | 15 31 |
| N 10 | 04 59 | 05 25 | 05 48 | 12 54 | 13 41 | 14 28 | 15 16 |
| 0 | 05 15 | 05 41 | 06 03 | 12 47 | 13 30 | 14 15 | 15 02 |
| S 10 | 05 30 | 05 55 | 06 18 | 12 39 | 13 20 | 14 03 | 14 48 |
| 20 | 05 43 | 06 10 | 06 34 | 12 31 | 13 10 | 13 50 | 14 33 |
| 30 | 05 57 | 06 26 | 06 52 | 12 22 | 12 58 | 13 35 | 14 16 |
| 35 | 06 04 | 06 35 | 07 02 | 12 17 | 12 51 | 13 27 | 14 06 |
| 40 | 06 11 | 06 45 | 07 14 | 12 11 | 12 43 | 13 17 | 13 55 |
| 45 | 06 20 | 06 56 | 07 28 | 12 05 | 12 33 | 13 05 | 13 42 |
| S 50 | 06 29 | 07 09 | 07 45 | 11 57 | 12 22 | 12 51 | 13 25 |
| 52 | 06 33 | 07 15 | 07 53 | 11 53 | 12 17 | 12 45 | 13 18 |
| 54 | 06 37 | 07 21 | 08 02 | 11 49 | 12 12 | 12 38 | 13 09 |
| 56 | 06 42 | 07 28 | 08 12 | 11 44 | 12 05 | 12 30 | 13 00 |
| 58 | 06 47 | 07 36 | 08 24 | 11 39 | 11 58 | 12 21 | 12 49 |
| S 60 | 06 52 | 07 46 | 08 37 | 11 34 | 11 50 | 12 11 | 12 37 |

### Sunset, Twilight and Moonset

| Lat. | Sunset | Civil | Naut. | Moonset 21 | 22 | 23 | 24 |
|---|---|---|---|---|---|---|---|
| N 72 | ☐ | ☐ | ☐ | 22 25 | 22 09 | 21 37 | ■ |
| N 70 | ☐ | ☐ | ☐ | 22 45 | 22 40 | 22 34 | 22 25 |
| 68 | 22 56 | //// | //// | 23 00 | 23 03 | 23 08 | 23 19 |
| 66 | 22 06 | //// | //// | 23 13 | 23 21 | 23 33 | 23 52 |
| 64 | 21 35 | //// | //// | 23 23 | 23 36 | 23 52 | 24 16 |
| 62 | 21 13 | 22 40 | //// | 23 32 | 23 48 | 24 08 | 00 08 |
| 60 | 20 55 | 22 04 | //// | 23 40 | 23 58 | 24 21 | 00 21 |
| N 58 | 20 39 | 21 39 | //// | 23 47 | 24 08 | 00 08 | 00 33 |
| 56 | 20 27 | 21 19 | 22 48 | 23 53 | 24 16 | 00 16 | 00 43 |
| 54 | 20 15 | 21 03 | 22 15 | 24 03 | 00 03 | 00 23 | 00 51 |
| 52 | 20 06 | 20 49 | 21 51 | 24 08 | 00 08 | 00 29 | 00 59 |
| 50 | 19 57 | 20 38 | 21 33 | 24 18 | 00 18 | 00 35 | 01 06 |
| 45 | 19 38 | 20 13 | 20 58 | 24 26 | 00 26 | 00 48 | 01 22 |
| N 40 | 19 23 | 19 55 | 20 34 | 24 26 | 00 26 | 00 58 | 01 34 |
| 35 | 19 11 | 19 39 | 20 14 | 00 00 | 00 33 | 01 07 | 01 45 |
| 30 | 19 00 | 19 26 | 19 58 | 00 04 | 00 39 | 01 15 | 01 54 |
| 20 | 18 41 | 19 05 | 19 33 | 00 12 | 00 49 | 01 29 | 02 10 |
| N 10 | 18 25 | 18 47 | 19 14 | 00 18 | 00 59 | 01 41 | 02 25 |
| 0 | 18 10 | 18 32 | 18 58 | 00 24 | 01 08 | 01 52 | 02 38 |
| S 10 | 17 55 | 18 17 | 18 43 | 00 30 | 01 16 | 02 03 | 02 51 |
| 20 | 17 39 | 18 03 | 18 30 | 00 37 | 01 26 | 02 15 | 03 05 |
| 30 | 17 21 | 17 47 | 18 16 | 00 44 | 01 37 | 02 29 | 03 22 |
| 35 | 17 11 | 17 38 | 18 09 | 00 48 | 01 43 | 02 37 | 03 31 |
| 40 | 16 59 | 17 29 | 18 02 | 00 53 | 01 50 | 02 46 | 03 42 |
| 45 | 16 45 | 17 18 | 17 54 | 00 59 | 01 58 | 02 57 | 03 55 |
| S 50 | 16 28 | 17 05 | 17 45 | 01 05 | 02 08 | 03 10 | 04 10 |
| 52 | 16 20 | 16 59 | 17 41 | 01 09 | 02 13 | 03 16 | 04 17 |
| 54 | 16 11 | 16 52 | 17 36 | 01 12 | 02 18 | 03 23 | 04 26 |
| 56 | 16 01 | 16 45 | 17 32 | 01 16 | 02 24 | 03 30 | 04 35 |
| 58 | 15 50 | 16 37 | 17 27 | 01 20 | 02 30 | 03 39 | 04 45 |
| S 60 | 15 36 | 16 28 | 17 21 | 01 25 | 02 37 | 03 49 | 04 57 |

### SUN and MOON

| Day | SUN Eqn. of Time 00h | 12h | Mer. Pass. | MOON Mer. Pass. Upper | Lower | Age | Phase |
|---|---|---|---|---|---|---|---|
| d | m s | m s | h m | h m | h m | d % | |
| 21 | 06 22 | 06 23 | 12 06 | 06 23 | 18 57 | 08 61 | ☽ |
| 22 | 06 24 | 06 26 | 12 06 | 19 41 | 07 19 | 09 70 | |
| 23 | 06 27 | 06 28 | 12 06 | 20 27 | 08 04 | 10 78 | |

*Figure 8–1.* GP tables, from the *Nautical Almanac*

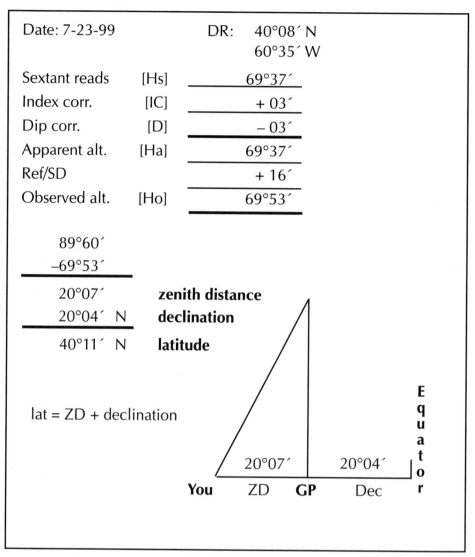

Date: 7-23-99                    DR:    40°08′ N
                                        60°35′ W

| Sextant reads | [Hs] | 69°37′ |
| Index corr. | [IC] | + 03′ |
| Dip corr. | [D] | – 03′ |
| Apparent alt. | [Ha] | 69°37′ |
| Ref/SD | | + 16′ |
| Observed alt. | [Ho] | 69°53′ |

89°60′
–69°53′

20°07′      **zenith distance**
20°04′  N   **declination**
40°11′  N   **latitude**

lat = ZD + declination

*Figure 8–2.* Work sheet for finding a noon sight and a sketch of the relative
locations of latitude, zenith distance, and declination when the sun is between you
and the equator

(20°07′) to the sun's latitude (20°04′ N). Thus, your latitude by direct
measurement is 40°11′ N, only 3′ north of your DR.

   This example deals with only one of the four possible positions
you can be in relative to the noonday sun: the sun is between you
and the equator.

   Figure 8-3 illustrates the situation if you and the sun reverse
positions. To find your latitude when you are between the noonday
sun and the equator you *subtract* the zenith distance from the GP's
latitude (the declination of the sun).

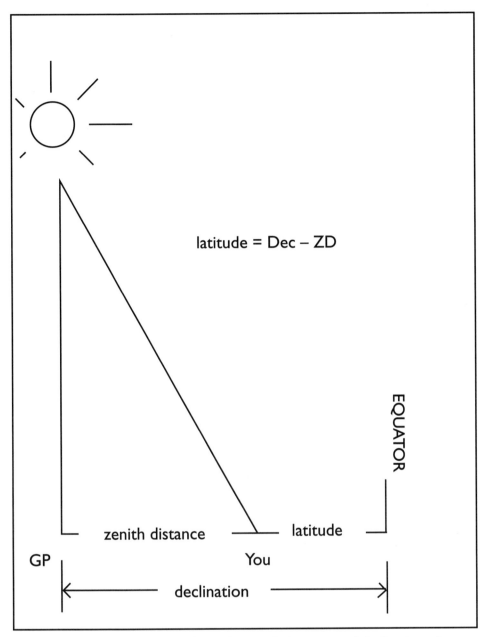

*Figure 8–3.* Relative locations of latitude, zenith distance, and declination when you are between the sun and the equator

When the equator is between you and the sun, as shown in figure 8-4, your latitude is the zenith distance *minus* the declination of the sun.

If you use sketches as I do, it is easy enough to see how to combine declination and zenith distance correctly, but it is a little cumbersome. A more common-sense approach is just to look at the

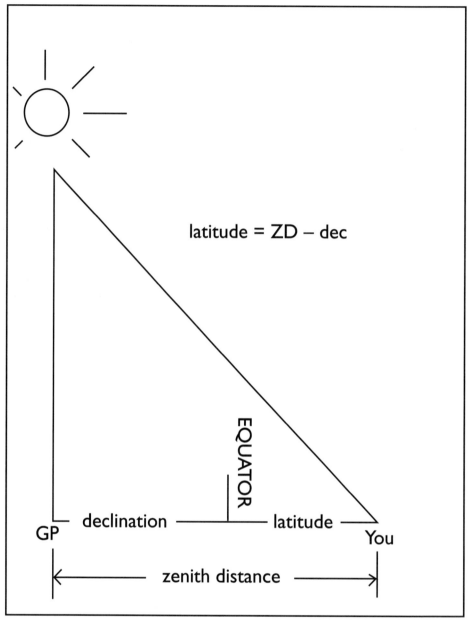

Figure 8–4. Relative locations of latitude, zenith distance, and declination when the equator is between you and the sun

numbers and see what you have to do to make them produce a latitude that is close to your DR. Remember, with a DR you never navigate from "lost"; you navigate from "the vicinity of the DR," an area you can usually cover with your thumb.

Finally, there is the very rare time when the sun passes virtually overhead—that is, when your latitude and the sun's declination are nearly the same. Here you get an observed altitude of 90°00´, which tells you your latitude and the declination are the same.

Actually, such a sight is virtually impossible to get because the sun is whizzing by from east to west and, as you swing the arc, you have to spin around in a complete circle. The closest I ever came to such a sight was during a summer passage from Bermuda to the Virgin Islands. I got an altitude of 89°40´. I put the GP on the chart and drew a circle with a 20´ radius around it. Since the boat was headed south and I was looking over the transom when I got the maximum altitude, I knew the GP was to the north and that the boat, therefore, had to be on the south side of the circle. Plotted, it confirmed the DR just fine (fig. 8-5).

Once you have established your latitude, draw it on your chart or plotting sheet and advance your morning sun line to it for a running fix. When you get your afternoon sun line (or an evening line from a planet), advance your noon latitude to it, and wrap your day up with another running fix.

Since noon occurs only once a day, you want to avoid missing it. The calculations are simple. All you need to do is take note of your DR longitude and look in the *Nautical Almanac.*

In the example, the longitude of the DR is 60°35´ W. The almanac shows that at 1600 GMT the sun's west longitude is 58°22.9´. So at 1600, the sun is a bit more than 2° east of your DR. It's unlikely your longitude will ever be 2° off, so you can start taking sights at 1600 GMT and not miss noon. If you want to allow yourself a bit more time, recall that it takes the sun 4 minutes to move across 1° of longitude and start taking sights at 1556 or earlier.

Another way to avoid missing noon is to watch the compass. When the sun gets close to a bearing of true south or north or the shadow cast by the vertical pin in the compass gets short, get out your sextant and get with it.

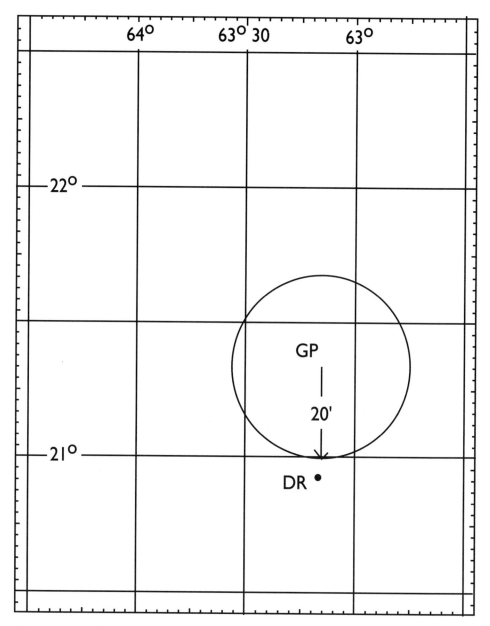

*Figure 8–5.* A plot of a nearly vertical (90°) sight relative to the DR

# Part II

⊙    ♃    ♂    ♄    ♀    ☆    ☽

# Neighbors: Navigation by the Planets

# 9

# Identification

The horizon is not the *only* element in celestial navigation, but it is the most important. If you can't see it, you can't take a sight.

How then can you take a sight of a star or a planet? It has to be dark before you can see enough stars to know which is which and to pick out the planets among the stars. But when it's dark, you can't reliably see the horizon.

The answer is that you don't take star or planet sights in the black of night. You take them at twilight, dawn or dusk. You take them in the gray time, after the sun sets or before it rises.

Imagine for a moment you are at sea at the end of a typical day in summer. The sky is blue; there are a few clouds. The sun reddens as it nears the horizon; as it touches, its lower edge gets a flat and smeary look (the refractive effect of 5,400 miles of air between you and the sun). Soon the sun is gone, and you are left looking at scattered pink clouds in a sky of milky gray.

The horizon is still very sharp. But where are the stars? You begin alternately to scan the sky and check the horizon. After a while, when you can just barely be sure you see the horizon, you spot a couple of points of light in the sky. "Star light, star bright," all right. But which ones are they? Until you can see the rest, the dimmer ones that shape the constellations, you can't tell. And by the time you can see those, the horizon is just a shadow. You can tell more or less where it is, but it isn't a line anymore; it's a blur.

There is no sense belaboring this point. Obviously, you need some way to identify stars and planets in advance, before the background stars appear and the horizon vanishes. Just as obviously, there must be ways to do so, because you hear celestial navigators yakking about "three-star fixes" ad nauseam. You will learn those ways in the chapters ahead. Meanwhile, there is an exception to working in the murk. One celestial body is so bright you can find it almost the instant the sun has set, well before anything else is visible so there is no chance of mistaken identity: the planet Venus. Only the sun and moon are brighter than Venus.

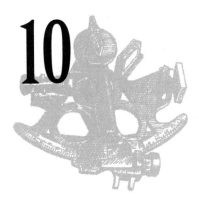

# 10

# Venus, Goddess of the Twilight

Venus is a planet about the size of our own, but much more brilliant. To celestial navigators her brightness ensures two things: instant identification and a clear horizon.

With stars, on the other hand, you have one or the other. As evening twilight deepens, the stars shine brighter, but the horizon fades. As sunrise approaches, the horizon clears, but the stars dissolve. Both situations leave navigators hastily grabbing sights in the few moments of twilight when a murky horizon and nebulous stars are balanced on the verge of obscurity. Venus, though, you can see while there's light enough on deck to read an almanac or a sight reduction table and time enough to set her down accurately on a sharp horizon. If you're solid with sun sights, Venus is one of the most comfortable bodies to sight in the full celestial suit of lights.

Venus' orbit lies between earth's and the sun, so the planet is visible when she is far enough out to one side or the other of the sun for the horizon to block the sun's dazzle. She's like the runner in a track meet you can only spot when he is in the outer turns because the guy in front of you is too big to argue with. When Venus is west of the sun, she comes over the horizon ahead of the sun in the darkness before dawn, and when she is east of the sun, the sun goes ahead of her below the horizon, leaving her as the first twinkle in the evening twilight.

Assume it is June 19, 1999; currently Venus is the evening star and will be right into August. You are a couple of days out from New England on your way to Bermuda. The cobalt blue water is a sure signal that you're in the Gulf Stream. The sun sets, and about twenty minutes later your eye is caught by a bright fleck in the western sky. It almost looks like a pearl. Soon it's a spark.

You lock on with your sextant, and as the sky and the water darken, you set the spark on the horizon, swing the arc, and look at your watch: 20-36-10. Your sextant reads 25°04′.

Now comes the hard part—the paper chase. Other than the raw sextant reading and the index error, the data for finding a position from Venus come from the inside front cover of the *Nautical Almanac* (fig. 4-3), rounded. As before, assume a height of eye of 9 feet, about average for a sailboat.

As far as refraction goes, Venus is a star, so you find the correction in the Stars and Planets table in the middle of the page. The number between 24°11′ and 25°14′ is −2.1′, which rounds to −2′ for the work sheet. Because Venus has a perceptible diameter (through a telescope) and her light rays are not strictly parallel, additional corrections are listed for different times of the year in the column just to the right of the refraction corrections. The maximum correction, though, is 0.5′ of arc in August, so you can ignore that table without undue peril. The result of this initial work is a real sight (Ho) of 25°01′.

Construction of the imaginary, comparison, or computed sight (Hc) begins with finding the GHA and declination of Venus at the time of the sextant shot. The GHA and declinations of the four navigational planets are listed on the left-hand white pages of the *Nautical Almanac* (fig. 4-1) in the same format as for the sun. The difference comes at the bottom of the column. There you see the hourly change in the declination *(d)*, as for the sun, and also a value *v*. This number is the amount that GHA varies from the table's standard rate of 15°.

Because Venus circles inside the earth's orbit, the planet's relative motions vary in direction as well as velocity. Sometimes Venus moves with the spin of the earth, sometimes against it. As a result, *v* can be negative. It's negligible most of the time, but it can get up to around 4′ of arc per hour, so you need to look at this value when

Date: 6-19-99                    DR:     38°03′ N
   (6-20 GMT)                             68°31′ W

Sextant reads     [Hs]         _____25°04′_____
Index corr.       [IC]         _____+ 02′_____
Dip corr.         [D]          _____− 03′_____
Apparent alt.     [Ha]         _____25°03′_____
Ref/SD                         + 02′
Observed alt.     [Ho]         _____25°01′_____

GHA  0000 UT   _131°26.3′_    Dec.  _N 18°29.8′_
+ 36m, 10s         9°02.5′             − 0.4′
**GHA**          _140°28.8′_    Dec.  _N 18°29.4′_
**GHA**          _140°29′_      Dec.  _N 18°29′_
(+ 360°?)
**AP longitude** −W  _− 68°29′ W_   **AP latitude = 38° N**
              +E
(− 360°?)
**LHA**              _72°00′_

Data for HO 249: lat. = 38°      ⟨Same⟩ | LHA = 72°  Dec. = 18°
                                   Contr

Figure 10–1. Work sheet solved for a Venus sight

you check the declination change and do a second mental interpolation if necessary. At the moment declination is decreasing 0.8′ per
hour, and GHA is increasing 0.3′ per hour.

Figure 10-1 is the work sheet filled out and solved for LHA and
the other data needed to use the sight reduction table *HO 249*. To
interpolate for the extra minutes and seconds of time, refer to the
table on the buff pages in the back of the almanac (fig. 4-2), using the
same column as for the sun—the one based on a rate of GHA change
of precisely 15° per hour. Interpolation for the extra GHA and the
declination change is accomplished mentally. You're about halfway
through the hour, but the GHA change of half 0.3′ isn't enough to
bother with; however, half 0.8′ subtracted from the declination of

18°29.8′ is just enough to keep from rounding to 18°30′. Keeping to the principle of working to the nearest minute of arc, I included it in the calculations, giving a declination on the work sheet of 18°29′ N.

The only trick to this example is that the navigator's watch is set to Eastern daylight time, which means that it's past midnight and therefore a new day in Greenwich. The GMT of the sight is 00-36-10, June 20.

If you take out a sight reduction table and plot the LOP for this sight, you find that you have an LOP that is very nearly a line of longitude because Venus is virtually west. (Comparing the LOP to your DR, you're also likely to find that the Gulf Stream has affected your position.)

# 11

# The Outer Planets

The other navigational planets—Mars, Jupiter, and Saturn—circle the sun beyond the earth. Although they are often brighter than the brightest stars, they are not as easy to locate as Venus. If Venus is like the runner, always in front of you as you face the track, Mars, Jupiter, and Saturn are like candy vendors, cruising the tiers above you. As they circle the stadium they can be in front of you, well to the right or left of you, or behind you. Because these planets can be more places, to find them you need more specific guidance than simply knowing they are above the horizon at twilight.

One way to locate the planets is to use the planet diagram printed on page 9 of the almanac (fig. 11-1). Essentially the diagram is a plot of the relative Greenwich hour angles of the planets and the sun through the year, with each square in the grid representing 1 hour of time, or 15° of GHA. The gray band through the middle is the area of the sun's dazzle. When a planet enters this band, it can't be seen. For example, if you look at the plot for Jupiter (the dashed line running diagonally from lower left to upper right), you see that it enters this zone in March and does not emerge until the end of April.

The way I prefer to use this chart is to imagine that the sun is on my meridian of longitude—that is, it is noon—and that I am facing it.

LOCAL MEAN TIME OF MERIDIAN PASSAGE

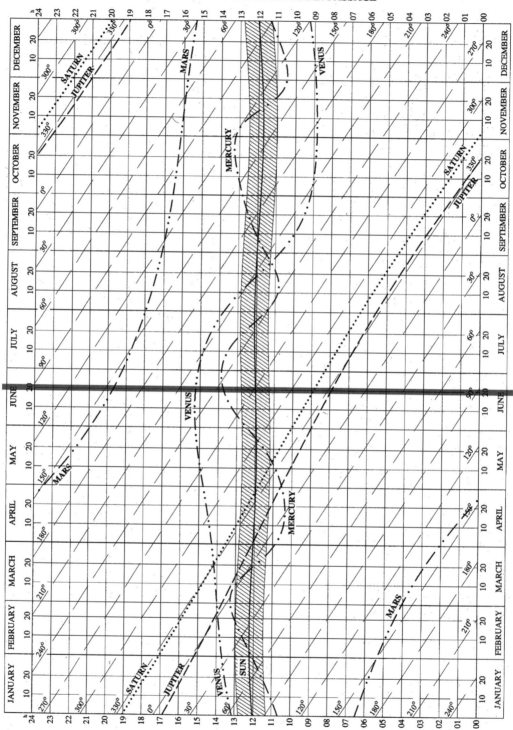

Figure 11–1. Planet diagram, 1999, from the Nautical Almanac

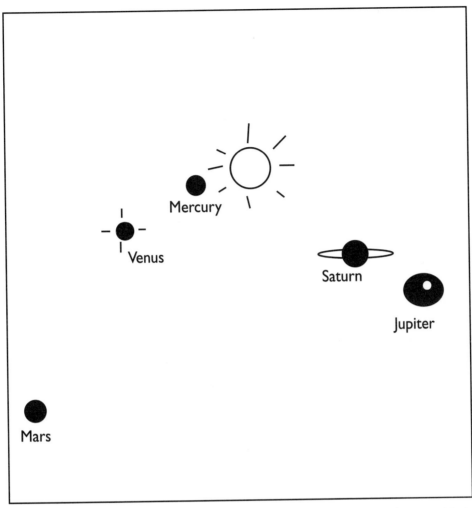

*Figure 11–2.* Sketch of the planets' locations relative to the sun, from data provided in the planet diagram, figure 11-1

That means if the sun is to my south, I look at the chart as it is presented here. East is left, and west is right. If the sun is to my north, I turn the chart upside down. That way east is right, and west is left.

For instance, imagine yourself looking at the sun at noon on June 20. The planets are lined up something like in the sketch in figure 11-2. You won't be able to see them because it is daylight, and depending on your latitude, some are below the horizon, but the drawing does show the big picture. As time passes, you can imagine the sun and planets moving west as a group and can see that Venus sets 3 hours after the sun does. By the same token, the sun rises 3 hours ahead of Venus. If you roll the planet diagram into a tube and rotate it westward, this sequence is even easier to visualize.

The amount of white space between a planet and the gray band that indicates the sun's glare gives a rough idea of how long the planet is above the horizon and where it is. You can see you never get much of a chance with Mercury, so its GHA and declination are not listed in the *Nautical Almanac*. However, turning to the example in the previous chapter, the sun set about 3 hours before Venus, which made the difference in their GHAs about 45°. In mid-latitudes in the summer, the sun sets in the northwest; 45° east of sunset is west, so that is where you would look for Venus.

Similarly, if you want to take morning sights of Saturn or Jupiter (3 and 4 hours, respectively, ahead of the sun according to the planet diagram), you need to get up some time before dawn and look to the east. In August you have to look more nearly south for these two planets, because at that time they are leading the sun by 6 hours (that is, 90° of GHA).

When you are planning to take a sight of a planet, you need to keep in mind its brightness. Otherwise, you may not spot it before the brightest stars begin to appear and cause possible confusion. You'll see a sparkle in the sky and think it is your planet. You'll take a sight, go below, and reduce it, but the LOP will make no sense at all, because you took the altitude of a star.

The brightness of the planets is the last bit of data that the almanac provides. Refer back to figure 4-1; the planet's brightness, or *magnitude,* is the number, plus or minus, that follows the planet name at the head of each column. You have most likely heard of first-magnitude stars, second-magnitude stars, and so on. Magnitude is one of those scientific scales where more means less, and every step on the scale means there is a whole lot of difference between what comes before or after.

Each step in magnitude corresponds to a difference in brightness of about 2.5 times the brightness of the previous step. Therefore, for example, Aldebaran, a star of magnitude 1.1, is about 2.5 times brighter than Nunki at 2.1, and Vega at 0.1 is about 2.5 times brighter than Aldebaran and about 6 times brighter than Nunki.

Again, the lower the magnitude, the brighter the star or planet, so celestial bodies with negative magnitudes are dazzling. The brightest star in the night skies is Sirius, the eye of Orion's dog: –1.6. By comparison, Venus is usually around –4 and occasionally approaches –5. The full moon is about –13 and the sun about –27.

The other planets wax and wane between positive and negative magnitudes depending on how far away they are from the earth, how they are oriented to the sun, and in the case of Saturn, which way the rings are facing. When you are looking for planets to use, check the magnitudes first to be sure you can spot them before the brighter stars appear. On June 20, 1999, for instance, Jupiter's magnitude is –2.2; Venus', –4.4, and Mars', –0.7, so they would be good bets; but a number of stars are close to Saturn's +0.4.

By the way, the almanac includes Mercury on the planet diagram (the sinuous line winding around the sun) even though it provides no sight data for this planet because Mercury is occasionally in conjunction with one of the four navigational planets (planets are in conjunction where the tracks cross).

If you do catch the wrong planet in your sights, the wild LOP should tip you off; providing you didn't get Mercury, go to the column for the other planet and rework the sight using its GHA and declination.

One final wrinkle to planets can be very handy in finding and using them. When a planet faces the sun across the earth, it is said to be in opposition. Its relative position is then like the full moon. The sun is shining full upon it, so it is bright. For example, Mars is in opposition around April 25, when its magnitude is –1.6, as bright as Sirius. Also, when a planet is in opposition, it rises when the sun sets, so you know where to look for it: rising in the east. Furthermore, it is up all night and sets in the west when the sun rises, so you can use it again in the morning. You can spot these times on the planet diagram by the planet's path crossing the left or right edge of the page (Mars in April, Jupiter and Saturn in October and early November).

What is especially appealing about this method of planet finding is being out under the starshine. Until you have been far at sea at night you have not seen a black sky. The stars seem very close, and there seem to be a stupendous number of them. On a clear night the glitter and sparkle of a huge constellation like Scorpio is actually a little scary. You might easily be charmed and changed from a navigator to an astrologer.

# 12

# The Edge of Night

The most scientific way to find any of the planets is to use the almanac and a sight reduction table to figure out in advance where the planet will be. This unromantic technique, employed by most practical navigators, is called *precomputation*. You don't see as much of the astral spectacle this way, but you get more sleep.

First, you need to know when dawn or evening will come upon you—that is, when the line that divides day from night will be at your longitude. This line is called the *terminator,* and if you have ever observed a half-moon you have an idea of how it looks on the earth. One-half of the earth is always in shadow; as the world turns, the terminator advances over land and sea at the same basic rate as everything else in the heavens: 15° of longitude per hour.

Since the edge of night is tangible and a factor in the practice of celestial navigation, its position is tabulated in the almanac. You won't find a table of hourly GHAs, like those for the sun and planets, because you don't take sextant shots of it (you use it to plan your shots—to get into the right playing field).

What the almanac does provide is a table that lists the GMT of the terminator at the longitude of Greenwich for latitudes between 60°S and 72°N on the middle day of each three-day period covered

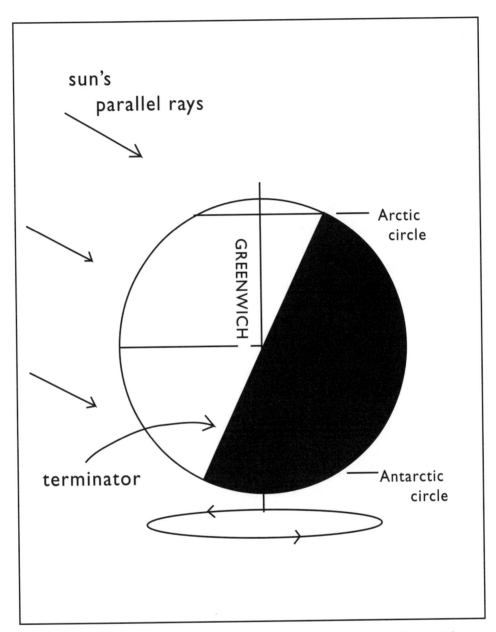

*Figure 12–1.* The sun's shadow as it falls across earth relative to the Greenwich meridian on the June solstice

by the almanac. Since you know the shadow moves westward from Greenwich at 15° per hour and you know your DR longitude, figuring out when the shadow will get to you is fairly straightforward.

Figure 12-1 shows the shadow as it appears at the June solstice. The upper and lower edges of night touch the Arctic and Antarctic circles in a way that leaves the Arctic light for 24 hours and the Antarctic dark for 24 hours. The main feature to notice, though, is that the shadow is not at the Greenwich meridian at the same time all over the world. The time varies by latitude. Thus, darkness is still far away in mid-northern latitudes, while the spinning earth has already carried the southern parts of the Greenwich meridian into the night. You can see this quite plainly in the sunset table for June 18, 19, and 20, 1999 (fig. 4-1, right-hand page). The sun sets at the meridian of Greenwich at latitude 45° N at 1950 GMT—almost 8:00 o'clock in the evening. Now look when the sun sets at 45° S: 1624 GMT—about 4:30 in the afternoon. (Of course, the shadow falls the other way around in December.)

Return now to the planning exercise. Assume you are on a trans-atlantic passage to England and want to know when the sun will set and the shadow fall, bringing the planets and stars into view. Your DR has the boat at 35° N, 60° W.

From the table in figure 4-1, you determine that the sun sets at latitude 35° N on the longitude of Greenwich at 1917 hours GMT. Since you are 60° west of the Greenwich meridian and the shadow moves 15° an hour, it will reach you 4 hours hence. So the sun will set aboard your boat at 2317 GMT.

Your DR latitude of 35° N is actually listed in the table, but if it isn't, eyeball interpolation is sufficient—remember, this exercise is just for planning purposes. For instance, if the DR is near 37° N, find the entry for 40° N. The time is 1932 GMT, 15 minutes later than at 35° N. Since 37° is two-fifths of the way between 35° and 40°, find two-fifths of 15 minutes, which is 6 minutes, and add it to 2317 for a sunset time of 2323 GMT.

Similarly, if your DR longitude is not a convenient multiple of fifteen, but 58° W, for example, you can use your knowledge that at the standard rate of 15° an hour, the sun covers 2° of longitude in 8 minutes of time. Thus, you subtract 8 minutes from 4 hours to get a time of sunset at 58° W of 3 hours and 52 minutes after sunset on the meridian of Greenwich. Therefore, at 37° N, 58° W, sunset arrives at 2315 GMT.

As an alternative to the computations in the preceding paragraph, you could recall another axiom of celestial navigation—there is always another table. In the back of the almanac, you will find the aptly named table Conversion of Arc to Time (fig. 12-2). To travel an arc of 58° (the next to last number in the first column), an object moving 15° per hour, like the shadow, takes 3 hours and 52 minutes. In the example, therefore, sunset occurs at approximately 2315 GMT

## CONVERSION OF ARC TO TIME

| 0°–59° | | 60°–119° | | 120°–179° | | 180°–239° | | 240°–299° | | 300°–359° | | 0'.00 | | 0'.25 | 0'.50 | 0'.75 |
|---|---|---|---|---|---|---|---|---|---|---|---|---|---|---|---|---|
| ° | h m | ° | h m | ° | h m | ° | h m | ° | h m | ° | h m | ' | m s | m s | m s | m s |
| 0 | 0 00 | 60 | 4 00 | 120 | 8 00 | 180 | 12 00 | 240 | 16 00 | 300 | 20 00 | 0 | 0 00 | 0 01 | 0 02 | 0 03 |
| 1 | 0 04 | 61 | 4 04 | 121 | 8 04 | 181 | 12 04 | 241 | 16 04 | 301 | 20 04 | 1 | 0 04 | 0 05 | 0 06 | 0 07 |
| 2 | 0 08 | 62 | 4 08 | 122 | 8 08 | 182 | 12 08 | 242 | 16 08 | 302 | 20 08 | 2 | 0 08 | 0 09 | 0 10 | 0 11 |
| 3 | 0 12 | 63 | 4 12 | 123 | 8 12 | 183 | 12 12 | 243 | 16 12 | 303 | 20 12 | 3 | 0 12 | 0 13 | 0 14 | 0 15 |
| 4 | 0 16 | 64 | 4 16 | 124 | 8 16 | 184 | 12 16 | 244 | 16 16 | 304 | 20 16 | 4 | 0 16 | 0 17 | 0 18 | 0 19 |
| 5 | 0 20 | 65 | 4 20 | 125 | 8 20 | 185 | 12 20 | 245 | 16 20 | 305 | 20 20 | 5 | 0 20 | 0 21 | 0 22 | 0 23 |
| 6 | 0 24 | 66 | 4 24 | 126 | 8 24 | 186 | 12 24 | 246 | 16 24 | 306 | 20 24 | 6 | 0 24 | 0 25 | 0 26 | 0 27 |
| 7 | 0 28 | 67 | 4 28 | 127 | 8 28 | 187 | 12 28 | 247 | 16 28 | 307 | 20 28 | 7 | 0 28 | 0 29 | 0 30 | 0 31 |
| 8 | 0 32 | 68 | 4 32 | 128 | 8 32 | 188 | 12 32 | 248 | 16 32 | 308 | 20 32 | 8 | 0 32 | 0 33 | 0 34 | 0 35 |
| 9 | 0 36 | 69 | 4 36 | 129 | 8 36 | 189 | 12 36 | 249 | 16 36 | 309 | 20 36 | 9 | 0 36 | 0 37 | 0 38 | 0 39 |
| 10 | 0 40 | 70 | 4 40 | 130 | 8 40 | 190 | 12 40 | 250 | 16 40 | 310 | 20 40 | 10 | 0 40 | 0 41 | 0 42 | 0 43 |
| 11 | 0 44 | 71 | 4 44 | 131 | 8 44 | 191 | 12 44 | 251 | 16 44 | 311 | 20 44 | 11 | 0 44 | 0 45 | 0 46 | 0 47 |
| 12 | 0 48 | 72 | 4 48 | 132 | 8 48 | 192 | 12 48 | 252 | 16 48 | 312 | 20 48 | 12 | 0 48 | 0 49 | 0 50 | 0 51 |
| 13 | 0 52 | 73 | 4 52 | 133 | 8 52 | 193 | 12 52 | 253 | 16 52 | 313 | 20 52 | 13 | 0 52 | 0 53 | 0 54 | 0 55 |
| 14 | 0 56 | 74 | 4 56 | 134 | 8 56 | 194 | 12 56 | 254 | 16 56 | 314 | 20 56 | 14 | 0 56 | 0 57 | 0 58 | 0 59 |
| 15 | 1 00 | 75 | 5 00 | 135 | 9 00 | 195 | 13 00 | 255 | 17 00 | 315 | 21 00 | 15 | 1 00 | 1 01 | 1 02 | 1 03 |
| 16 | 1 04 | 76 | 5 04 | 136 | 9 04 | 196 | 13 04 | 256 | 17 04 | 316 | 21 04 | 16 | 1 04 | 1 05 | 1 06 | 1 07 |
| 17 | 1 08 | 77 | 5 08 | 137 | 9 08 | 197 | 13 08 | 257 | 17 08 | 317 | 21 08 | 17 | 1 08 | 1 09 | 1 10 | 1 11 |
| 18 | 1 12 | 78 | 5 12 | 138 | 9 12 | 198 | 13 12 | 258 | 17 12 | 318 | 21 12 | 18 | 1 12 | 1 13 | 1 14 | 1 15 |
| 19 | 1 16 | 79 | 5 16 | 139 | 9 16 | 199 | 13 16 | 259 | 17 16 | 319 | 21 16 | 19 | 1 16 | 1 17 | 1 18 | 1 19 |
| 20 | 1 20 | 80 | 5 20 | 140 | 9 20 | 200 | 13 20 | 260 | 17 20 | 320 | 21 20 | 20 | 1 20 | 1 21 | 1 22 | 1 23 |
| 21 | 1 24 | 81 | 5 24 | 141 | 9 24 | 201 | 13 24 | 261 | 17 24 | 321 | 21 24 | 21 | 1 24 | 1 25 | 1 26 | 1 27 |
| 22 | 1 28 | 82 | 5 28 | 142 | 9 28 | 202 | 13 28 | 262 | 17 28 | 322 | 21 28 | 22 | 1 28 | 1 29 | 1 30 | 1 31 |
| 23 | 1 32 | 83 | 5 32 | 143 | 9 32 | 203 | 13 32 | 263 | 17 32 | 323 | 21 32 | 23 | 1 32 | 1 33 | 1 34 | 1 35 |
| 24 | 1 36 | 84 | 5 36 | 144 | 9 36 | 204 | 13 36 | 264 | 17 36 | 324 | 21 36 | 24 | 1 36 | 1 37 | 1 38 | 1 39 |
| 25 | 1 40 | 85 | 5 40 | 145 | 9 40 | 205 | 13 40 | 265 | 17 40 | 325 | 21 40 | 25 | 1 40 | 1 41 | 1 42 | 1 43 |
| 26 | 1 44 | 86 | 5 44 | 146 | 9 44 | 206 | 13 44 | 266 | 17 44 | 326 | 21 44 | 26 | 1 44 | 1 45 | 1 46 | 1 47 |
| 27 | 1 48 | 87 | 5 48 | 147 | 9 48 | 207 | 13 48 | 267 | 17 48 | 327 | 21 48 | 27 | 1 48 | 1 49 | 1 50 | 1 51 |
| 28 | 1 52 | 88 | 5 52 | 148 | 9 52 | 208 | 13 52 | 268 | 17 52 | 328 | 21 52 | 28 | 1 52 | 1 53 | 1 54 | 1 55 |
| 29 | 1 56 | 89 | 5 56 | 149 | 9 56 | 209 | 13 56 | 269 | 17 56 | 329 | 21 56 | 29 | 1 56 | 1 57 | 1 58 | 1 59 |
| 30 | 2 00 | 90 | 6 00 | 150 | 10 00 | 210 | 14 00 | 270 | 18 00 | 330 | 22 00 | 30 | 2 00 | 2 01 | 2 02 | 2 03 |
| 31 | 2 04 | 91 | 6 04 | 151 | 10 04 | 211 | 14 04 | 271 | 18 04 | 331 | 22 04 | 31 | 2 04 | 2 05 | 2 06 | 2 07 |
| 32 | 2 08 | 92 | 6 08 | 152 | 10 08 | 212 | 14 08 | 272 | 18 08 | 332 | 22 08 | 32 | 2 08 | 2 09 | 2 10 | 2 11 |
| 33 | 2 12 | 93 | 6 12 | 153 | 10 12 | 213 | 14 12 | 273 | 18 12 | 333 | 22 12 | 33 | 2 12 | 2 13 | 2 14 | 2 15 |
| 34 | 2 16 | 94 | 6 16 | 154 | 10 16 | 214 | 14 16 | 274 | 18 16 | 334 | 22 16 | 34 | 2 16 | 2 17 | 2 18 | 2 19 |
| 35 | 2 20 | 95 | 6 20 | 155 | 10 20 | 215 | 14 20 | 275 | 18 20 | 335 | 22 20 | 35 | 2 20 | 2 21 | 2 22 | 2 23 |
| 36 | 2 24 | 96 | 6 24 | 156 | 10 24 | 216 | 14 24 | 276 | 18 24 | 336 | 22 24 | 36 | 2 24 | 2 25 | 2 26 | 2 27 |
| 37 | 2 28 | 97 | 6 28 | 157 | 10 28 | 217 | 14 28 | 277 | 18 28 | 337 | 22 28 | 37 | 2 28 | 2 29 | 2 30 | 2 31 |
| 38 | 2 32 | 98 | 6 32 | 158 | 10 32 | 218 | 14 32 | 278 | 18 32 | 338 | 22 32 | 38 | 2 32 | 2 33 | 2 34 | 2 35 |
| 39 | 2 36 | 99 | 6 36 | 159 | 10 36 | 219 | 14 36 | 279 | 18 36 | 339 | 22 36 | 39 | 2 36 | 2 37 | 2 38 | 2 39 |
| 40 | 2 40 | 100 | 6 40 | 160 | 10 40 | 220 | 14 40 | 280 | 18 40 | 340 | 22 40 | 40 | 2 40 | 2 41 | 2 42 | 2 43 |
| 41 | 2 44 | 101 | 6 44 | 161 | 10 44 | 221 | 14 44 | 281 | 18 44 | 341 | 22 44 | 41 | 2 44 | 2 45 | 2 46 | 2 47 |
| 42 | 2 48 | 102 | 6 48 | 162 | 10 48 | 222 | 14 48 | 282 | 18 48 | 342 | 22 48 | 42 | 2 48 | 2 49 | 2 50 | 2 51 |
| 43 | 2 52 | 103 | 6 52 | 163 | 10 52 | 223 | 14 52 | 283 | 18 52 | 343 | 22 52 | 43 | 2 52 | 2 53 | 2 54 | 2 55 |
| 44 | 2 56 | 104 | 6 56 | 164 | 10 56 | 224 | 14 56 | 284 | 18 56 | 344 | 22 56 | 44 | 2 56 | 2 57 | 2 58 | 2 59 |
| 45 | 3 00 | 105 | 7 00 | 165 | 11 00 | 225 | 15 00 | 285 | 19 00 | 345 | 23 00 | 45 | 3 00 | 3 01 | 3 02 | 3 03 |
| 46 | 3 04 | 106 | 7 04 | 166 | 11 04 | 226 | 15 04 | 286 | 19 04 | 346 | 23 04 | 46 | 3 04 | 3 05 | 3 06 | 3 07 |
| 47 | 3 08 | 107 | 7 08 | 167 | 11 08 | 227 | 15 08 | 287 | 19 08 | 347 | 23 08 | 47 | 3 08 | 3 09 | 3 10 | 3 11 |
| 48 | 3 12 | 108 | 7 12 | 168 | 11 12 | 228 | 15 12 | 288 | 19 12 | 348 | 23 12 | 48 | 3 12 | 3 13 | 3 14 | 3 15 |
| 49 | 3 16 | 109 | 7 16 | 169 | 11 16 | 229 | 15 16 | 289 | 19 16 | 349 | 23 16 | 49 | 3 16 | 3 17 | 3 18 | 3 19 |
| 50 | 3 20 | 110 | 7 20 | 170 | 11 20 | 230 | 15 20 | 290 | 19 20 | 350 | 23 20 | 50 | 3 20 | 3 21 | 3 22 | 3 23 |
| 51 | 3 24 | 111 | 7 24 | 171 | 11 24 | 231 | 15 24 | 291 | 19 24 | 351 | 23 24 | 51 | 3 24 | 3 25 | 3 26 | 3 27 |
| 52 | 3 28 | 112 | 7 28 | 172 | 11 28 | 232 | 15 28 | 292 | 19 28 | 352 | 23 28 | 52 | 3 28 | 3 29 | 3 30 | 3 31 |
| 53 | 3 32 | 113 | 7 32 | 173 | 11 32 | 233 | 15 32 | 293 | 19 32 | 353 | 23 32 | 53 | 3 32 | 3 33 | 3 34 | 3 35 |
| 54 | 3 36 | 114 | 7 36 | 174 | 11 36 | 234 | 15 36 | 294 | 19 36 | 354 | 23 36 | 54 | 3 36 | 3 37 | 3 38 | 3 39 |
| 55 | 3 40 | 115 | 7 40 | 175 | 11 40 | 235 | 15 40 | 295 | 19 40 | 355 | 23 40 | 55 | 3 40 | 3 41 | 3 42 | 3 43 |
| 56 | 3 44 | 116 | 7 44 | 176 | 11 44 | 236 | 15 44 | 296 | 19 44 | 356 | 23 44 | 56 | 3 44 | 3 45 | 3 46 | 3 47 |
| 57 | 3 48 | 117 | 7 48 | 177 | 11 48 | 237 | 15 48 | 297 | 19 48 | 357 | 23 48 | 57 | 3 48 | 3 49 | 3 50 | 3 51 |
| 58 | 3 52 | 118 | 7 52 | 178 | 11 52 | 238 | 15 52 | 298 | 19 52 | 358 | 23 52 | 58 | 3 52 | 3 53 | 3 54 | 3 55 |
| 59 | 3 56 | 119 | 7 56 | 179 | 11 56 | 239 | 15 56 | 299 | 19 56 | 359 | 23 56 | 59 | 3 56 | 3 57 | 3 58 | 3 59 |

The above table is for converting expressions in arc to their equivalent in time ; its main use in this Almanac is for the conversion of longitude for application to L.M.T. (*added* if *west*, *subtracted* if *east*) to give G.M.T. or vice versa, particularly in the case of sunrise, sunset, etc.

*Figure 12–2.* Table to convert degrees and minutes of arc into hours and minutes of time, from the *Nautical Almanac*

(1917 at 35° N, plus 6 minutes for 37° N, plus 3 hours, 52 minutes for the shadow to travel 58° of longitude). Naturally, this result is the same as that you arrived at earlier by interpolation.

So far, I have been talking about this edge of night as though it were a blade that drops across earth like a guillotine. Of course, that's not so. Earth's air splinters sunlight and sprinkles the bits into the gloom, so the terminator has a fuzzy edge. This period when the sky turns from silver to sable and the stars from pearls to diamonds is called twilight. Twilight is the time for sights of planets and stars.

Technically, there are three gradations of twilight: civil, nautical, and astronomical. Roughly, the differences can be characterized as follows: civil, light enough to see the horizon and bright stars; nautical, too dark to see the horizon without a 7×50 telescope; astronomical, hopelessly stygian. Obviously for most celestial navigators, working hours are during civil twilight. The other two twilights are of academic interest only.

In the *Nautical Almanac* tables of civil and nautical twilights are printed alongside the tables for sunrise and sunset. The times listed are based on the adopted convention that the moment of civil twilight occurs when the sun is 6° below the horizon—that is, when the great-circle distance between you and the sun's GP is 96°. For practical purposes in clear weather, this time is about the middle of the period in which you can hope to see the planets, the brighter stars, *and* the horizon at the same time.

You should always be on deck before civil twilight. If you aren't, you may miss your opportunity for sights. In the evening as civil twilight passes, it gets darker and you run the risk of losing the horizon; in the morning it gets lighter and you run the risk of losing the planet or star. If you have ever stood the last watch of the night, you know that there is a time before dawn when you suddenly realize you can see your hands again. If you, the navigator, are not already on deck, it's helpful to ask the early morning watch to come and get you when this event occurs.

You can figure the time of civil twilight by noting the difference between the times for civil twilight and sunset or sunrise and applying this difference to the time you have already figured for sunrise or sunset. Alternatively, you can figure it by taking the time in the table to be the time of the event at the Greenwich meridian and proceeding as you did for the sunset calculation, converting your longitude into time and adding it to the time of civil twilight in the table.

Once again, assume it is June 19, 1999. You notice from the planet diagram in the previous chapter (fig. 11-1) that Mars is about 5 hours east of Venus. That kind of spread in their hour angles should mean their LOPs will cross at a good angle and give you an accurate fix.

You estimate your DR by evening will be about 25° N, 65° W.

By interpolation, the sunset/twilight table in figure 4-1 gives you a civil twilight for 25° N at Greenwich of 1918.

According to the arc/time conversion table, it takes twilight 4 hours, 20 minutes to travel to 65° W. Therefore, GMT of civil twilight for your expected DR on the evening of June 19, 1999, is 1918 plus 0420, or 2338 GMT.

Turning now to the Mars column in the almanac (fig. 4-1), you find that at 2300, GHA is 48°55.9´ and declination is 10°48.1´ S.

Since the time of civil twilight (2338) is 38 minutes later than the base data in the almanac for 2300, the GHA of Mars increases 9°30´ (fig. 4-2, value at 37 minutes, 60 seconds). At the approximate time of civil twilight, then, the GHA of Mars is 58°25.9´. Adding 360° so that you can subtract your anticipated DR longitude of 65° W gives an LHA of 353°25.9´, which you round to 353°, since this is a planning exercise.

If you now look in the sight reduction table (fig. 7-5) for latitude 25°, declination [0°–14°] contrary name to latitude, and round off the declination to 11°, you find that on June 19, 1999, Mars, with an LHA of 353° and a declination of 11°, has a computed altitude of 53°22´ and a bearing of 168°.

That's about as close as you need to calculate for planning purposes. After getting a couple of shots of Venus, set your sextant for 53°22´. The odds are good that Mars will be in your scope, and you will end your day with a nice sharp fix.

# Part III

☉　♃　♂　♄　♀　☆　☾

# The Astral Archipelago:
# Navigation by the Stars

# 13

# A Handful of Stars

On a clear night about two thousand stars are visible without a telescope. Galileo started counting the others in 1611, and his successors haven't found the last one yet. Every time astronomers make a bigger telescope, they uncover more stars.

Unlike astronomers, celestial navigators need to see the horizon and stars simultaneously, which limits the useful stars pretty much to those of first and second magnitude. Over the years, usage has created an official canon of fifty-seven stars known as the "Selected Stars" or the "Navigational Stars."

The names, numbers, and magnitudes of this stellar bunch are printed in the *Nautical Almanac* on a loose bookmark of light cardboard (fig. 13-1). On the left side of this sheet the stars are listed in alphabetical order; on the right, by their assigned numbers. Alpheratz is star 1; Markab is 57.

Each body in the heavens has a Greenwich hour angle and a declination, and it is the job of the almanac to provide navigators with this information. If you look at the bookmark you will see a column of declinations, but you won't find one headed GHA. The reason for this omission is that the stars do not change position

## INDEX TO SELECTED STARS, 1999

| Name | No | Mag | SHA | Dec | | No | Name | Mag | SHA | Dec |
|------|----|-----|-----|-----|-|----|------|-----|-----|-----|
| Acamar | 7 | 3·1 | 315 | S 40 | | 1 | Alpheratz | 2·2 | 358 | N 29 |
| Achernar | 5 | 0·6 | 336 | S 57 | | 2 | Ankaa | 2·4 | 353 | S 42 |
| Acrux | 30 | 1·1 | 173 | S 63 | | 3 | Schedar | 2·5 | 350 | N 57 |
| Adhara | 19 | 1·6 | 255 | S 29 | | 4 | Diphda | 2·2 | 349 | S 18 |
| Aldebaran | 10 | 1·1 | 291 | N 17 | | 5 | Achernar | 0·6 | 336 | S 57 |
| Alioth | 32 | 1·7 | 167 | N 56 | | 6 | Hamal | 2·2 | 328 | N 23 |
| Alkaid | 34 | 1·9 | 153 | N 49 | | 7 | Acamar | 3·1 | 315 | S 40 |
| Al Na'ir | 55 | 2·2 | 28 | S 47 | | 8 | Menkar | 2·8 | 314 | N 4 |
| Alnilam | 15 | 1·8 | 276 | S 1 | | 9 | Mirfak | 1·9 | 309 | N 50 |
| Alphard | 25 | 2·2 | 218 | S 9 | | 10 | Aldebaran | 1·1 | 291 | N 17 |
| Alphecca | 41 | 2·3 | 126 | N 27 | | 11 | Rigel | 0·3 | 281 | S 8 |
| Alpheratz | 1 | 2·2 | 358 | N 29 | | 12 | Capella | 0·2 | 281 | N 46 |
| Altair | 51 | 0·9 | 62 | N 9 | | 13 | Bellatrix | 1·7 | 279 | N 6 |
| Ankaa | 2 | 2·4 | 353 | S 42 | | 14 | Elnath | 1·8 | 278 | N 29 |
| Antares | 42 | 1·2 | 113 | S 26 | | 15 | Alnilam | 1·8 | 276 | S 1 |
| Arcturus | 37 | 0·2 | 146 | N 19 | | 16 | Betelgeuse | Var.* | 271 | N 7 |
| Atria | 43 | 1·9 | 108 | S 69 | | 17 | Canopus | −0·9 | 264 | S 53 |
| Avior | 22 | 1·7 | 234 | S 60 | | 18 | Sirius | −1·6 | 259 | S 17 |
| Bellatrix | 13 | 1·7 | 279 | N 6 | | 19 | Adhara | 1·6 | 255 | S 29 |
| Betelgeuse | 16 | Var.* | 271 | N 7 | | 20 | Procyon | 0·5 | 245 | N 5 |
| Canopus | 17 | −0·9 | 264 | S 53 | | 21 | Pollux | 1·2 | 244 | N 28 |
| Capella | 12 | 0·2 | 281 | N 46 | | 22 | Avior | 1·7 | 234 | S 60 |
| Deneb | 53 | 1·3 | 50 | N 45 | | 23 | Suhail | 2·2 | 223 | S 43 |
| Denebola | 28 | 2·2 | 183 | N 15 | | 24 | Miaplacidus | 1·8 | 222 | S 70 |
| Diphda | 4 | 2·2 | 349 | S 18 | | 25 | Alphard | 2·2 | 218 | S 9 |
| Dubhe | 27 | 2·0 | 194 | N 62 | | 26 | Regulus | 1·3 | 208 | N 12 |
| Elnath | 14 | 1·8 | 278 | N 29 | | 27 | Dubhe | 2·0 | 194 | N 62 |
| Eltanin | 47 | 2·4 | 91 | N 51 | | 28 | Denebola | 2·2 | 183 | N 15 |
| Enif | 54 | 2·5 | 34 | N 10 | | 29 | Gienah | 2·8 | 176 | S 18 |
| Fomalhaut | 56 | 1·3 | 16 | S 30 | | 30 | Acrux | 1·1 | 173 | S 63 |
| Gacrux | 31 | 1·6 | 172 | S 57 | | 31 | Gacrux | 1·6 | 172 | S 57 |
| Gienah | 29 | 2·8 | 176 | S 18 | | 32 | Alioth | 1·7 | 167 | N 56 |
| Hadar | 35 | 0·9 | 149 | S 60 | | 33 | Spica | 1·2 | 159 | S 11 |
| Hamal | 6 | 2·2 | 328 | N 23 | | 34 | Alkaid | 1·9 | 153 | N 49 |
| Kaus Australis | 48 | 2·0 | 84 | S 34 | | 35 | Hadar | 0·9 | 149 | S 60 |
| Kochab | 40 | 2·2 | 137 | N 74 | | 36 | Menkent | 2·3 | 148 | S 36 |
| Markab | 57 | 2·6 | 14 | N 15 | | 37 | Arcturus | 0·2 | 146 | N 19 |
| Menkar | 8 | 2·8 | 314 | N 4 | | 38 | Rigil Kentaurus | 0·1 | 140 | S 61 |
| Menkent | 36 | 2·3 | 148 | S 36 | | 39 | Zubenelgenubi | 2·9 | 137 | S 16 |
| Miaplacidus | 24 | 1·8 | 222 | S 70 | | 40 | Kochab | 2·2 | 137 | N 74 |
| Mirfak | 9 | 1·9 | 309 | N 50 | | 41 | Alphecca | 2·3 | 126 | N 27 |
| Nunki | 50 | 2·1 | 76 | S 26 | | 42 | Antares | 1·2 | 113 | S 26 |
| Peacock | 52 | 2·1 | 54 | S 57 | | 43 | Atria | 1·9 | 108 | S 69 |
| Pollux | 21 | 1·2 | 244 | N 28 | | 44 | Sabik | 2·6 | 102 | S 16 |
| Procyon | 20 | 0·5 | 245 | N 5 | | 45 | Shaula | 1·7 | 97 | S 37 |
| Rasalhague | 46 | 2·1 | 96 | N 13 | | 46 | Rasalhague | 2·1 | 96 | N 13 |
| Regulus | 26 | 1·3 | 208 | N 12 | | 47 | Eltanin | 2·4 | 91 | N 51 |
| Rigel | 11 | 0·3 | 281 | S 8 | | 48 | Kaus Australis | 2·0 | 84 | S 34 |
| Rigil Kentaurus | 38 | 0·1 | 140 | S 61 | | 49 | Vega | 0·1 | 81 | N 39 |
| Sabik | 44 | 2·6 | 102 | S 16 | | 50 | Nunki | 2·1 | 76 | S 26 |
| Schedar | 3 | 2·5 | 350 | N 57 | | 51 | Altair | 0·9 | 62 | N 9 |
| Shaula | 45 | 1·7 | 97 | S 37 | | 52 | Peacock | 2·1 | 54 | S 57 |
| Sirius | 18 | −1·6 | 259 | S 17 | | 53 | Deneb | 1·3 | 50 | N 45 |
| Spica | 33 | 1·2 | 159 | S 11 | | 54 | Enif | 2·5 | 34 | N 10 |
| Suhail | 23 | 2·2 | 223 | S 43 | | 55 | Al Na'ir | 2·2 | 28 | S 47 |
| Vega | 49 | 0·1 | 81 | N 39 | | 56 | Fomalhaut | 1·3 | 16 | S 30 |
| Zubenelgenubi | 39 | 2·9 | 137 | S 16 | | 57 | Markab | 2·6 | 14 | N 15 |

*0·1 — 1·2

*Figure 13–1.* Table of magnitude, sidereal hour angle, and declination of the fifty-seven navigational stars, from the *Nautical Almanac* bookmark

relative to one another. From earth, the stars appear to be pasted on the inside of a black sphere.

The stars visible today are the same ones the ancient Arab astronomers saw and identified; in many cases even the names have remained the same (just run your eye down the list on the bookmark). The patterns form the same constellations the Greeks drew and named more than two thousand years ago.

The practical effect of this stasis among the stars is that it is unnecessary for the almanac to list a GHA for each and every star. Since the stars are fixed relative to one another, the spacing of their astral longitudes cannot be changing. Therefore, if you have a list of the meridians of all the stars and are given the GHA of the meridian of any one star, you can figure out the GHA of any other star.

What you need from the almanac, then, is a GHA column for one star and a list of the longitudes and declinations of the others. And that is exactly what the almanac provides.

Refer once again to figure 4-1. Near the left margin is the GHA column for a reference star called Aries. It looks much like the other main columns in the almanac except that it does not have an adjacent list of declinations. That's because Aries' declination is 0°; this star is always directly above the equator.

In fact, Aries is not a star at all. Aries is a point on the black astral sphere—a benchmark in the sky, if you will—located directly over the spot on the earth where the sun crosses the equator on the day of the March equinox.

From this starting point the almanac makers calculate what is called the *sidereal hour angle* (SHA) of each star—the angular distance from the meridian of Aries to the meridian of the star. Like any other hour angle, sidereal hour angle is measured *westward* from its benchmark. Greenwich hour angle is measured westward from Greenwich; local hour angle is measured westward from the AP; sidereal hour angle is measured westward from Aries.

For example, the brightest star in the night skies is Sirius (magnitude –1.6). Referring to the alphabetical, left-hand side of the bookmark, note that the SHA of Sirius is 259°—that is, at any given moment the GP of Sirius is 259° west of Aries (fig. 13-2).

What a navigator needs to know to use a star, of course, is not its SHA but its GHA, so the next step is to figure out how to get from

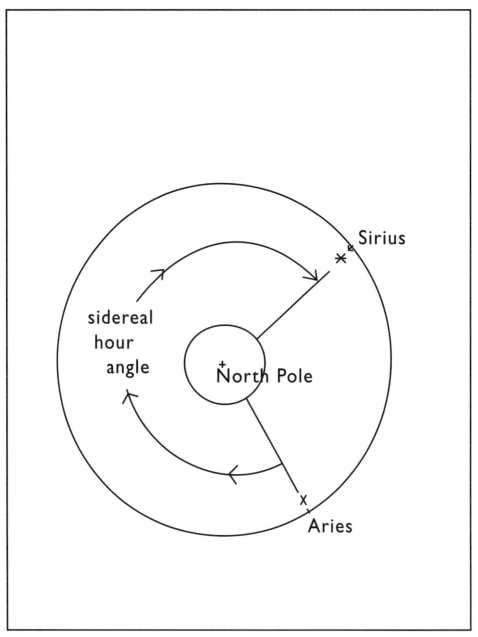

*Figure 13–2.* The relative locations of Sirius and Aries as determined by SHA

SHA to GHA. Look at figure 13-3. The GHA of Aries is about 45° in this sketch; Aries is about 3 hours west of Greenwich. If Sirius is 259° west of Aries, it is pretty obvious that the GHA of Sirius is 45° plus 259°, or 304°. The formula is simple: the GHA of a star equals the GHA of Aries plus the SHA of the star.

You may have noticed that the bookmark from the almanac gives the sidereal hour angles and declinations in integral degrees, and

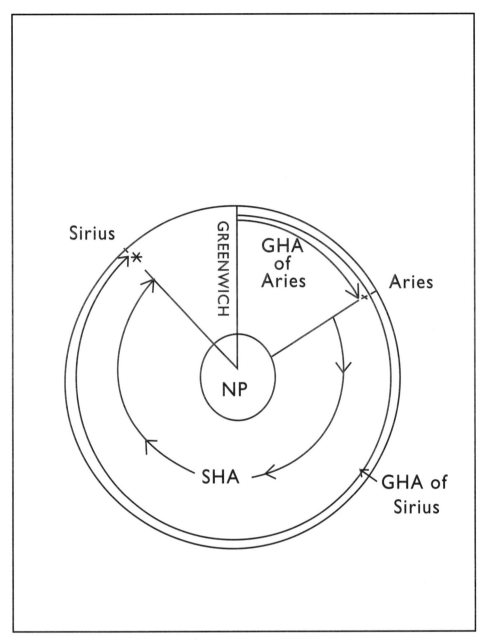

*Figure 13–3.* Finding the GHA of a star

you know enough about celestial by now to know that this is a field in which minutiae always lurk. And so it is with the stars. The minutes and decimals of their exact SHAs and declinations are tabulated on each of the left-hand pages in the *Nautical Almanac* in the wide column next to the spine (fig. 4-1). Here you can see that the SHA of Sirius is not 259° exactly, but 258°43.6′, and its declination is not 17° S, but 16°43.0′ S. For rough planning purposes, the bookmark data serve, but when you take a sight, those missing 11´ in the SHA and the 18´ in the declination make a considerable difference.

Star sights can be planned just as planet sights were in the previous chapter. Look again at the planet diagram (fig. 11-1), and notice the light, dashed lines slanting across the page. Those are sidereal hour angles, spaced 30° apart and labeled at each end. Suppose you want to find which stars are available to cross with a morning sight of Jupiter on June 20, 1999 (the line for this date is highlighted). Scan along the June 20 line until you come to the slanting line for SHA 30°, about 4 hours to Jupiter's right. Then turn to the bookmark, look in the list, and find star number 54, whose SHA is 34. The magnitude of this star, Enif, however, is only 2.5, dimmer than that of the North Star. Just above it on the list, though, is number 53, Deneb, a first-magnitude star, and above Deneb is a really bright star, number 51, Altair, magnitude 0.9.

Select either Altair or Deneb, make a note of the SHA and declination given in the bookmark, figure the time of twilight, look up the GHA of Aries for that time, add the SHA of the star, and find its computed altitude and bearing from the sight reduction table. The much-talked-about virtue of stars is that you can get nearly simultaneous sights of several and so have a fix. So you have to repeat these planning steps for several more stars.

Then, once you take the actual sights, go back to the almanac, determine the LHA of Aries for the time of the sights, look up the SHA and declination of each star, form the GHA of each star, find the LHA of each star, and then enter a sight reduction table to find the computed altitude and bearing of each star.

If you know the constellations, one dodge is to get up well before dawn, pick out two or more bright stars, and take sights until you have a horizon. But this process won't work for evening stars, because by the time you can identify the constellations, it is so dark the horizon is gone.

There must be a better way.

There is, and it is *HO 249*, Volume 1, *Sight Reduction Tables for Air Navigation (Selected Stars)*, the book with the red spine. If you hope to navigate by the stars from a small boat with any degree of grace or aplomb, get this book and do not let anybody ever take it away.

*Selected Stars* takes advantage of the fact that your position relative to all the stars is uniquely determined by the position of Aries relative to you (the LHA of Aries). In other words, for any given LHA of Aries, there is only one place each of the stars can be. They are, for all practical purposes, fixed relative to one another. They're stuck to the inside of a titanic sphere, and the position of Aries relative to you tells how far the sphere has turned and where each and every one of the stars has to be.

*Selected Stars* is arranged as follows: For every latitude from 69° N to 69° S two facing pages list the seven best stars for every integral degree of LHA of Aries. For latitudes higher than 70° N and S, there is only one page, and LHA of Aries is tabulated for every *whole* degree, because the longitudes have converged so much that 2° covers the same distance 1° does at mid-latitudes. Figure 13-4 shows two typical pages that might be used by temperate-latitude voyagers—the ones for latitude 25° N.

Assume you are on a passage from San Francisco to Hawaii. It is June 19, 1999, about 2 hours to sunset, and your DR is 25° N, 150° W. From the sunset/twilight table of the daily pages (fig. 4-1), the time, by interpolation, of evening civil twilight at Greenwich is 1918 GMT. Since you are 150° west of Greenwich, it takes the shadow 10 hours to reach you; civil twilight at your longitude is at 2918 GMT, a time that makes no sense, but obviously means evening twilight arrives 5 hours and 18 minutes into the next day, or at 0518 GMT, June 20.

From the Aries column for 0500, June 20:

> GHA Aries = 342°58.1′
> +18 minutes = 4°30.7′
> GHA Aries = 347°28.8′
> −AP Lon W = 150°28.8′
> LHA Aries = 197°

If you now look at the pages for 25° N in the *Selected Stars* table (fig. 13-4) and scan the columns for LHA Aries (the symbol for Aries, the Ram, looks like a Y with down-turned arms), you find 197° in the upper left of the right-hand page. Printed in the seven columns to its right are the seven best stars for your assumed position at the time of civil twilight on June 19, 1999. They are Kochab, Vega, Rasalhague, Antares, Spica, Regulus, and Dubhe.

The stars whose names are printed in capital letters (Vega, Antares, Spica, and Regulus) are first-magnitude stars, so those are likely

## LAT 25°N                  LAT 25°N

*(A dense tabular page from HO 249, vol. 1, giving Hc and Zn values of selected stars for each LHA of Aries at latitude 25°N. The table is organized into two halves (left and right), each with columns labeled Hc and Zn under sets of named stars. Representative star-name header rows down the columns include, for the left half: Schedar, CAPELLA, ALDEBARAN, Diphda, FOMALHAUT, ALTAIR, DENEB; CAPELLA, ALDEBARAN, RIGEL, Diphda, FOMALHAUT, Enif, DENEB; CAPELLA, ALDEBARAN, RIGEL, Acamar, Diphda, Alpheratz, DENEB; CAPELLA, POLLUX, PROCYON, SIRIUS, Acamar, Diphda, Alpheratz; CAPELLA, PROCYON, SIRIUS, RIGEL, Diphda, Hamal, Mirfak; CAPELLA, Dubhe, POLLUX, PROCYON, SIRIUS, RIGEL, Hamal. For the right half: Dubhe, REGULUS, Alphard, SIRIUS, RIGEL, ALDEBARAN, CAPELLA; Dubhe, REGULUS, Alphard, SIRIUS, RIGEL, ALDEBARAN, CAPELLA; Dubhe, ARCTURUS, SPICA, Alphard, SIRIUS, BETELGEUSE, CAPELLA; Dubhe, ARCTURUS, SPICA, Alphard, SIRIUS, POLLUX, CAPELLA; Dubhe, Alkaid, ARCTURUS, SPICA, Alphard, PROCYON, POLLUX. The leftmost column of each half is labeled LHA ♈.)*

*Figure 13–4.* For LHAs of Aries at latitude 25°N, the Hc and Zn of selected stars, from *HO 249*, vol. 1 (Selected Stars)

LAT 25°N

| LHA ♈ | Hc Zn | Hc Zn | Hc Zn | Hc Zn | Hc Zn | Hc Zn | Hc Zn |
|---|---|---|---|---|---|---|---|
| | ◆ Alkaid | Alphecca | ◆ SPICA | Gienah | REGULUS | ◆ POLLUX | Dubhe |
| 180 | 57 56 034 | 42 02 076 | 48 18 148 | 47 17 174 | 60 35 249 | 33 36 288 | 52 02 349 |
| 181 | 58 26 033 | 42 55 076 | 48 47 149 | 47 22 176 | 59 45 250 | 32 44 288 | 51 52 349 |
| 182 | 58 55 032 | 43 48 076 | 49 14 150 | 47 25 177 | 58 53 251 | 31 53 289 | 51 40 348 |
| 183 | 59 24 031 | 44 40 076 | 49 41 152 | 47 27 179 | 58 02 252 | 31 01 289 | 51 29 347 |
| 184 | 59 52 030 | 45 33 077 | 50 06 153 | 47 27 180 | 57 10 252 | 30 10 289 | 51 16 346 |
| 185 | 60 19 029 | 46 26 077 | 50 30 154 | 47 27 181 | 56 18 253 | 29 19 289 | 51 03 346 |
| 186 | 60 45 028 | 47 19 077 | 50 53 156 | 47 25 183 | 55 26 254 | 28 27 290 | 50 49 345 |
| 187 | 61 10 027 | 48 12 077 | 51 15 157 | 47 21 184 | 54 34 255 | 27 36 290 | 50 35 344 |
| 188 | 61 35 026 | 49 05 077 | 51 35 159 | 47 17 186 | 53 41 256 | 26 45 290 | 50 20 344 |
| 189 | 61 59 025 | 49 58 078 | 51 54 160 | 47 10 187 | 52 48 256 | 25 54 290 | 50 05 343 |
| 190 | 62 21 024 | 50 51 078 | 52 12 162 | 47 03 188 | 51 55 257 | 25 03 291 | 49 49 343 |
| 191 | 62 43 023 | 51 44 078 | 52 28 163 | 46 54 190 | 51 02 258 | 24 13 291 | 49 32 342 |
| 192 | 63 04 022 | 52 38 078 | 52 43 165 | 46 44 191 | 50 09 258 | 23 22 291 | 49 15 341 |
| 193 | 63 23 020 | 53 31 078 | 52 57 166 | 46 33 193 | 49 16 259 | 22 31 292 | 48 58 341 |
| 194 | 63 42 019 | 54 24 078 | 53 09 168 | 46 21 194 | 48 22 260 | 21 41 292 | 48 40 340 |
| | ◆ Kochab | VEGA | Rasalhague | ◆ ANTARES | SPICA | ◆ REGULUS | Dubhe |
| 195 | 38 44 009 | 19 37 055 | 24 23 087 | 17 55 132 | 53 19 170 | 47 29 260 | 48 21 340 |
| 196 | 38 53 009 | 20 22 056 | 25 17 088 | 18 35 132 | 53 28 171 | 46 35 261 | 48 02 339 |
| 197 | 39 01 009 | 21 07 056 | 26 11 088 | 19 15 133 | 53 36 173 | 45 41 261 | 47 42 339 |
| 198 | 39 09 008 | 21 52 056 | 27 06 088 | 19 55 134 | 53 42 175 | 44 48 262 | 47 22 338 |
| 199 | 39 17 008 | 22 37 056 | 28 00 089 | 20 34 134 | 53 46 176 | 43 54 262 | 47 02 338 |
| 200 | 39 25 008 | 23 22 057 | 28 54 089 | 21 12 135 | 53 49 178 | 43 00 263 | 46 41 337 |
| 201 | 39 32 008 | 24 08 057 | 29 49 089 | 21 51 136 | 53 50 180 | 42 06 264 | 46 20 337 |
| 202 | 39 39 007 | 24 53 057 | 30 43 090 | 22 28 136 | 53 50 181 | 41 12 264 | 45 58 336 |
| 203 | 39 46 007 | 25 39 057 | 31 38 090 | 23 05 137 | 53 48 183 | 40 18 265 | 45 36 336 |
| 204 | 39 52 007 | 26 25 057 | 32 32 091 | 23 42 138 | 53 45 184 | 39 23 265 | 45 14 336 |
| 205 | 39 58 006 | 27 10 057 | 33 26 091 | 24 18 139 | 53 40 186 | 38 29 265 | 44 51 335 |
| 206 | 40 04 006 | 27 56 058 | 34 21 092 | 24 54 139 | 53 33 188 | 37 35 266 | 44 28 335 |
| 207 | 40 09 006 | 28 42 058 | 35 15 092 | 25 29 140 | 53 25 189 | 36 41 266 | 44 05 334 |
| 208 | 40 14 005 | 29 28 058 | 36 09 092 | 26 04 141 | 53 15 191 | 35 47 267 | 43 41 334 |
| 209 | 40 19 005 | 30 14 058 | 37 04 093 | 26 38 142 | 53 04 193 | 34 52 267 | 43 17 334 |
| | ◆ Kochab | VEGA | Rasalhague | ◆ ANTARES | SPICA | ◆ REGULUS | Dubhe |
| 210 | 40 23 005 | 31 01 058 | 37 58 093 | 27 12 142 | 52 51 194 | 33 58 268 | 42 53 333 |
| 211 | 40 27 004 | 31 47 058 | 38 52 094 | 27 45 143 | 52 37 196 | 33 04 268 | 42 28 333 |
| 212 | 40 31 004 | 32 33 059 | 39 46 094 | 28 17 144 | 52 22 197 | 32 09 269 | 42 04 333 |
| 213 | 40 35 003 | 33 20 059 | 40 41 095 | 28 49 145 | 52 05 199 | 31 15 269 | 41 38 332 |
| 214 | 40 38 003 | 34 06 059 | 41 35 095 | 29 20 146 | 51 47 200 | 30 20 270 | 41 13 332 |
| 215 | 40 41 003 | 34 53 059 | 42 29 096 | 29 50 146 | 51 27 202 | 29 26 270 | 40 48 332 |
| 216 | 40 43 002 | 35 39 059 | 43 23 096 | 30 20 147 | 51 06 203 | 28 32 270 | 40 22 332 |
| 217 | 40 45 002 | 36 26 059 | 44 17 097 | 30 49 148 | 50 44 205 | 27 37 271 | 39 56 331 |
| 218 | 40 47 002 | 37 12 059 | 45 11 097 | 31 17 149 | 50 20 206 | 26 43 271 | 39 30 331 |
| 219 | 40 48 001 | 37 59 059 | 46 05 098 | 31 45 150 | 49 56 208 | 25 49 272 | 39 03 331 |
| 220 | 40 49 001 | 38 46 059 | 46 59 099 | 32 11 151 | 49 30 209 | 24 54 272 | 38 37 331 |
| 221 | 40 50 001 | 39 33 059 | 47 52 099 | 32 37 152 | 49 03 210 | 24 00 272 | 38 10 330 |
| 222 | 40 51 000 | 40 19 059 | 48 46 100 | 33 03 153 | 48 35 212 | 23 06 273 | 37 43 330 |
| 223 | 40 51 000 | 41 06 059 | 49 40 100 | 33 27 154 | 48 06 213 | 22 11 273 | 37 16 330 |
| 224 | 40 50 000 | 41 53 059 | 50 33 101 | 33 51 155 | 47 36 214 | 21 17 274 | 36 49 330 |
| | VEGA | ◆ ALTAIR | Nunki | ANTARES | ◆ SPICA | Denebola | ◆ Alkaid |
| 225 | 42 40 059 | 19 22 089 | 13 30 128 | 34 14 156 | 47 05 215 | 44 08 266 | 61 53 335 |
| 226 | 43 26 059 | 20 16 089 | 14 13 128 | 34 36 157 | 46 33 217 | 43 13 267 | 61 29 333 |
| 227 | 44 13 059 | 21 10 090 | 14 55 129 | 34 57 158 | 46 00 218 | 42 19 267 | 61 05 332 |
| 228 | 45 00 059 | 22 05 090 | 15 37 130 | 35 17 159 | 45 26 219 | 41 25 268 | 60 39 331 |
| 229 | 45 47 059 | 22 59 091 | 16 19 130 | 35 36 160 | 44 52 220 | 40 30 268 | 60 13 330 |
| 230 | 46 33 059 | 23 53 091 | 17 00 131 | 35 55 161 | 44 17 221 | 39 36 269 | 59 45 329 |
| 231 | 47 20 059 | 24 48 092 | 17 41 131 | 36 12 162 | 43 40 222 | 38 42 269 | 59 17 329 |
| 232 | 48 07 059 | 25 42 092 | 18 22 132 | 36 29 163 | 43 03 223 | 37 47 269 | 58 49 328 |
| 233 | 48 53 059 | 26 37 092 | 19 02 133 | 36 44 164 | 42 26 224 | 36 53 270 | 58 19 327 |
| 234 | 49 40 059 | 27 31 093 | 19 42 133 | 36 59 165 | 41 47 225 | 35 59 270 | 57 49 326 |
| 235 | 50 26 059 | 28 25 093 | 20 21 134 | 37 12 166 | 41 09 226 | 35 04 271 | 57 19 325 |
| 236 | 51 13 058 | 29 19 094 | 21 00 135 | 37 25 167 | 40 29 227 | 34 10 271 | 56 47 325 |
| 237 | 51 59 058 | 30 14 094 | 21 39 135 | 37 36 168 | 39 49 228 | 33 15 271 | 56 16 324 |
| 238 | 52 45 058 | 31 08 095 | 22 17 136 | 37 47 169 | 39 08 229 | 32 21 272 | 55 43 323 |
| 239 | 53 31 058 | 32 02 095 | 22 54 137 | 37 56 171 | 38 26 230 | 31 27 272 | 55 10 323 |
| | ◆ VEGA | ALTAIR | Nunki | ◆ ANTARES | SPICA | ARCTURUS | ◆ Alkaid |
| 240 | 54 17 058 | 32 56 096 | 23 31 137 | 38 05 172 | 37 45 231 | 65 11 262 | 54 37 322 |
| 241 | 55 03 057 | 33 50 096 | 24 08 138 | 38 12 173 | 37 02 232 | 64 17 262 | 54 04 321 |
| 242 | 55 49 057 | 34 44 097 | 24 44 139 | 38 19 174 | 36 19 233 | 63 23 263 | 53 30 321 |
| 243 | 56 34 057 | 35 38 097 | 25 19 140 | 38 24 175 | 35 36 233 | 62 29 264 | 52 55 320 |
| 244 | 57 20 056 | 36 32 098 | 25 54 140 | 38 28 176 | 34 52 234 | 61 35 264 | 52 20 320 |
| 245 | 58 05 056 | 37 26 098 | 26 29 141 | 38 31 177 | 34 08 235 | 60 41 265 | 51 45 319 |
| 246 | 58 50 056 | 38 20 099 | 27 03 142 | 38 33 178 | 33 23 236 | 59 47 265 | 51 10 319 |
| 247 | 59 35 055 | 39 14 099 | 27 36 143 | 38 34 180 | 32 38 236 | 58 53 266 | 50 34 319 |
| 248 | 60 19 055 | 40 07 100 | 28 08 143 | 38 34 181 | 31 52 237 | 57 58 266 | 49 58 318 |
| 249 | 61 03 054 | 41 01 100 | 28 40 144 | 38 33 182 | 31 06 238 | 57 04 267 | 49 21 318 |
| 250 | 61 47 054 | 41 54 101 | 29 12 145 | 38 30 183 | 30 20 239 | 56 10 267 | 48 45 317 |
| 251 | 62 31 053 | 42 47 102 | 29 43 146 | 38 27 184 | 29 33 239 | 55 15 268 | 48 08 317 |
| 252 | 63 14 052 | 43 41 102 | 30 13 147 | 38 22 185 | 28 46 240 | 54 21 268 | 47 31 317 |
| 253 | 63 57 052 | 44 34 103 | 30 42 148 | 38 17 186 | 27 59 241 | 53 27 269 | 46 53 317 |
| 254 | 64 40 051 | 45 27 103 | 31 11 149 | 38 10 188 | 27 12 241 | 52 32 269 | 46 16 316 |
| | ◆ DENEB | ALTAIR | ◆ Nunki | ANTARES | SPICA | ◆ ARCTURUS | Alkaid |
| 255 | 41 31 051 | 46 20 104 | 31 39 149 | 38 02 189 | 26 24 242 | 51 38 270 | 45 38 316 |
| 256 | 42 13 051 | 47 12 105 | 32 06 150 | 37 54 190 | 25 36 243 | 50 44 270 | 45 00 316 |
| 257 | 42 55 050 | 48 05 105 | 32 32 151 | 37 44 191 | 24 47 243 | 49 49 271 | 44 22 316 |
| 258 | 43 37 050 | 48 57 106 | 32 58 152 | 37 33 192 | 23 59 244 | 48 55 271 | 43 44 315 |
| 259 | 44 18 050 | 49 49 107 | 33 23 153 | 37 21 193 | 23 10 244 | 48 00 271 | 43 06 315 |
| 260 | 45 00 050 | 50 41 108 | 33 47 154 | 37 08 194 | 22 20 245 | 47 06 272 | 42 28 315 |
| 261 | 45 42 050 | 51 33 108 | 34 10 155 | 36 54 195 | 21 31 246 | 46 12 272 | 41 49 315 |
| 262 | 46 23 050 | 52 25 109 | 34 33 156 | 36 40 196 | 20 41 246 | 45 17 273 | 41 11 315 |
| 263 | 47 05 049 | 53 16 110 | 34 54 157 | 36 24 197 | 19 52 247 | 44 23 273 | 40 32 315 |
| 264 | 47 46 049 | 54 07 111 | 35 15 158 | 36 07 199 | 19 02 247 | 43 29 273 | 39 53 314 |
| 265 | 48 27 049 | 54 58 112 | 35 35 159 | 35 49 200 | 18 11 248 | 42 35 274 | 39 14 314 |
| 266 | 49 08 049 | 55 48 113 | 35 54 160 | 35 31 201 | 17 21 248 | 41 40 274 | 38 35 314 |
| 267 | 49 49 048 | 56 38 114 | 36 12 161 | 35 11 202 | 16 30 249 | 40 46 274 | 37 57 314 |
| 268 | 50 30 048 | 57 28 114 | 36 29 162 | 34 51 203 | 15 39 249 | 39 52 275 | 37 18 314 |
| 269 | 51 10 048 | 58 17 116 | 36 45 163 | 34 29 204 | 14 48 250 | 38 58 275 | 36 38 314 |

LAT 25°N

| LHA ♈ | Hc Zn | Hc Zn | Hc Zn | Hc Zn | Hc Zn | Hc Zn | Hc Zn |
|---|---|---|---|---|---|---|---|
| | ◆ DENEB | Enif | ◆ Nunki | ANTARES | ◆ ARCTURUS | Alkaid | Kochab |
| 270 | 51 50 048 | 34 50 095 | 37 00 164 | 34 07 205 | 38 04 275 | 35 59 314 | 35 03 346 |
| 271 | 52 30 047 | 35 44 096 | 37 14 166 | 33 44 206 | 37 09 276 | 35 20 314 | 34 50 346 |
| 272 | 53 10 047 | 36 38 096 | 37 27 167 | 33 20 207 | 36 15 276 | 34 41 314 | 34 36 345 |
| 273 | 53 49 046 | 37 32 097 | 37 39 168 | 32 55 207 | 35 21 277 | 34 02 314 | 34 22 345 |
| 274 | 54 29 046 | 38 26 097 | 37 50 169 | 32 30 208 | 34 27 277 | 33 23 314 | 34 08 345 |
| 275 | 55 07 045 | 39 20 098 | 38 00 170 | 32 03 209 | 33 33 277 | 32 44 314 | 33 54 345 |
| 276 | 55 46 045 | 40 14 098 | 38 09 171 | 31 36 210 | 32 39 278 | 32 05 314 | 33 40 345 |
| 277 | 56 24 044 | 41 08 099 | 38 17 172 | 31 09 211 | 31 46 278 | 31 26 314 | 33 26 345 |
| 278 | 57 02 044 | 42 01 100 | 38 24 173 | 30 40 212 | 30 52 278 | 30 47 314 | 33 11 344 |
| 279 | 57 39 043 | 42 55 100 | 38 30 174 | 30 11 213 | 29 58 279 | 30 08 314 | 32 56 344 |
| 280 | 58 16 043 | 43 48 101 | 38 34 176 | 29 41 214 | 29 04 279 | 29 29 314 | 32 42 344 |
| 281 | 58 53 042 | 44 42 101 | 38 38 177 | 29 10 215 | 28 10 279 | 28 50 314 | 32 27 344 |
| 282 | 59 29 041 | 45 35 102 | 38 40 178 | 28 39 215 | 27 17 280 | 28 11 314 | 32 12 344 |
| 283 | 60 05 040 | 46 28 102 | 38 42 179 | 28 07 216 | 26 23 280 | 27 32 314 | 31 57 344 |
| 284 | 60 39 040 | 47 21 103 | 38 42 180 | 27 35 217 | 25 30 280 | 26 53 315 | 31 41 344 |
| | DENEB | ◆ Alpheratz | FOMALHAUT | ◆ Nunki | ANTARES | ◆ ARCTURUS | Kochab |
| 285 | 61 14 039 | 22 29 067 | 11 04 130 | 38 41 181 | 27 02 218 | 24 36 281 | 31 26 344 |
| 286 | 61 48 038 | 23 19 067 | 11 46 131 | 38 40 183 | 26 28 219 | 23 43 281 | 31 10 343 |
| 287 | 62 21 037 | 24 09 068 | 12 26 131 | 38 37 184 | 25 54 219 | 22 50 281 | 30 55 343 |
| 288 | 62 53 036 | 24 59 068 | 13 07 132 | 38 33 185 | 25 19 220 | 21 56 282 | 30 39 343 |
| 289 | 63 24 035 | 25 50 068 | 13 47 133 | 38 28 186 | 24 44 221 | 21 03 282 | 30 24 343 |
| 290 | 63 55 034 | 26 41 069 | 14 27 133 | 38 21 187 | 24 08 222 | 20 10 282 | 30 08 343 |
| 291 | 64 25 033 | 27 31 069 | 15 07 134 | 38 14 188 | 23 31 222 | 19 17 283 | 29 52 343 |
| 292 | 64 54 031 | 28 22 069 | 15 46 134 | 38 06 189 | 22 54 223 | 18 24 283 | 29 36 343 |
| 293 | 65 22 030 | 29 13 069 | 16 25 135 | 37 57 190 | 22 17 224 | 17 31 283 | 29 20 343 |
| 294 | 65 49 029 | 30 04 070 | 17 03 136 | 37 46 192 | 21 39 224 | 16 38 284 | 29 04 343 |
| 295 | 66 14 028 | 30 55 070 | 17 41 136 | 37 35 193 | 21 01 225 | 15 45 284 | 28 48 343 |
| 296 | 66 39 026 | 31 46 070 | 18 18 137 | 37 22 194 | 20 22 226 | 14 53 285 | 28 32 343 |
| 297 | 67 02 025 | 32 37 070 | 18 55 137 | 37 09 195 | 19 43 226 | 14 00 285 | 28 15 343 |
| 298 | 67 24 023 | 33 28 070 | 19 32 138 | 36 54 196 | 19 03 227 | 13 08 285 | 27 59 343 |
| 299 | 67 45 021 | 34 19 071 | 20 08 139 | 36 39 197 | 18 23 228 | 12 15 286 | 27 43 343 |
| | ◆ DENEB | Schedar | Alpheratz | ◆ FOMALHAUT | Nunki | ◆ Rasalhague | VEGA |
| 300 | 68 04 020 | 31 30 037 | 35 11 071 | 20 44 139 | 36 23 198 | 53 37 257 | 67 43 313 |
| 301 | 68 22 018 | 32 03 037 | 36 02 071 | 21 19 140 | 36 05 199 | 52 44 257 | 67 03 312 |
| 302 | 68 38 016 | 32 36 037 | 36 53 071 | 21 53 141 | 35 47 200 | 51 51 258 | 66 22 311 |
| 303 | 68 52 014 | 33 09 037 | 37 45 071 | 22 27 142 | 35 28 201 | 50 58 259 | 65 41 310 |
| 304 | 69 05 013 | 33 42 037 | 38 37 072 | 23 01 142 | 35 08 202 | 50 05 259 | 64 59 309 |
| 305 | 69 16 011 | 34 15 037 | 39 28 072 | 23 34 143 | 34 47 203 | 49 11 260 | 64 17 309 |
| 306 | 69 25 009 | 34 48 037 | 40 20 072 | 24 06 144 | 34 25 204 | 48 18 261 | 63 34 308 |
| 307 | 69 32 007 | 35 21 037 | 41 12 072 | 24 38 144 | 34 02 205 | 47 24 261 | 62 51 307 |
| 308 | 69 38 005 | 35 53 037 | 42 04 072 | 25 10 145 | 33 38 206 | 46 30 262 | 62 08 307 |
| 309 | 69 41 003 | 36 26 037 | 42 55 073 | 25 40 146 | 33 14 207 | 45 36 262 | 61 24 306 |
| 310 | 69 43 001 | 36 59 037 | 43 47 073 | 26 10 147 | 32 49 208 | 44 42 263 | 60 40 306 |
| 311 | 69 43 359 | 37 31 037 | 44 39 073 | 26 40 148 | 32 23 209 | 43 48 263 | 59 56 305 |
| 312 | 69 41 357 | 38 03 036 | 45 31 073 | 27 09 148 | 31 56 210 | 42 54 264 | 59 11 305 |
| 313 | 69 36 355 | 38 36 036 | 46 23 073 | 27 37 149 | 31 29 211 | 42 00 264 | 58 26 304 |
| 314 | 69 30 353 | 39 08 036 | 47 15 073 | 28 04 150 | 31 00 212 | 41 06 265 | 57 41 304 |
| | ◆ Alpheratz | Diphda | ◆ FOMALHAUT | ALTAIR | Rasalhague | ◆ VEGA | DENEB |
| 315 | 48 08 074 | 20 40 123 | 28 31 151 | 66 56 229 | 40 12 265 | 56 56 303 | 69 23 351 |
| 316 | 49 00 074 | 21 25 123 | 28 57 152 | 66 15 230 | 39 18 266 | 56 10 303 | 69 13 349 |
| 317 | 49 52 074 | 22 10 124 | 29 22 153 | 65 33 232 | 38 23 266 | 55 24 303 | 69 01 347 |
| 318 | 50 44 074 | 22 55 125 | 29 47 154 | 64 49 234 | 37 29 267 | 54 39 302 | 68 48 345 |
| 319 | 51 36 074 | 23 40 125 | 30 11 154 | 64 05 235 | 36 35 267 | 53 53 302 | 68 33 343 |
| 320 | 52 29 074 | 24 24 126 | 30 34 155 | 63 20 237 | 35 40 268 | 53 07 302 | 68 17 341 |
| 321 | 53 21 074 | 25 08 127 | 30 56 156 | 62 34 238 | 34 46 268 | 52 21 302 | 67 59 340 |
| 322 | 54 13 074 | 25 52 127 | 31 18 157 | 61 48 239 | 33 52 269 | 51 34 302 | 67 39 338 |
| 323 | 55 06 074 | 26 35 128 | 31 38 158 | 61 01 241 | 32 57 269 | 50 48 301 | 67 18 336 |
| 324 | 55 58 074 | 27 17 129 | 31 58 159 | 60 13 242 | 32 03 269 | 50 01 301 | 66 56 335 |
| 325 | 56 51 075 | 28 00 129 | 32 17 160 | 59 25 243 | 31 09 270 | 49 15 301 | 66 32 333 |
| 326 | 57 43 075 | 28 42 130 | 32 35 161 | 58 36 244 | 30 14 270 | 48 28 301 | 66 07 332 |
| 327 | 58 35 075 | 29 23 131 | 32 53 162 | 57 47 245 | 29 20 271 | 47 42 301 | 65 41 331 |
| 328 | 59 28 075 | 30 04 132 | 33 09 163 | 56 57 246 | 28 25 271 | 46 55 301 | 65 14 329 |
| 329 | 60 20 075 | 30 44 132 | 33 25 164 | 56 08 247 | 27 31 272 | 46 08 301 | 64 46 328 |
| | ◆ Mirfak | Hamal | Diphda | ◆ FOMALHAUT | ALTAIR | ◆ VEGA | DENEB |
| 330 | 24 26 044 | 34 08 078 | 31 24 133 | 33 39 165 | 55 17 248 | 45 22 301 | 64 17 327 |
| 331 | 25 04 045 | 35 02 078 | 32 04 134 | 33 53 166 | 54 27 249 | 44 35 301 | 63 47 326 |
| 332 | 25 42 045 | 35 55 078 | 32 43 135 | 34 06 167 | 53 36 250 | 43 48 301 | 63 16 325 |
| 333 | 26 21 045 | 36 48 078 | 33 21 136 | 34 17 168 | 52 45 251 | 43 02 301 | 62 44 324 |
| 334 | 26 59 045 | 37 41 079 | 33 59 136 | 34 28 169 | 51 53 251 | 42 15 301 | 62 11 323 |
| 335 | 27 37 045 | 38 35 079 | 34 36 137 | 34 38 170 | 51 02 252 | 41 28 301 | 61 38 322 |
| 336 | 28 16 045 | 39 28 079 | 35 12 138 | 34 47 171 | 50 10 253 | 40 41 301 | 61 04 321 |
| 337 | 28 54 045 | 40 22 080 | 35 48 139 | 34 55 172 | 49 18 254 | 39 54 301 | 60 30 320 |
| 338 | 29 33 045 | 41 15 080 | 36 23 140 | 35 02 173 | 48 25 254 | 39 08 301 | 59 54 319 |
| 339 | 30 11 045 | 42 09 080 | 36 58 141 | 35 08 174 | 47 33 255 | 38 21 301 | 59 19 319 |
| 340 | 30 50 045 | 43 02 080 | 37 32 142 | 35 13 175 | 46 40 256 | 37 34 301 | 58 43 318 |
| 341 | 31 29 045 | 43 56 081 | 38 05 143 | 35 17 176 | 45 47 256 | 36 48 301 | 58 06 317 |
| 342 | 32 07 045 | 44 50 081 | 38 37 144 | 35 20 177 | 44 55 257 | 36 01 301 | 57 29 317 |
| 343 | 32 46 045 | 45 43 081 | 39 09 145 | 35 22 178 | 44 02 258 | 35 14 301 | 56 51 316 |
| 344 | 33 25 045 | 46 37 082 | 39 40 146 | 35 23 180 | 43 08 258 | 34 28 301 | 56 13 315 |
| | Schedar | CAPELLA | ◆ ALDEBARAN | Diphda | ◆ FOMALHAUT | ALTAIR | ◆ DENEB |
| 345 | 53 37 023 | 14 58 046 | 12 12 077 | 40 10 147 | 35 22 181 | 42 15 259 | 55 35 315 |
| 346 | 53 58 023 | 15 37 046 | 13 05 078 | 40 39 148 | 35 21 182 | 41 22 259 | 54 56 314 |
| 347 | 54 18 022 | 16 16 046 | 13 58 078 | 41 07 149 | 35 19 183 | 40 28 260 | 54 17 314 |
| 348 | 54 38 021 | 16 55 047 | 14 51 078 | 41 34 150 | 35 16 184 | 39 35 261 | 53 38 314 |
| 349 | 54 57 020 | 17 35 047 | 15 44 079 | 42 01 151 | 35 12 185 | 38 41 261 | 52 59 313 |
| 350 | 55 16 019 | 18 15 047 | 16 38 079 | 42 26 153 | 35 07 186 | 37 47 262 | 52 19 313 |
| 351 | 55 34 019 | 18 55 047 | 17 31 080 | 42 51 154 | 35 01 187 | 36 53 262 | 51 39 312 |
| 352 | 55 51 018 | 19 35 047 | 18 25 080 | 43 14 155 | 34 54 188 | 35 59 263 | 50 58 312 |
| 353 | 56 07 017 | 20 15 048 | 19 18 080 | 43 37 156 | 34 46 189 | 35 05 263 | 50 18 312 |
| 354 | 56 22 016 | 20 55 048 | 20 12 081 | 43 58 157 | 34 36 190 | 34 11 264 | 49 37 311 |
| 355 | 56 37 015 | 21 35 048 | 21 06 081 | 44 19 159 | 34 26 191 | 33 17 264 | 48 56 311 |
| 356 | 56 51 014 | 22 16 048 | 21 59 081 | 44 38 160 | 34 15 192 | 32 23 265 | 48 15 311 |
| 357 | 57 04 013 | 22 56 048 | 22 53 082 | 44 56 161 | 34 03 193 | 31 29 265 | 47 34 311 |
| 358 | 57 16 012 | 23 37 049 | 23 47 082 | 45 13 162 | 33 51 194 | 30 35 266 | 46 53 310 |
| 359 | 57 27 011 | 24 18 049 | 24 41 082 | 45 29 164 | 33 37 195 | 29 41 266 | 46 12 310 |

*Figure 13–4 (continued).*

the easiest to spot. The diamonds above the star names indicate the stars that have the most suitable spread in bearings for good crossing angles of their LOPs in a three-star fix. Frankly, though, I have found it is usually best to pick two of the brightest stars, so long as their bearings have a good enough spread, and then concentrate on getting several sights of each, rather than trying to get a lot of single shots. With multiple shots of two stars you can average the altitudes and times.

This approach reduces the pressure, too, because when you are doing star sights either the stars are fading or the horizon is. In this example, Vega in the northeast and Antares in the southeast are good picks. Both stars are very bright, and the bearing spread is a little over 50°. Or you could pick Spica and Regulus, where the bearing spread is nearly 90°, but in the evening I prefer to shoot to the east, opposite the sun, because that's where the edge of nightfall is closest and, therefore, where the stars first appear.

One thing to note about this table is that the number next to the computed altitude is the true bearing (Zn) of the star, not the azimuth angle (Z). So what you do now is make a note of the Hc and Zn of each star you plan to shoot, go on deck, set your sextant to that altitude, and as twilight comes, point the instrument toward Zn. Waggle the sextant around and the star will appear. Set it on the horizon. Take the time. Take a couple more sights and then reset for the other star and do the same.

Once you have the actual sights and their times, get the GHA of Aries from the almanac for the actual times of the sights, take an assumed position for each that eliminates the extra minutes of GHA to give you an integral LHA, just as in any other sight, and go into the table with that LHA. Take out Hc and Zn, compare Hc and Ho, and go to the plotting sheet.

Figures 13-5 and 13-6 show sights of Vega and Antares, using the *Selected Stars* table. Notice that the stars were shot a bit before the planned time of 0518, which means that the Hc and Zn are looked up on the lines for LHA of Aries of 195° (Vega) and 196° (Antares). Antares, by the way, is reddish and is considered the heart of one of the few constellations that truly look like what they are named for. After your work, come on deck in the full night and face the blaze of a gigantic glittering Scorpion.

Remember that in using *Selected Stars* you need to find only the LHA of Aries. There is no need to look up the SHAs or declinations

| | | |
|---|---|---|
| Date: 6-20-99 | VEGA | DR: 25°15′ N |
| (Greenwich) | | 150°11′ W |

| | | |
|---|---|---|
| Sextant reads | [Hs] | 20°03′ |
| Index corr. | [IC] | + 02′ |
| Dip corr. | [D] | – 03′ |
| Apparent alt. | [Ha] | 20°02′ |
| Ref/SD | | – 03′ |
| Observed alt. | [Ho] | 19°59′ |

| | |
|---|---|
| GHA   0500 UT | 342°58.1′ |
| + 10m, 03s | 2°31.2′ |
| **GHA** | 345°29.3′ |
| **GHA** | 345°29′ |
| (+ 360°?) | |

**AP longitude** $^{-W}_{+E}$   –150°29′ W        **AP latitude = 25° N**
(– 360°?)

**LHA**        195°

Data for HO 249:   lat. = 25° N   LHA = 195°
Data from HO 249:  Hc = 19°37′    Zn = 055°

**Hc**    19°37′
**Ho**    19°59′

        22′   Toward        **Zn = 055°**
              Away

*Figure 13–5.* Work sheet for a sight of the star Vega

of the stars because those are fixed and plugged into the computer formulas that generated the table. Because there is no declination component, there is no crisscross or other interpolation table. For the same reason, there is no contrary/same distinction to be made. A page of computed altitudes and bearings is simply calculated for each degree of north and south latitude. True bearing is tabulated, not azimuth angle, so there are no cute little mnemonics cluttering the top and bottom corners of the pages.

Date: 6-20-99          ANTARES      DR: 25°15′ N
        (Greenwich)                 150°11′ W

| | | |
|---|---|---|
| Sextant reads | [Hs] | 18°41′ |
| Index corr. | [IC] | + 02′ |
| Dip corr. | [D] | – 03′ |
| Apparent alt. | [Ha] | 18°40′ |
| Ref/SD | | – 03′ |
| Observed alt. | [Ho] | 18°37′ |

GHA  0500 UT    342°58.1′
+ 14m, 05s        3°31.8′
**GHA**          346°29.9′
**GHA**          346°30′
(+ 360°?)

**AP longitude** $\begin{smallmatrix}-W\\+E\end{smallmatrix}$  –150°30′ W          **AP latitude = 25° N**
(– 360°?)

**LHA**          196°

Data for HO 249:   lat. = 25° N   LHA = 196°
Data from HO 249:  Hc = 18°35′    Zn = 132°

**Hc**    18°35′
**Ho**    18°37′
        02′ (Toward)                **Zn = 132°**
              Away

*Figure 13–6.* Work sheet for a sight of the star Antares

There is one thing about the stars, or rather Aries, though, that is like the planets (brace yourself, here comes another table): the GHA of Aries changes a little faster than the basic rate of 15° per hour, so there is a *v* correction. It amounts to about 2.5′ of arc per hour and is constant, unlike that of the planets. In the interests of strict precision, the *Nautical Almanac* provides a separate column labeled Aries in the GHA interpolation table (fig. 4-2). If you compare the bottom of the columns for the sun and Aries, you see that in 37 minutes of time the sun travels 9°15′ whereas Aries advances 9°16.5′. In the figuring for the LHA of Aries at 0518, note that in 18 minutes of time, Aries goes 4°30.7′, whereas the sun goes 4°30′ exactly.

A final feature about *Selected Stars* is that, unlike the white- and blue-spined volumes, it slowly goes out of date because the earth does not spin perfectly, but wobbles like a top winding down. However, a table in the back informs you how much and in what direction to move the fix or single LOP. It's called Correction for Precession and Nutation, and the maximum correction doesn't reach 3′ of arc until the year 2003.

In sum, *Selected Stars* is both the star finder for planning purposes *and* the sight reduction table once a sight has been taken. The only entry data are the LHA of Aries and the latitude of the AP. Given an LHA of Aries and a latitude, the table immediately tells you the seven best stars for that latitude and time, identifies the first magnitude ones by capitalizing their names, and indicates which three have the optimum bearings by tagging them with a diamond shape.

Would that the other sight reduction tables could do so much with so little.

# 14

# The Pole Star

Having dealt with yet another tome of numbers, you will probably find taking sights of the North Star something of a relief. As with the noon sight, you can drop spherical trig and deal in plane geometry.

Polaris, as the North Star is referred to in the almanac, is virtually over the North Pole of our planet. If it were exactly over the pole, taking its altitude would give your latitude without further fuss (fig. 14-1). If you were at the pole, the star's altitude, directly overhead, would be 90°, equal to your latitude; likewise, if you were at the equator, the star's altitude, on the horizon, would be 0°, equal to your latitude.

In fact, the North Star travels in a little circle around the pole, the radius of which is about three-quarters of a degree (44′). That value is great enough to make a significant difference in your latitude, but small enough to produce a simple correction table (fig. 14-2), which is printed in the back of *Selected Stars.* To enter the table, you need only the LHA of Aries (again, shown as the astrological symbol of the Ram).

So, the theory and the table involved in this sight are not much of a problem. What is difficult is finding the star before the horizon vanishes. Polaris is dim (magnitude 2.1). The North Star has a saving

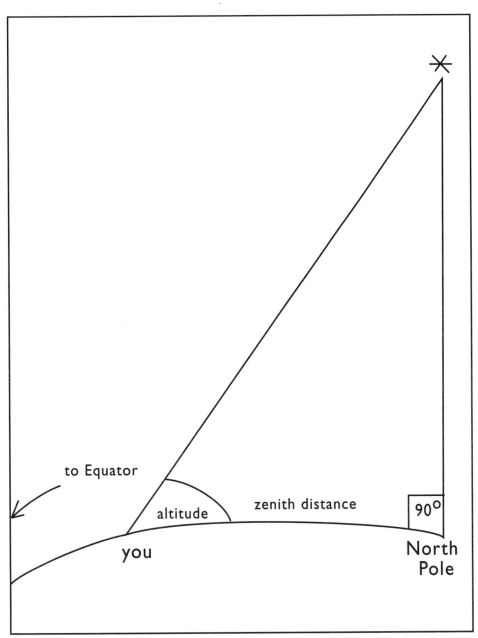

*Figure 14–1.* The relationship between the North Star's altitude and your latitude

grace, however. It shines alone in a blank patch of sky over the Arctic Ocean, so it is possible to spot it and get your sextant on it while the horizon is still visible (usually on the dark side of just barely but usable, nonetheless).

One way to find Polaris is to follow the outer edge of the bowl of the Big Dipper (fig. 14-3). The problem with this method is that the stars in the Dipper are not much brighter than Polaris. By the time

**TABLE 6 — CORRECTION (Q) FOR POLARIS**

| LHA ϓ | Q | LHA ϓ | Q | LHA ϓ | Q | LHA ϓ | Q | LHA ϓ | Q | LHA ϓ | Q | LHA ϓ | Q | LHA ϓ | Q |
|---|---|---|---|---|---|---|---|---|---|---|---|---|---|---|---|
| 359 47 | −35 | 87 32 | −28 | 123 09 | − 3 | 156 56 | +22 | 237 58 | +41 | 286 26 | +16 | 319 33 | − 9 | 357 45 | −34 |
| 1 55 | −36 | 89 12 | −27 | 124 27 | − 2 | 158 27 | +23 | 241 31 | +40 | 287 50 | +15 | 320 53 | −10 | 359 47 | −35 |
| 4 09 | −37 | 90 50 | −26 | 125 45 | − 1 | 159 58 | +24 | 244 38 | +39 | 289 13 | +14 | 322 13 | −11 | 1 55 | −36 |
| 6 31 | −38 | 92 27 | −25 | 127 03 | 0 | 161 32 | +25 | 247 26 | +38 | 290 36 | +13 | 323 33 | −12 | 4 09 | −37 |
| 9 04 | −39 | 94 01 | −24 | 128 22 | + 1 | 163 06 | +26 | 250 01 | +37 | 291 57 | +12 | 324 54 | −13 | 6 31 | −38 |
| 11 51 | −40 | 95 33 | −23 | 129 40 | + 2 | 164 43 | +27 | 252 25 | +36 | 293 18 | +11 | 326 15 | −14 | 9 04 | −39 |
| 14 55 | −41 | 97 04 | −22 | 130 58 | + 3 | 166 22 | +28 | 254 41 | +35 | 294 39 | +10 | 327 38 | −15 | 11 51 | −40 |
| 18 26 | −42 | 98 34 | −21 | 132 16 | + 4 | 168 04 | +29 | 256 49 | +34 | 295 59 | + 9 | 329 00 | −16 | 14 55 | −41 |
| 22 42 | −43 | 100 03 | −20 | 133 34 | + 5 | 169 48 | +30 | 258 53 | +33 | 297 19 | + 8 | 330 24 | −17 | 18 26 | −42 |
| 28 41 | −44 | 101 30 | −19 | 134 53 | + 6 | 171 34 | +31 | 260 51 | +32 | 298 38 | + 7 | 331 48 | −18 | 22 42 | −43 |
| 47 28 | −43 | 102 56 | −18 | 136 12 | + 7 | 173 25 | +32 | 262 44 | +31 | 299 57 | + 6 | 333 13 | −19 | 28 41 | −44 |
| 53 27 | −42 | 104 21 | −17 | 137 31 | + 8 | 175 18 | +33 | 264 35 | +30 | 301 16 | + 5 | 334 39 | −20 | 47 28 | −43 |
| 57 43 | −41 | 105 45 | −16 | 138 50 | + 9 | 177 16 | +34 | 266 21 | +29 | 302 35 | + 4 | 336 06 | −21 | 53 27 | −42 |
| 61 14 | −40 | 107 09 | −15 | 140 10 | +10 | 179 20 | +35 | 268 05 | +28 | 303 53 | + 3 | 337 35 | −22 | 57 43 | −41 |
| 64 18 | −39 | 108 31 | −14 | 141 30 | +11 | 181 28 | +36 | 269 47 | +27 | 305 11 | + 2 | 339 05 | −23 | 61 14 | −40 |
| 67 05 | −38 | 109 54 | −13 | 142 51 | +12 | 183 44 | +37 | 271 26 | +26 | 306 29 | + 1 | 340 36 | −24 | 64 18 | −39 |
| 69 38 | −37 | 111 15 | −12 | 144 12 | +13 | 186 08 | +38 | 273 03 | +25 | 307 47 | 0 | 342 08 | −25 | 67 05 | −38 |
| 72 00 | −36 | 112 36 | −11 | 145 33 | +14 | 188 43 | +39 | 274 37 | +24 | 309 06 | − 1 | 343 42 | −26 | 69 38 | −37 |
| 74 14 | −35 | 113 56 | −10 | 146 56 | +15 | 191 31 | +40 | 276 11 | +23 | 310 24 | − 2 | 345 19 | −27 | 72 00 | −36 |
| 76 22 | −34 | 115 16 | − 9 | 148 19 | +16 | 194 38 | +40 | 277 42 | +22 | 311 42 | − 3 | 346 57 | −28 | 74 14 | −35 |
| 78 24 | −33 | 116 36 | − 8 | 149 43 | +17 | 198 11 | +41 | 279 13 | +21 | 313 00 | − 4 | 348 37 | −29 | 76 22 | −34 |
| 80 21 | −32 | 117 55 | − 7 | 151 07 | +18 | 202 30 | +42 | 280 42 | +20 | 314 18 | − 5 | 350 20 | −30 | 78 24 | −33 |
| 82 14 | −31 | 119 14 | − 6 | 152 33 | +19 | 208 34 | +43 | 282 09 | +19 | 315 37 | − 6 | 352 06 | −31 | 80 21 | −32 |
| 84 03 | −30 | 120 32 | − 5 | 154 00 | +20 | 227 35 | +44 | 283 36 | +18 | 316 55 | − 7 | 353 55 | −32 | 82 14 | −31 |
| 85 49 | −29 | 121 51 | − 4 | 155 27 | +21 | 233 39 | +43 | 285 02 | +17 | 318 14 | − 8 | 355 48 | −33 | 84 03 | −30 |
| 87 32 | | 123 09 | | 156 56 | | 237 58 | +42 | 286 26 | | 319 33 | | 357 45 | | 85 49 | |

The above table, which does *not* include refraction, gives the quantity Q to be applied to the corrected sextant altitude of *Polaris* to give the latitude of the observer. In critical cases ascend.

Polaris: Mag. 2.1, SHA 321° 55′, Dec N 89° 15′.9

*Figure 14–2.* Correction table for the movement of Polaris around the North Pole, from *HO 249,* vol. 1

you have found it, the horizon may be gone. Another way to locate Polaris is to face north and look at the appropriate altitude. Since the altitude of the star is equal to your latitude, the number of degrees in your DR latitude is the altitude of the portion of the sky you want to scan. (To measure an approximate angle, use the out-stretched hand-spans trick described in chapter 2.)

The best way to find Polaris is to do all of the above and get your sextant into the act, too. Set your sextant to your DR latitude. Use your hand to locate the approximate area in the sky. Put the telescope to your eye, and swing it around. Take it down. See if you can spot the Dipper. Go back and forth like this for a bit until you find it. When you have the North Star in your scope, bring it down to the horizon, take the time, and read the sextant. Then go ahead as in any other sight. Apply the corrections for index error, dip, and refraction to get Ho. Now look up the GHA of Aries in the almanac, and figure out the LHA of Aries. Then go to the table and apply the correction.

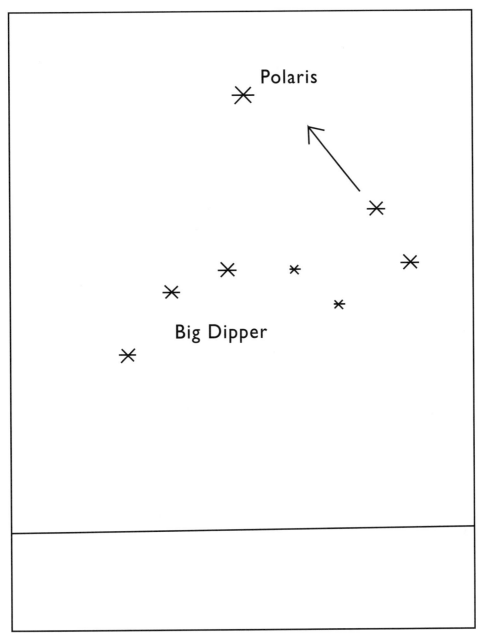

*Figure 14–3.* Relative locations of Polaris and the constellation known as the Big Dipper

For instance, if you add Polaris to your sights in the previous chapter, the LHA of Aries is probably between 194°38′ and 198°11′, so you add 41′ to Ho and have your latitude, which you can use to cross-check the other star sights, advance for a running fix with a late-afternoon sun line, or just let stand alone as a final check on your DR before turning in for the night or reporting for duty in the galley.

# Part IV

☉ ♃ ♂ ♄ ♀ ☆ ☾

# Luna:
# Navigation by the Moon

# 15

# The Moon

Compared to the other celestial bodies the moon really whizzes around. The moon accomplishes in one month what it takes the sun a year and many of the planets decades or centuries to do—it makes a complete circuit around its orbit.

High velocity is not confined to the moon, of course. All bodies in the heavens are spinning along their orbits at incredible speeds. But all these other bodies are millions or billions of miles from earth, so they *seem* to move slowly, as a jet does when it is high in the sky. The motions of celestial bodies are also not truly smooth. Orbits are ellipses, not perfect circles, so at any moment celestial bodies are either speeding up or slowing down. Planets and moons wobble around on their axes like cheap toy gyroscopes. They *totter* along their paths like a bunch of old sots, appearing as sober citizens only because they are seen across illimitable space.

The moon, however, is close to earth—a mere couple of hundred thousand miles off—and the vagaries of its orbit are only too evident. The upshot is that the *Nautical Almanac* has a hard time keeping track. The basic reason for the difficulty is that the almanac calculates the instantaneous *hourly* position of celestial bodies, which works fine for the stars, sun, and planets because their GHA and declinations run along at steady rates or change quite slowly. The maximum rate of change of the sun's declination, for example, is 1′ per hour, and its GHA varies so little (0.3′ per hour, maximum) from the adopted rate of 15° per hour that the difference is negligible when interpolating. And finally, the *v* correction to the 15° per hour GHA rate for the planets and Aries is so small you can do the interpolation mentally, so small that if you forget it, you aren't seriously embarrassed.

In the case of the moon, however, the basic rate of the GHA varies from hour to hour and is sometimes greater than 15′. You need to interpolate, and you need another table. The declination behaves the same way, increasing or decreasing by 15′ per hour or more. This means more work for the navigator.

The moon's proximity to earth is the source of another complication for celestial navigators (and of another table, naturally). This complicating factor is called parallax. To understand parallax you need to understand celestial navigation's true geometry, which was discovered more than two thousand years ago in Alexandria, Egypt.

Back then, Alexandria had a huge library, so the city was a natural focal point for the world's scholars, among them a Greek named Eratosthenes (circa 200 BC). He belonged to a group that had pretty well concluded the earth was spherical, and he wanted to know how big it was.

Eratosthenes had heard that at noon on the day of the summer solstice the sun was reflected from the water in the bottom of a certain well in the city of Syene. Syene, now called Aswan, is far to the south of Alexandria. He caught the next caravan to see for himself the sun in the well. He saw the sun and also noted that by camel the trip took fifty days each way. He translated camel-days into the unit of distance he customarily worked with—the *stadium*—and calculated 4,307 stadia (about 430 nautical miles) as the distance between the two cities.

In Alexandria, Eratosthenes had observed that the obelisks and statues cast shadows at noon on the day of the solstice. The fact that the sun lighted the bottom of a well in Syene on that same day, as he verified, meant the sun was vertically overhead there. He also noted that in Syene at noon on the day of the solstice, the statues cast no shadows.

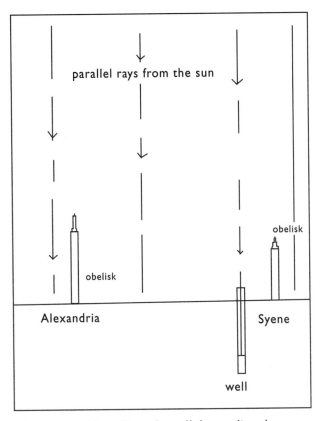

*Figure 15–1.* The effect of parallel rays directly
above vertical objects on a flat surface

To Eratosthenes, shadows in Alexandria and the lack of them in
Syene was further proof of the curvature of the earth. Moreover, his
sense of the scale of the natural world was that the sun was so far
away its rays struck the earth at the same angle everywhere—that is,
the rays were parallel. This being the case, in order to have shadows
in Alexandria and none in Syene, Alexandria would have to be tilted
relative to Syene (figs. 15-1, 15-2).

With his preliminary work complete, Eratosthenes waited in
Alexandria for the next summer solstice. On that day he went out late
in the morning and kept watch on the shadow cast by an obelisk
whose height he knew. As the sun rose toward noon, the shadow
shortened; he followed it, making successive marks on the pavement.
When the shadow started to lengthen again, he knew it was noon.
He measured the length of the shadow; and basic trig gave him the

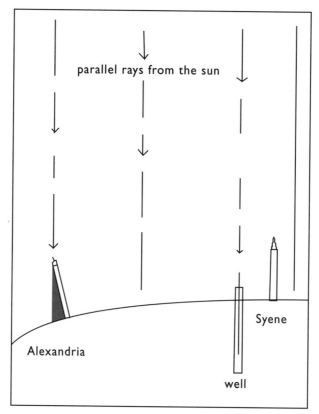

*Figure 15–2.* The effect of parallel rays directly above vertical objects on a rounded surface

interior angles: the one at the top was 7°30´, the bottom, 82°30´ (fig. 15-3).

Now Eratosthenes drew a picture (fig. 15-4). He showed the earth as a circle, as though viewed from the side. He indicated two parallel rays of the sun, one striking Syene vertically, the other hitting Alexandria aslant. He labeled the angles in his drawing and saw that the angle formed at the center of the earth between his obelisk and the well was the same as angle *B* at the top of his shadow-based triangle: 7°30´. That meant the arc of the earth between the obelisk and the well was also 7°30´. And he knew personally the length of that arc: fifty camel-days, or 4,307 stadia. Therefore, 7°30´ of arc on the surface of the earth equaled a distance he knew. Again, that distance was about 430 modern nautical miles.

Now, 7°30´ is one forty-eighth of a complete 360°, so Eratosthenes had established that the distance between Alexandria and Syene was one forty-eighth of the total distance around the world.

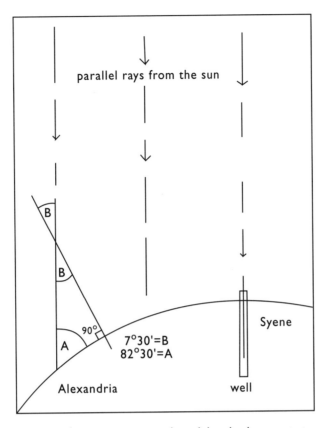

*Figure 15–3.* Measuring angles of the shadow cast at Alexandria at the summer solstice

According to Eratosthenes, then, the girth of the earth was 2,400 camel-days, or 206,740 stadia, or 20,640 nautical miles, a value that is only about five percent less than the generally accepted modern one of 21,600 nautical miles.

In any case, as far as celestial navigation goes, Eratosthenes' way of measuring the earth is the equivalent of the wheel. It's the *sine qua non* of celestial navigation.

If you take another look at figure 15-4, you can easily imagine that Syene is a GP and Alexandria your boat. The angle Eratosthenes called *A* is the angle you measure with your sextant when you take a sight. Angle *B* is what you get when you subtract your observed altitude from 90°. It is equal to the arc of the earth between the GP and your boat because it is equal to angle *C* at the center of the earth.

It's now obvious that the simple vertical triangle you have been using is a fiction, though a mighty useful one. Yours is the triangle

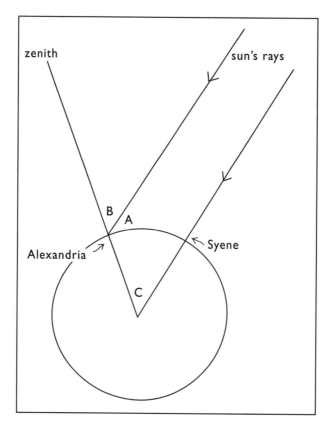

*Figure 15–4.* Measuring the circumference of earth

Alexandria–Sun–Syene, an impossible triangle because its two sides meet only at the infinitely distant sun. But it is a token of the universal geometry that makes celestial go and a useful mnemonic; it's easy to remember that as you approach a GP by 1 mile the altitude goes up 1´, which is something that takes a little study to see in Eratosthenes' sliced-earth picture. In any case, the key to understanding this great discovery is the equivalence of angles *C* and *B*.

Angle *B*, by the way, is called the *zenith distance*, the angular span between the point vertically over your head and your line of sight to the sun. It is equal in degrees to the great-circle arc between the GP and you, which is what you have been calling the zenith distance.

Quite obviously, Eratosthenes' method of measuring the earth and the utility of celestial navigation depend on the angle at the center of the earth being equal to the zenith distance, and that requires parallel rays. For the sun, planets, and stars, the light rays that intersect earth are parallel. For the moon, they are distinctly not, as figure 15-5 shows.

The difference (angle *P)* between a parallel ray and an actual ray from the moon is the *parallax.* It is 0° at an altitude of 90° and around 1° when the moon is on the horizon. It makes the sextant angle *smaller* than it would be if the rays were parallel.

Now that you have a notion of the three difficulties of using the moon (extra interpolating for the rates of change of GHA and of declination plus correction for parallax), here's the advantage: For about half the month, the moon is in the sky the same time as the sun, so you can often get a daytime fix from simultaneous sights of the two. Usually, this opportunity comes during the moon's quarter phases, when you see a half-moon in the sky or in the little diagram in the lower right corner of the almanac page. You can quite easily tell if a fix is possible by pointing at the sun and moon and looking at the angle between your arms. If it's generous, you can get a daytime fix with a hard horizon.

Here's an example. You're on a passage to Honolulu. It is late afternoon, June 19, 1999; your DR is 45°21′ N, 135°34′ W. There is a half-moon to the east, and the bearing spread between it and the sun looks to be about 60°, so you haul out your sextant and get sights of both.

The moon sight is 42°23′ at 17-36-12 by your watch, which is set to Pacific daylight time, so GMT is 24-36-12, or 36 minutes, 12 seconds past midnight, June 20.

Turning to the *Nautical Almanac* (fig. 4-1), a glance at the moon columns just to the right of the sun's on the right-hand page immediately confirms the need for additional calculations. Instead of the usual two columns for GHA and declination, the moon has five.

The first column is Greenwich hour angle; the one alongside it labeled *v* is the variation of GHA from a basic rate of 14°19′ per hour. Unlike *v* for planets, *v* for the moon is always positive.

The next two columns are declination and *d,* which stands here for the hourly change in the moon's declination (*d* is a general mathematical symbol for a small change and is used in lots of contexts; in the sight reduction tables, for example, it is the little number with the plus or minus sign between Hc and Z, the change in altitude for 1° change in declination). Here, *d* can be positive or negative, and as

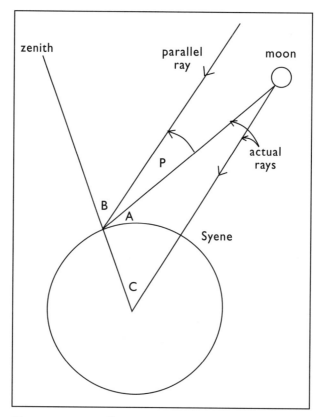

*Figure 15–5.* Parallax (P), the difference between the angle of parallel moon rays and actual moon rays

you do with the sun, you figure out which it is by looking down the declination column to the next hour. In this example, on June 20, 1999, between 00 and 01 hours, the declination of the moon *decreases* 10.3´.

The fifth column, headed HP, which stands for horizontal parallax, is the amount of parallax when the moon is on the horizon—that is, when its altitude is 0°.

Finally, at the bottom of the moon column are values for its semi-diameter for the three days covered by each page of the almanac.

Now continue to work your sight by taking out the moon data: For 00 hours on June 20, 1999, GHA is 96°18.5´; *v* is 13.1´; declination is 6°56.5´ N and is *decreasing* 10.3´ per hour; and HP is 56.3´.

Now look at the excerpt from the almanac interpolation table (fig. 4-2) and find the column for the moon. In 36 minutes and 12 seconds the GHA of the moon increases 8°38.3´. That's 36 minutes and 12 seconds of the basic rate of change of the moon's GHA in an hour (14°19´). The $v$ value of 13.1´, however, means that during this particular hour the GHA of the moon is changing 13.1´ more per hour than the base rate, so you have to get 36 minutes worth of 13.1´ and add it as well as 8°38.3´ to 96°18.5´ to get the GHA of the moon at the time of the sight.

If you look to the right of the moon's column on the interpolation table, you see three more columns of numbers, headed $v$ or $d$. In these three columns are all the possible values $v$ or $d$ can have. Look through these three columns until you find 13.1´ (about a quarter way down the outside column). Now look to the right, and you will see 8.0´. That's 36 minutes worth of a $v$ rate of 13.1´ per hour. You don't interpolate $v$ or $d$ for seconds (thank goodness!).

This part of the table is also used to interpolate $d$, the hourly change in the declination, 10.3´ in this case. It's in the middle column, about a quarter of the way from the bottom, and the value alongside 10.3´ is 6.3´. Remember, this 6.3´ is *subtracted* from the declination, because the almanac shows declination decreasing with the passage of time.

The adjustments to the sextant altitude for refraction, semi-diameter, and parallax of the moon are handled by a table that combines all three. It is printed in two halves on the inside back covers of the almanac. The section that deals with altitudes from 35°00´ to 89°50´ is reproduced as figure 15-6.

To use the table, first look in the upper section for the altitude nearest the apparent altitude of the sight of 42°23´. The closest value in the table is 42°20´ (look down the column headed 40°–44°), in the block for 42°. The correction listed is 52.2´. Next, look all the way down this same column into the section headed L U. The sight is of the lower limb (edge) of the moon, so look down the L part of the column until you come to the parallax value for the hour of the sight, 56.3´. This value is not tabulated, so use 56.4 and write down the value there: 3.7´. Round up to 4.0´ (04´) for the work sheet (fig. 15-7).

These corrections are always positive, even if you shoot the upper limb of the moon; but in that case you find the second correction in the U column, and you also *subtract* 30´ to compensate for the fact that the table assumes a lower-limb shot and factors in a

## ALTITUDE CORRECTION TABLES 35°–90°—MOON

| App. Alt. | 35°–39° Corrⁿ | 40°–44° Corrⁿ | 45°–49° Corrⁿ | 50°–54° Corrⁿ | 55°–59° Corrⁿ | 60°–64° Corrⁿ | 65°–69° Corrⁿ | 70°–74° Corrⁿ | 75°–79° Corrⁿ | 80°–84° Corrⁿ | 85°–89° Corrⁿ | App. Alt. |
|---|---|---|---|---|---|---|---|---|---|---|---|---|
| 00 | 35 56.5 | 40 53.7 | 45 50.5 | 50 46.9 | 55 43.1 | 60 38.9 | 65 34.6 | 70 30.1 | 75 25.3 | 80 20.5 | 85 15.6 | 00 |
| 10 | 56.4 | 53.6 | 50.4 | 46.8 | 42.9 | 38.8 | 34.4 | 29.9 | 25.2 | 20.4 | 15.5 | 10 |
| 20 | 56.3 | 53.5 | 50.2 | 46.7 | 42.8 | 38.7 | 34.3 | 29.7 | 25.0 | 20.2 | 15.3 | 20 |
| 30 | 56.2 | 53.4 | 50.1 | 46.5 | 42.7 | 38.5 | 34.1 | 29.6 | 24.9 | 20.0 | 15.1 | 30 |
| 40 | 56.2 | 53.3 | 50.0 | 46.4 | 42.5 | 38.4 | 34.0 | 29.4 | 24.7 | 19.9 | 15.0 | 40 |
| 50 | 56.1 | 53.2 | 49.9 | 46.3 | 42.4 | 38.2 | 33.8 | 29.3 | 24.5 | 19.7 | 14.8 | 50 |
| 00 | 36 56.0 | 41 53.1 | 46 49.8 | 51 46.2 | 56 42.3 | 61 38.1 | 66 33.7 | 71 29.1 | 76 24.4 | 81 19.6 | 86 14.6 | 00 |
| 10 | 55.9 | 53.0 | 49.7 | 46.0 | 42.1 | 37.9 | 33.5 | 29.0 | 24.2 | 19.4 | 14.5 | 10 |
| 20 | 55.8 | 52.8 | 49.5 | 45.9 | 42.0 | 37.8 | 33.4 | 28.8 | 24.1 | 19.2 | 14.3 | 20 |
| 30 | 55.7 | 52.7 | 49.4 | 45.8 | 41.8 | 37.7 | 33.2 | 28.7 | 23.9 | 19.1 | 14.1 | 30 |
| 40 | 55.6 | 52.6 | 49.3 | 45.7 | 41.7 | 37.5 | 33.1 | 28.5 | 23.8 | 18.9 | 14.0 | 40 |
| 50 | 55.5 | 52.5 | 49.2 | 45.5 | 41.6 | 37.4 | 32.9 | 28.3 | 23.6 | 18.7 | 13.8 | 50 |
| 00 | 37 55.4 | 42 52.4 | 47 49.1 | 52 45.4 | 57 41.4 | 62 37.2 | 67 32.8 | 72 28.2 | 77 23.4 | 82 18.6 | 87 13.7 | 00 |
| 10 | 55.3 | 52.3 | 49.0 | 45.3 | 41.3 | 37.1 | 32.6 | 28.0 | 23.3 | 18.4 | 13.5 | 10 |
| 20 | 55.2 | 52.2 | 48.8 | 45.2 | 41.2 | 36.9 | 32.5 | 27.9 | 23.1 | 18.2 | 13.3 | 20 |
| 30 | 55.1 | 52.1 | 48.7 | 45.0 | 41.0 | 36.8 | 32.3 | 27.7 | 22.9 | 18.1 | 13.2 | 30 |
| 40 | 55.0 | 52.0 | 48.6 | 44.9 | 40.9 | 36.6 | 32.2 | 27.6 | 22.8 | 17.9 | 13.0 | 40 |
| 50 | 55.0 | 51.9 | 48.5 | 44.8 | 40.8 | 36.5 | 32.0 | 27.4 | 22.6 | 17.8 | 12.8 | 50 |
| 00 | 38 54.9 | 43 51.8 | 48 48.4 | 53 44.6 | 58 40.6 | 63 36.4 | 68 31.9 | 73 27.2 | 78 22.5 | 83 17.6 | 88 12.7 | 00 |
| 10 | 54.8 | 51.7 | 48.2 | 44.5 | 40.5 | 36.2 | 31.7 | 27.1 | 22.3 | 17.4 | 12.5 | 10 |
| 20 | 54.7 | 51.6 | 48.1 | 44.4 | 40.3 | 36.1 | 31.6 | 26.9 | 22.1 | 17.3 | 12.3 | 20 |
| 30 | 54.6 | 51.5 | 48.0 | 44.2 | 40.2 | 35.9 | 31.4 | 26.8 | 22.0 | 17.1 | 12.2 | 30 |
| 40 | 54.5 | 51.4 | 47.9 | 44.1 | 40.1 | 35.8 | 31.3 | 26.6 | 21.8 | 16.9 | 12.0 | 40 |
| 50 | 54.4 | 51.2 | 47.8 | 44.0 | 39.9 | 35.6 | 31.1 | 26.5 | 21.7 | 16.8 | 11.8 | 50 |
| 00 | 39 54.3 | 44 51.1 | 49 47.6 | 54 43.9 | 59 39.8 | 64 35.5 | 69 31.0 | 74 26.3 | 79 21.5 | 84 16.6 | 89 11.7 | 00 |
| 10 | 54.2 | 51.0 | 47.5 | 43.7 | 39.6 | 35.3 | 30.8 | 26.1 | 21.3 | 16.5 | 11.5 | 10 |
| 20 | 54.1 | 50.9 | 47.4 | 43.6 | 39.5 | 35.2 | 30.7 | 26.0 | 21.2 | 16.3 | 11.4 | 20 |
| 30 | 54.0 | 50.8 | 47.3 | 43.5 | 39.4 | 35.0 | 30.5 | 25.8 | 21.0 | 16.1 | 11.2 | 30 |
| 40 | 53.9 | 50.7 | 47.2 | 43.3 | 39.2 | 34.9 | 30.4 | 25.7 | 20.9 | 16.0 | 11.0 | 40 |
| 50 | 53.8 | 50.6 | 47.0 | 43.2 | 39.1 | 34.7 | 30.2 | 25.5 | 20.7 | 15.8 | 10.9 | 50 |

| H.P. | L U | L U | L U | L U | L U | L U | L U | L U | L U | L U | L U | H.P. |
|---|---|---|---|---|---|---|---|---|---|---|---|---|
| 54.0 | 1.1 1.7 | 1.3 1.9 | 1.5 2.1 | 1.7 2.4 | 2.0 2.6 | 2.3 2.9 | 2.6 3.2 | 2.9 3.5 | 3.2 3.8 | 3.5 4.1 | 3.8 4.5 | 54.0 |
| 54.3 | 1.4 1.8 | 1.6 2.0 | 1.8 2.2 | 2.0 2.5 | 2.3 2.7 | 2.5 3.0 | 2.8 3.2 | 3.0 3.5 | 3.3 3.8 | 3.6 4.1 | 3.9 4.4 | 54.3 |
| 54.6 | 1.7 2.0 | 1.9 2.2 | 2.1 2.4 | 2.3 2.6 | 2.5 2.8 | 2.7 3.0 | 3.0 3.3 | 3.2 3.5 | 3.5 3.8 | 3.7 4.1 | 4.0 4.3 | 54.6 |
| 54.9 | 2.0 2.2 | 2.2 2.3 | 2.3 2.5 | 2.5 2.7 | 2.7 2.9 | 2.9 3.1 | 3.2 3.3 | 3.4 3.5 | 3.6 3.8 | 3.9 4.0 | 4.1 4.3 | 54.9 |
| 55.2 | 2.3 2.3 | 2.5 2.4 | 2.6 2.6 | 2.8 2.8 | 3.0 2.9 | 3.2 3.1 | 3.4 3.3 | 3.6 3.5 | 3.8 3.7 | 4.0 4.0 | 4.2 4.2 | 55.2 |
| 55.5 | 2.7 2.5 | 2.8 2.6 | 2.9 2.7 | 3.1 2.9 | 3.2 3.0 | 3.4 3.2 | 3.6 3.4 | 3.7 3.5 | 3.9 3.7 | 4.1 3.9 | 4.3 4.1 | 55.5 |
| 55.8 | 3.0 2.6 | 3.1 2.7 | 3.2 2.8 | 3.3 3.0 | 3.5 3.1 | 3.6 3.3 | 3.8 3.4 | 3.9 3.6 | 4.1 3.7 | 4.2 3.9 | 4.4 4.0 | 55.8 |
| 56.1 | 3.3 2.8 | 3.4 2.9 | 3.5 3.0 | 3.6 3.1 | 3.7 3.2 | 3.8 3.3 | 4.0 3.4 | 4.1 3.6 | 4.2 3.7 | 4.3 3.8 | 4.5 4.0 | 56.1 |
| 56.4 | 3.6 2.9 | 3.7 3.0 | 3.8 3.1 | 3.9 3.2 | 3.9 3.3 | 4.0 3.4 | 4.1 3.5 | 4.3 3.6 | 4.4 3.7 | 4.5 3.8 | 4.6 3.9 | 56.4 |
| 56.7 | 3.9 3.1 | 4.0 3.1 | 4.1 3.2 | 4.1 3.3 | 4.2 3.3 | 4.3 3.4 | 4.3 3.5 | 4.4 3.6 | 4.5 3.7 | 4.6 3.8 | 4.7 3.8 | 56.7 |
| 57.0 | 4.3 3.2 | 4.3 3.3 | 4.3 3.3 | 4.4 3.4 | 4.4 3.4 | 4.5 3.5 | 4.5 3.5 | 4.6 3.6 | 4.7 3.6 | 4.7 3.7 | 4.8 3.8 | 57.0 |
| 57.3 | 4.6 3.4 | 4.6 3.4 | 4.6 3.4 | 4.6 3.5 | 4.7 3.5 | 4.7 3.5 | 4.7 3.6 | 4.8 3.6 | 4.8 3.6 | 4.8 3.7 | 4.9 3.7 | 57.3 |
| 57.6 | 4.9 3.6 | 4.9 3.6 | 4.9 3.6 | 4.9 3.6 | 4.9 3.6 | 4.9 3.6 | 4.9 3.6 | 4.9 3.6 | 5.0 3.6 | 5.0 3.6 | 5.0 3.6 | 57.6 |
| 57.9 | 5.2 3.7 | 5.2 3.7 | 5.2 3.7 | 5.2 3.7 | 5.2 3.7 | 5.1 3.6 | 5.1 3.6 | 5.1 3.6 | 5.1 3.6 | 5.1 3.6 | 5.1 3.6 | 57.9 |
| 58.2 | 5.5 3.9 | 5.5 3.8 | 5.5 3.8 | 5.4 3.8 | 5.4 3.7 | 5.4 3.7 | 5.3 3.7 | 5.3 3.6 | 5.2 3.6 | 5.2 3.5 | 5.2 3.5 | 58.2 |
| 58.5 | 5.9 4.0 | 5.8 4.0 | 5.8 3.9 | 5.7 3.9 | 5.6 3.8 | 5.6 3.8 | 5.5 3.7 | 5.5 3.6 | 5.4 3.6 | 5.3 3.5 | 5.3 3.4 | 58.5 |
| 58.8 | 6.2 4.2 | 6.1 4.1 | 6.0 4.1 | 6.0 4.0 | 5.9 3.9 | 5.8 3.8 | 5.7 3.7 | 5.6 3.6 | 5.5 3.5 | 5.4 3.5 | 5.3 3.4 | 58.8 |
| 59.1 | 6.5 4.3 | 6.4 4.3 | 6.3 4.2 | 6.2 4.1 | 6.1 4.0 | 6.0 3.9 | 5.9 3.8 | 5.8 3.6 | 5.7 3.5 | 5.6 3.4 | 5.4 3.3 | 59.1 |
| 59.4 | 6.8 4.5 | 6.7 4.4 | 6.6 4.3 | 6.5 4.2 | 6.4 4.1 | 6.2 3.9 | 6.1 3.8 | 6.0 3.7 | 5.8 3.5 | 5.7 3.4 | 5.5 3.2 | 59.4 |
| 59.7 | 7.1 4.6 | 7.0 4.5 | 6.9 4.4 | 6.8 4.3 | 6.6 4.1 | 6.5 4.0 | 6.3 3.8 | 6.2 3.7 | 6.0 3.5 | 5.8 3.3 | 5.6 3.2 | 59.7 |
| 60.0 | 7.5 4.8 | 7.3 4.7 | 7.2 4.5 | 7.0 4.4 | 6.9 4.2 | 6.7 4.0 | 6.5 3.9 | 6.3 3.7 | 6.1 3.5 | 5.9 3.3 | 5.7 3.1 | 60.0 |
| 60.3 | 7.8 5.0 | 7.6 4.8 | 7.5 4.7 | 7.3 4.5 | 7.1 4.3 | 6.9 4.1 | 6.7 3.9 | 6.5 3.7 | 6.3 3.5 | 6.0 3.2 | 5.8 3.0 | 60.3 |
| 60.6 | 8.1 5.1 | 7.9 5.0 | 7.7 4.8 | 7.6 4.6 | 7.3 4.4 | 7.1 4.2 | 6.9 3.9 | 6.7 3.7 | 6.4 3.4 | 6.2 3.2 | 5.9 2.9 | 60.6 |
| 60.9 | 8.4 5.3 | 8.2 5.1 | 8.0 4.9 | 7.8 4.7 | 7.6 4.5 | 7.3 4.2 | 7.1 4.0 | 6.8 3.7 | 6.6 3.4 | 6.3 3.2 | 6.0 2.9 | 60.9 |
| 61.2 | 3.7 5.4 | 8.5 5.2 | 8.3 5.0 | 8.1 4.8 | 7.8 4.5 | 7.6 4.3 | 7.3 4.0 | 7.0 3.7 | 6.7 3.4 | 6.4 3.1 | 6.1 2.8 | 61.2 |
| 61.5 | 9.1 5.6 | 8.8 5.4 | 8.6 5.1 | 8.3 4.9 | 8.1 4.6 | 7.8 4.3 | 7.5 4.0 | 7.2 3.7 | 6.9 3.4 | 6.5 3.1 | 6.2 2.7 | 61.5 |

*Figure 15–6.* Table for correcting sextant altitude for refraction, semidiameter, and parallax of the moon, from the *Nautical Almanac*

Date: 6-20-99          MOON          DR: 45°21′ N
         (Greenwich)                  135°34′ W

| Sextant reads | (Hs) | 42°23′ |
| Index corr. | (IC) | + 03′ |
| Dip corr. | (D) | – 03′ |
| Apparent alt. | (Ha) | 42°23′ |
| Main corr | | + 52′ |
| L - U corr | | + 04′ |
| if U – 30′ | | – – |
| Observed alt. | (Ho) | 43°19′ |

| 6-20  00 UT | 96°19′ | Dec.  N 6°57′ |
| + 36m, 12s | 8°38′ | – – |
| + v | 08′ | d      –06′ |
| **GHA** | **105°05′** | Dec.  N 6°51′ |
| (± 360°?) | + 360°00′ | |
| **GHA** | **465°05′** | |

**AP longitude** $_{+E}^{-W}$ –135°05′ W        AP latitude = 45° N

**LHA**                      330°00′

**Data for HO 249:** lat. = 45° N   LHA = 330°   Dec. = 6° same name

*Figure 15–7.* Work sheet for a moon sight

semidiameter of 15′. There is a note to this effect on the half of the table that covers altitudes to 35°, but I include it on the work sheet, too, as one more reminder.

The extra paperwork involved in moon sights is the main reason many navigators don't do them. That's a shame, because it means passing up many chances for multiple daytime fixes from two bodies whose identification can never be in doubt.

# Afterword: Accuracy

If navigation has a patron saint in Ariadne, it also has a resident siren. Her name is Accuracy.

Because celestial navigation makes use of two exact sciences—astronomy and spherical trigonometry—it's natural enough to assume it produces results of analogous precision. The tools reinforce this assumption.

You open the *Nautical Almanac* and see GHA and declination calculated to the tenth of a minute of arc. Adjacent to the micrometer drums of sextants are scales called verniers that allow you to read sextant measurement to a tenth of a minute also.

To an astronomer with a telescope rooted in reinforced concrete and a clock that clicks when an atom sneezes, a decimal part of a minute is a meaningful unit. But can it be to a sailor with a quartz wristwatch and a hand-held sextant, swaying along on the surface of an undulating sea?

The nub of these remarks is that practical navigators cannot let the precision of the data in the tables lure them to believe their results are likely to be at that level or even anywhere near it. The tables are made for many users, surveyors and astronomers among them. They have instruments that can measure to a decimal of a minute of arc and time; navigators don't.

For instance, the other currently published sight reduction table (HO 229) gives altitudes to the tenth of a minute, while a pencil line on a typical plotting sheet is two or three times that thick.

Recall also that an LOP is a straight line standing in for a curved piece of an entire circle around a GP, that the chart or plotting sheet is a flat surface standing in for a piece of a sphere, that the earth is not in fact the perfect sphere assumed by the navigational triangle, and you can see that there is a limit to the accuracy you can reasonably expect.

A fairly common opinion among practicing navigators is that LOPs are not *lines*, but *bands*—ribbons about two nautical miles wide. The few times that I have been able to check a celestial fix with a loran or a satnav position, I have found one coordinate agreeing exactly and the other about two miles different; either the latitudes of the fixes were two miles apart, while the longitudes agreed, or vice versa. So that consensus seems valid to me.

However, since the best fix I have ever been able to produce with a top-line metal sextant under ideal circumstances was one mile from a known position (a micrometer drum plastic sextant was two miles off and the cheapest plastic sextant, four), I think two miles is optimistic. Personally, I never expect my celestial LOPs or fixes to be within three miles of my actual position, and I always keep a close watch on the depthfinder and the horizon when coming to a landfall.

I arrive at that number of three miles by considering that there is likely to be slop to the extent of about one minute of arc in each of the five steps in every sight: taking it, timing it, getting its almanac data, reducing it, plotting it. Of course, some of the errors are one way and some the other, so there are countervailing and canceling effects. That's the reason I cut the probable error from five minutes of arc to three. If your celestial has you within five miles of a charted danger, though, common sense says *get on deck* and stay there until you have spotted the hazard or put it surely astern.

Once in a while, the compensating effects can give you a shock. In the 1978 Newport–Bermuda Race I was plotting the result of a round of sights on four stars and saw that the LOPs were not going to make the usual open figure I expected; the lines just seemed to be going every which way. I grabbed my sextant and ran on deck to get a shot of the North Star, thinking that at least I would have a latitude, but I was too late. The horizon was as black as the sky. So sitting down at the chart table again, I finished the plotting and found the reason the LOPs had looked so strange to me. They crossed at the same point! All four of them. The skipper happened to come below at that moment and was mightily impressed, but my mind boggles at the number of countervailing errors that produced that plotted point.

Thinking about it now, after the passage of some twenty years, there was something strange about that entire trip. All of my subsequent star triangles measured only two miles on a side whereas I usually expect seven to ten miles on a side. Perhaps it was the perfect conditions—the stars without a twinkle; smooth seas; light winds; a large, heavy boat. A dead calm fell the last night out, and at two in the morning I sat on the cabin top and took star sights because the moon over my shoulders lit the horizon off one side of the boat.

Official navigational wisdom has it that sights such as these (taken within an arc of 180° ) are suspect; but again the triangles were tiny and virtually on top of the DR. Maybe it wasn't the weather or the boat. Maybe it wasn't the calm—perhaps it was a time warp. Whatever it was, such celestial delights never came my way again.

The saving grace of celestial navigation is that most landfalls can be seen from far greater distances than five or even ten miles (sea buoys can be seen from three in clear conditions). It is a matter of common practice, common sense, and good seamanship for the navigator to arrange to come at the land from the safest direction.

Having said this much about the limits of celestial navigation, it's time take a look at some of the ways to get the most out of it—to ensure you get the best results the art can give you. As you well know by now, there are two sights in celestial navigation—the actual sight and the computed sight—so it seems logical to discuss them in turn.

Naturally enough, the greatest single source of error in the actual sight is the taker. Measuring the angle of a moving object from a moving platform requires skill, and the more you do it, the better you get. One proven way to improve the actual sight is to take more than one. A pretty standard practice among navigators is to "take five and average." With a calculator capable of dealing directly in hours, minutes, and seconds of time and in degrees, minutes, and tenths of minutes of arc, averaging is virtually painless. If you do your calculations with pencil and paper the main thing to remember is that you carry the one into the degrees column after the minutes of arc total *sixty*—not *one hundred* as in conventional base-ten arithmetic.

With any sort of decent metal sextant, instrument error is unlikely to be much of a factor, but checking your sextant at the outset of any trip is only common sense. In the course of a passage, index error is the next source to track. It's good practice to check it at both the beginning and end of a round of sights and average any difference. You don't normally find a difference when you use a metal sextant, but you are quite likely to when the sextant is made of plastic.

Beyond operator and index errors, the other factors that affect the sight are refraction and, in the case of the moon and sun, semi-diameter. Refraction can inject errors of a minute or so, especially at low altitudes on very hot or cold days. The *Nautical Almanac* provides tables to correct for unusual atmospheric conditions. Extremes of temperature and humidity at sea are rare, but they do exist—in the middle of the Gulf Stream on a glorious (that is, very high barometric pressure) day, for instance.

The final action you can take to improve accuracy in the actual sight is keep it between 10° and 70°. Low altitudes are most sensitive to aberrant refraction, and high altitudes mean the GP is close to you and the edge of the circle around the GP is more heavily curved, so the LOP your sight generates becomes a less accurate stand-in.

As a practical matter, your sights fall within this range naturally. If you are using the sun, by the time you get yourself up and organized in the morning, the sun is most likely higher than 10° above the horizon. If you are using stars, the atmosphere cuts the brightness of those near the horizon, so you won't be able to see them anyway. Taking sights above 70° makes you feel like you are leaning over backwards, so you naturally tend to avoid them, too. "Moderation in all things" is a pretty fair philosophy in navigation as well as in many other areas of life.

Turning now to the computed sight, the first place for errors to enter is with the time. If you time your sights yourself, you are more likely to get it right than if someone else holds the watch, especially if the watch or chronometer has hands. Unless they are really thinking about it, people concentrating on the hands of a clock almost invariably get the time wrong by one or five minutes. Even if you are not averaging your sights, this potential problem is another reason to take more than one; the time-taker is more likely to notice a mistake. No matter how you approach time-taking, though, there is going to be some lag between the instant you have the body balanced on the horizon and the moment you or your helper checks the timepiece and writes down the time. (Some navigators subtract as many as five seconds from their noted time to allow for this time gap, but I've always taken it as I've seen it.)

When you enter the almanac, a useful practice is to make a line under the value you take out. If you have to check your work because the DR says your LOP just doesn't make sense, you know right away whether you got the wrong data to start. Also, it helps you keep track of the days.

When it comes to sight reduction, the most accurate benchmark is your DR. It's closer to where you really are than the AP is likely to be, and therefore, an LOP through the DR will vary the least from the curvature of the circle around the GP. Working from the DR means, of course, that you have to use the basic formulas and a calculator, a programmed navigational calculator, or one of the logarithmic methods such as HO 208 or 211. A calculator or HO 211 also boosts the accuracy in another way. It lets you use the actual declination of the moment of the sight and therefore avoids the potential error of doing a linear interpolation of something that is not always changing in a straightforward way.

This generally happens when your latitude and the declination of the body are close and the LHA is within 30° of your meridian. What this means in practical terms is that the body's altitude is high: 70° or more. Here again is a reason for moderation.

When using any book of tables, I've found it generally useful to leaf through any explanatory material. Often there's good additional information. For instance, at the tail end of *Selected Stars,* there's a long-term almanac of the stars, and at the end of the other two volumes of *HO 249,* there are long-term almanacs of the sun. The *Nautical Almanac* includes directions for using it the next year. It also provides star charts, a sight-reduction table, and the formulas to let you do sight reduction with a basic scientific calculator. By the way, save your almanacs; when they are exactly four years out of date, the sun and Aries columns are again usable for practical purposes. (This is not true, alas, for the moon and the planet columns.)

As far as plotting sheets and plotting go, it is best to work to the largest scale you find convenient; awkwardness can introduce lots of errors. The scale on the sheets that come with preprinted latitudes and longitudes is very generous, but I've found the sheets awkward to use because most of the boats I've sailed on have had fairly small navigation tables. Some didn't have any; aboard those boats I worked with photocopies of the VP-OS universal sheets reduced to standard letter size, 8 1/2 by 11 inches. If you must have a larger scale, the "Universal Plotting Sheet" can be expanded by making your ruled meridians and the preprinted latitudes 30′ apart instead of 1°. That way, each tick on the latitude scale is half a nautical mile instead of a whole nautical mile.

The availability of preprogrammed navigational calculators (specialized computers, really) has increased a natural inclination for navigators to think in terms of fixes only. As a result, often individual LOPs are not plotted because the calculator can compute a running fix from a subsequent sight; the latitude and longitude of the resulting fix are then put on the passage chart, bypassing the plot altogether. If you think about it a bit, this is an odd way to proceed because a single LOP is the most accurate information a sight can ever produce. It is the minimum product of celestial navigation; it has the fewest parts, so it is the most reliable. Combining it with other LOPs only injects their uncertainties. When you combine two LOPs for a running fix, for example, you mix errors in the distance run into the final result. A calculator may be able to give you a fix to the precision of three decimal points, but the numbers may be punctilious garbage and not as useful as any one of the LOPs that went into it. Quite often a single LOP gives you all the information you need.

For instance, if you are nearing a landfall and it's been a long time between sights, you may get an LOP that happens to fall across the land or close to it (as with your approach to the Bahamas in the example in chapter 7). To find the land you simply run along the line. If the line doesn't strike the land, you sail on, advancing the line, until it does; then you change course and sail along the new line. The same technique can be used if you are trying to *avoid* a landfall—a reef or very low island, for instance.

Beyond this application of the lone LOP, there are two special cases that can be very useful. If you take a sight when a body is abeam, the LOP tells you how far you are to the left or right of your intended track—especially helpful when you are trying to clear a cape or a patch of outlying shoal water. Likewise, a shot of a body ahead or astern checks up on the distance run and helps keep you from being overly optimistic or unduly gloomy about your progress.

This subject of the utility of fixes versus LOPs is an interesting one historically, because until the middle of the nineteenth century, celestial navigators also thought exclusively in terms of fixes. Instead of computing an altitude, navigators used their observed altitudes as input for another formula of spherical trigonometry, one that gave them a longitude to cross with a latitude—that is, a fix. The accuracy of their calculation, however, depended on an accurate latitude, so if the distance run since the last noon sight was questionable, so was the fix—a situation exactly analogous to the uncertainty inherent in any modern running fix. This weakness was known, of course, and it goes a long way to explain the sanctity of the noon sight in those days: A good latitude was essential to accurate results from the formula.

All this changed, however, at ten o'clock in the morning, December 18, 1837, when Thomas H. Sumner, the master of an American sailing ship, discovered the celestial LOP. Captain Sumner's ship arrived in the channel between Ireland and England in heavy weather. Ireland was a lee shore somewhere over the horizon to the west, and Sumner needed a positive landfall before easing off to run north up St. George's Channel toward his destination, Greenock, near Glasgow. Here's the story in the captain's words:

> Having sailed from Charleston 25th November, 1837, bound to Greenock, a series of heavy gales from the Westward promised a quick passage; after passing the Azores, the wind prevailed from the Southward, with thick weather; after passing Longitude 21° W., no observation was had until near the land, but soundings were had not far, as was supposed, from the edge of the Bank. The weather was now more boisterous and very thick; and the wind still Southerly; arriving about midnight 17th December, within 40 miles, by dead reckoning, of Tusker light, the wind hauled S.E. true, making the Irish coast a lee shore; the ship was then kept close to the wind, and several tacks made to preserve her position as nearly as possible until daylight, when, nothing being in sight, she was kept on E.N.E. under short sail with heavy gales. At about 10 A.M. an altitude of the sun was observed, and the Chronometer time noted; but having run so far without any observation, it was plain the Latitude by dead reckoning was liable to error, and could not be entirely relied on.
>
> Using, however, this Latitude, in finding the Longitude by Chronometer, it was found to put the ship 15' of Longitude E. of the position by dead reckoning; which in Latitude 52° N. is 9 nautical miles; this seemed to agree tolerably well with the dead reckoning; but feeling doubtful of the Latitude, the observation was tried with a Latitude 10' further N.; finding this placed the ship E.N.E. 27 nautical miles, of the former position, it was tried again with a Latitude 20' N. of the dead reckoning; this also placed the ship still further E.N.E. and still 27 *nautical miles* further; these three positions were then seen to lie in the direction of *Small's light*. It then at once appeared that the observed altitude must have happened at all

the three points and at Small's light, and at the ship, at the same instant of time; and it followed, that Small's light must bear E.N.E., if the Chronometer was right. Having been convinced of this truth, the ship was kept on her course, E.N.E., the wind being still S.E., and in less than an hour Small's light was made bearing E.N.E. 1/2 E., and close aboard.

Whew! It's the classic mariner's nightmare—a lee shore and a lousy day. But this one produced a revelation that completely changed the practice of celestial navigation. Sumner's method of navigating by celestial LOPs was quickly adopted by navigators all over the world and came to be called the "new navigation."

Today, navigation by LOPs *is* celestial navigation, but it's useful to remember how the LOP came about and not to think solely in terms of *crossed* LOPs—that is, fixes. A humble LOP can restore your confidence wonderfully—just ask Captain Sumner.

For practical purposes, I think the way to get the most out of celestial navigation can be stated in five rules.

1. Take five and average.
2. *Non decimalis carborundum.* (Don't drown in the decimals.)
3. Keep your altitudes between 10° and 70°.
4. Use a calculator for sight reduction from your DR.
5. Don't pass up a sight because it doesn't fit the rules.

In all of this, there is a law of diminishing returns. Frequently the navigator is cook and skipper and mechanic too, and it's often a matter of judgment whether it is worth spending an hour to get a result that may be a mile or two closer to the truth or whether a fifteen-minute cut at it is sufficient. Usually the closer you are to land, the more closely you want to know your position. No matter how fine you slice it, though, when you are at sea you are on a voyage between one place now sunk beneath the waters and another still to rise from it. You won't know exactly where you are until you find the land (whence, no doubt, the phrase "being at sea"). A navigator is not an astronomer; extremes of accuracy are not the main goal—a safe arrival is.

In any case, after all the arcs have been swung, all the altitudes calculated, all the intercepts laid off, and all the LOPs plotted, celestial navigation will be what it has always been: the high art of the useful approximation.

# Index

*Note: Page numbers in italics refer to illustrations, tables, and work sheets.*